Selling Public Enterprises

Selling Public Enterprises

A Cost-Benefit
Methodology

Leroy P. Jones, Pankaj Tandon,
Ingo Vogelsang

The MIT Press
Cambridge, Massachusetts
London, England

This book was set in Palatino by Asco Trade Typesetting Ltd., and printed and bound in the United States of America.

Library of Congress Cataloging-in-Publication Data

Jones, Leroy P.
    Selling public enterprises: a cost-benefit methodology / Leroy P. Jones, Pankaj Tandon, Ingo Vogelsang.
        p.   cm.
    Includes bibliographical references (p.   ) and index.
    ISBN 0-262-10041-X
    1. Government business enterprises—Cost effectiveness. 2. Government ownership—Cost effectiveness. 3. Government business enterprises—Valuation.
    4. Privatization—Cost effectiveness. I. Tandon, Pankaj. II. Vogelsang, Ingo.
    III. Title.
    HD3845.6.J663   1990
    350.009′2—dc20   90-6244
                                                                          CIP

Contents

List of Tables

List of Figures

Acknowledgments

Much of this material was originally prepared for the World Bank (IBRD) as "The Economics of Divestiture: Ex-Ante Valuation and Ex-Post Evaluation." Most of chapter 9 was originally prepared for the International Center for Economic Growth (ICEG) as "The Political Economy of Public Enterprise Divestiture." We are grateful to the IBRD, ICEG, and the Boston University Public Enterprise Program for financial support. Martine Gavinet and Jeff Huther provided capable and cheerful research, word-processing, graphics, and bibliographic assistance, without which the project never could have been completed. We would like to thank Ahmed Galal, John Nellis, Mary Shirley, Geri Sicat, Terry Vaughn, Ray Vernon, and anonymous referees for helpful suggestions.

1   An Economic Approach to Divestiture

1.1   Divestiture of Public Enterprise

This book is about public enterprise divestiture. *Public enterprise*[1] means public production[2] for private consumption.[3] *Divestiture* means to get rid of, in this case by sale to the private sector.[4] Our approach, however, is not descriptive but analytic.

Our goal is to begin to do for the government's *dis*-investment decision what the project evaluation literature has done for the *in*vestment decision: that is, to provide an analytic framework for systematically identifying and evaluating the costs and benefits of a particular decision and comparing the results with alternative policies. We are not so naive as to believe that such a technocratic approach to decision-making will *supplant* ideological and political elements; however, neither are we so cynical as to believe that it cannot *supplement* those elements. Our premise is not that technocratic input will create a perfect decision, only a better one: a decision-maker is likely to achieve political ends or indulge ideological predilections at less economic cost if fully informed of the economic consequences of various policy packages. Readers unsympathetic to this view may want to stop here; for the sympathetic, the balance of this chapter provides an overview of our approach.

1.2   Divestiture: Stylized Facts and Analytical Tools

Our concern with dis-investment rather than investment follows from a fundamental change in the revealed preferences of the world's governments. There has been a marked discontinuity in postwar world economic history: in the 1980s the public enterprise sector contracted or remained the same in almost all countries; prior to that, it expanded or remained the same in almost all countries in almost all subperiods. Such a bald statement obviously must admit important exceptions (for example, the divestiture of British Steel in 1953 or Korean Airlines in 1968) and complicate matters further with qualifications (for example, restricting the assertion to policy-generated change, recognizing that the sector can shrink absolutely as a result of recession and shrink relatively if large public-dominated sectors— read oil—are hit disproportionately).

Nonetheless, the generalization is surprisingly robust across the world's 200-odd countries, be they socialist, less-developed countries (LDCs), or more-developed countries (MDCs). Among MDCs, the United Kingdom, Japan, and France are the best-known examples, but others have also pursued such policies with some zeal (including the Federal Republic of Germany, Canada, and New Zealand). Among socialist countries, the most dramatic changes have been in the broader area of privatization, but a lot has happened in the narrower sphere of divestiture as well (recent events in Eastern Europe are most striking in this regard). In the LDCs, substantial divestitures[5] have thus far been extremely limited (Chile and Mexico), but most countries have announced major programs (with notable exceptions such as India, Indonesia, and Brazil), many countries have sold significant numbers of small firms (Bangladesh and Pakistan), and most have shifted the balance of entry of new firms toward the private sector, resulting in relative shrinking at the margin, even where actual divestiture has not occurred.

It is not our intention to document these assertions, but their validity will be readily apparent to the informed observer of the international public enterprise scene, and they are well documented in a variety of sources cited in our bibliography. Here we merely wish to note that the shift in the world's behavior has yet to be matched by a shift in analytic methods.

This is by no means to suggest that the divestiture phenomenon has been ignored in the literature: the length of our bibliography testifies to the contrary, and more studies continue to appear.[6] What has been ignored is the potential use of the cost-benefit approach, where gains and losses are measured in the applied-welfare-economics tradition.

We therefore apply an intermediate level of technology and examine only a piece of the divestiture pie. The whole pie would include the broad, rich, and diverse range of the versal tradition as represented by the volumes edited by Vernon and by Suleiman and Waterbury[7] as well as the narrow technical virtuosity of the formal modeling tradition as represented by the works of Bös and of Shapiro and Willig.[8] Also in the intermediate range, but far broader than our benefit/cost framework, is the eclectic work of Vickers and Yarrow.[9] The utility of our particular approach can perhaps be seen by considering the basic economic elements of the divestiture decision.

1.3   The Role of Valuation and Price

As an explanation of the slow pace of divestiture policies in many countries, the following couplet elicits knowing smiles and nods of agreement:

If a public enterprise is making money,
   the government won't sell it;
if it's losing money, the private
   sector won't buy it.

Unfortunately, the widespread initial appeal of this quote can be attributed only to the dominance of political over economic logic because it represents a fundamental misunderstanding of the economics of divestiture.

If this logic operated in the private sector, then the *Wall Street Journal* would be considerably thinner than it is. On the one hand, profitable firms are regularly relinquished because the price offered exceeds what the seller expects to earn in future profits. On the other hand, even chronically unprofitable firms can be sold at a positive price if the buyer believes that a management turnaround will create future profits. In short, (1) assets are sold when buyers and sellers value them differently, thus creating a positive-sum game where both parties can gain; and (2) the selling price of the asset is the intervening variable that allocates the benefits of the game. Whether a firm is profitable or unprofitable is secondary, since it is the *difference* in the valuation that makes a trade possible, not the *level* of the valuation. There is room for a deal if the seller can run an enterprise to yield 20 percent while the buyer could run it to earn 25 percent.[10] If, however, buyer and seller value a firm identically, then no deal can be struck, as there is no gain to be had from trading, and any transaction costs will create a negative-sum game. In sum, it is *divergence* of valuation that facilitates sale the *identity* of valuation that retards it.

If government preferences and management styles differ considerably from those in the private sector, then differential valuations are likely to be large; hence the sale of a public enterprise should be easier than the sale of a private enterprise. For example, if—as is commonly held—public enterprises are less cost-efficient than their private brethren, then the magnitude of the positive-sum game should be larger, and the sale should be easier, as compared with a private-to-private transaction where efficiency—and hence value—differentials are smaller. Because public-to-private transactions are in practice notoriously more difficult to consummate, we have a paradox. Resolution is found in both political and economic spheres.

One political problem follows from point (2). Even if the potential gains are great, how are they to be divided between the two parties? In a purely private transaction, the distribution depends on the degree of competition in the market for the shares: with many potential buyers, the seller might be expected to reap most of the benefits; with only one potential buyer, something in the vicinity of 50/50 might be reasonable, but the exact division will vary with the relative negotiating skills of the two parties. Matters are much more complicated in the politically charged atmosphere of a public sale, where accusations of "giving away the national patrimony," favoritism, and corruption are likely. Such political factors can override economic logic and make negotiation of the sale price a difficult exercise at best.

There are, however, economic obstacles as well. Public enterprises typically operate in highly imperfect markets. If the government chooses not to exploit a monopolistic or oligopolistic position, but the private buyer plans to do so, then he or she will value the enterprise more highly even in the absence of efficiency differentials. The government may nonetheless be reluctant to sell because it is concerned with the welfare of consumers (or workers, or suppliers) after the sale. Analytically, the problem is that the government seller cares about the operation of the enterprise *after* the sale, so we must introduce a third value into the calculation to reflect the social value of the enterprise after divestiture.[11] A private seller does not care about the operation of the enterprise after the sale, but the government seller, as fiduciary for all of society's interests, must care. The introduction of this third element into the divestiture calculus makes the economics of public divestiture fundamentally different from private divestiture.

There is a good deal more to it than this, of course. At this point we merely suggest that the economics of public divestiture are rather more complicated than those of private divestiture, and that to our knowledge they have been nowhere spelled out.[12] The purpose of this book is therefore to identify the relationships among, and the determinants of, the sale price and the three fundamental values of the firm.

More broadly, it is hoped that focusing on price and value will shed some technocratic light on three fundamental divestiture questions:

1. Should the public enterprise be sold?
2. To whom should it be sold?
3. At what price should it be sold?

1.4 Market Failures versus Organizational Failures

Are not the three questions internally inconsistent? Is not the entire goal of divestiture to make greater use of decentralized market forces? And does it not follow that if an enterprise is to be divested, the price and the buyer should be determined by impartial market forces, rather than by government technocrats?

More concretely, should not the institutional model for divestiture be British Columbia, where:[13]

1. Shares in companies to be divested were consolidated into a single company (British Columbia Resources Investments Corporation—BCRIC);

2. Some shares in BCRIC were distributed without cost to the "public" at the rate of five shares per resident, others were sold at the offering rate ($6), and the remainder were retained by the provincial government and;

3. Therefore, shares were valued by the stock market.

The purity and sophistication of this model is to be admired, on both political and economic grounds. On the political side, by taking seriously the notion that the "public" is the ultimate owner of a public enterprise, and by distributing shares accordingly, accusations of favoritism and inequity are neutralized. On the economic side, creation of a market with large numbers of buyers and sellers avoids any governmental discretion in deciding buyer or price.

Although we commend the British Columbia model for the consideration of any government structuring a divestiture plan, we suggest that its direct applications may be limited. Many—if not most—real-world divestitures are motivated at least in part by deficit reduction considerations. Thus any political gains from distributing shares are likely to be offset by political losses from raising taxes or reducing critical expenditures. Even in a surplus context, the alternative to giving away the enterprise is tax reduction or expenditure expansion, and the question becomes, Would we gain more politically and/or economically by transferring income via giveaways, lower taxes, or higher subsidies? The answer, of course, is "it depends," but given the fiscal alternatives, it is not surprising that the British Columbia experiment has not (to our knowledge) been repeated in other MDCs, even where the sale was made to diversified investors via the stock market. Once the government wants the revenue, then the pricing problem returns, since the initial offering price must somehow be set.

In LDCs, matters are further complicated by the underdevelopment of capital markets in general and of the stock market in particular.[14] Thin capital markets and information gaps make market valuations an imperfect matter at best, and at worst result in artificial manipulations.

Even more critical is the control issue. As we shall emphasize later, there is little to be gained from divestiture unless enterprise behavior changes in the direction of cost efficiency and heightened entrepreneurial initiative. The question is whether in an LDC context management is likely to alter its conduct significantly when controlled by a large number of diversified shareholders, as opposed to the government shareholder. In short, will an LDC capital market exercise financial discipline over the firm? Even if you believe it will, will LDC investors believe this and be willing to bet their savings on it? We suspect that many LDC governments will answer in the negative and instead rely on selling controlling interests to a single individual, company, or group.

Even when selling to a single buyer, however, one could still rely on market mechanisms to set the price, through competitive bidding. Here again, the problem of thin capital markets poses a problem. How many bidders are you likely to get? What is the probability that they will collude? In such an environment it is only prudent for the government to do a bit of homework in setting its own reservation price and in estimating a reasonable offer price for the private sector so as to enhance its own negotiating position.

In sum, we suggest that in the LDC context, the pure market mechanism of divestiture will often fail because divestiture will not generate a large number of informed and competitive bidders. It follows that the government or its representatives will need to take an active role in valuing the assets and setting the price.[15]

Saying the government *should* undertake a particular task is of course rather different from saying it *can* do it. The market-failure limitations on market mechanisms are paralleled by the organization-failure limits on government actions. Determining the value of a firm is a complex effort at best, requiring knowledge of a host of unknowable future events. Is the government really capable of doing this? Further, even if the technocrats could do it, would the politicians listen? Is it not the case that the three fundamental questions will ultimately be answered on political grounds, with technocratic analysis being either ignored or merely used as justification for what the powers-that-be wanted to do in the first place?

The foregoing class of criticisms can of course be applied to any technocratic approach to public policy decision-making. Knowing the relevant divestiture values is not going to ensure the right divestiture decision any more than knowing the marginal cost of electricity is going to ensure that such a price is actually charged, nor is knowing the net present social value of a project going to ensure that the right investment decision occurs. Furthermore, given measurement problems, we are never going to "know" the relevant technocratic values with great precision. Nonetheless, while giving full recognition to the political and ideological elements of public policy decisions, the goal of a technocratic approach is to inform the discussion by a careful detailing of the factors to be considered and to reduce the scope for political discretion by quantifying the outer bounds of the costs and benefits.

What distinguishes the divestiture decision from the investment or pricing decision is neither the role of politics nor the inability to provide a perfect answer. Rather, the difference is that the economics of divestiture have nowhere been systematically worked out.

1.5 Approach

In pursuit of this goal, we adopt an approach aimed at the educated practitioner rather than either the high theorist or the "who-needs-a-study?" lay person. The aim is to provide a resource for those who actually have to go to the field and propose a selling price for the enterprise or conduct an evaluation after the sale. We therefore need to strike a balance between theoretical rigor and practical applicability.

On the one hand are proponents of what may be called the "Wall Street" school of divestiture, who view the sale of a public enterprise as fundamentally the same as the sale of a private enterprise and therefore think that all you need to do is hire a "Big Eight" accounting firm. While this approach is relatively easy to apply (which might explain its widespread use), we argue that it isn't enough. It captures the value of the enterprise to potential buyers but ignores the interests of consumers, workers, and others who must be safeguarded by the government. Thus, for example, we believe that demand curves have some slope, that quantities vary with prices, and that therefore the government should be concerned with changes in consumer surplus when evaluating divestiture decisions. In a like manner, the government should be concerned with the fiscal impact of the divestiture and its impact on workers and others.

But where does one draw the line in introducing further complications? Here, pure theorists would step in and say that the only "right" way to do the analysis is to build a general equilibrium model of the whole economy and then allow all the secondary and tertiary impacts of the divestiture to work themselves out through this model. Whereas we might agree with this principle, we reject it as impractical. Instead, we follow the tradition adopted in cost-benefit analysis, which is to use a partial equilibrium approach with the introduction of many shadow multipliers that serve as proxies for many of the general equilibrium effects that are otherwise left out. This approach is not only practical but correct so long as the changes generated by divestiture are not large enough to change the values of the multipliers by more than the error in their estimation. The approach therefore is generally acceptable as long as the divestiture under analysis is "small" relative to the whole economy. If a country is truly expected to divest much of a large public sector over a short period of time, then a formal general equilibrium approach may become necessary. In general, then, we try to take the insights of theory as far as they are likely to be usable in empirical field work, and no further.

Our approach is also eclectic. Economists tend to be preoccupied with the behavioral changes accompanying divestiture, whereas financial analysts focus on valuation issues. We try to look at the interdependency of both.

1.6   Overview

We begin by laying out the relationships between the various prices and values and the way in which they jointly determine the answers to the fundamental divestiture questions (chapter 2). Subsequent sections investigate the determination of the values in increasingly complex environments. Chapter 3 details the considerations involved in deciding the relative value of funds in government and private hands. Chapter 4 deals with the simplest possible case of competitive equilibrium where all prices are "right" and there are no differences between public and private behavior. Here the focus is empirical, and considerable attention is given to extracting relevant data from the accounting records of an actual enterprise. In later sections we see how the respective valuations of this same firm change as we introduce additional complexities.

The first complexity involves the fundamental trade-off between increased cost efficiency and possible exercise of market power by the divested enterprise (chapter 5). The second complexity is the presence of price regulation, indirect taxes, and other factors creating a gap between market and shadow prices (chapter 6). The third complexity is the presence of positive and negative synergies between the buyer and the acquiring firm (chapter 7). The fourth complexity is income distribution; because various classes in society are affected differently by divestiture, incorporation of distributional effects into the model is essential in its own right and also provides a link to the political economy of the process (chapter 9).

To achieve clarity, each of these complexities is introduced on a (largely) ceteris paribus basis. In chapter 8, however, most pieces of the methodology are combined in a Lotus 1-2-3 template, which allows testing for the sensitivity to the various assumptions, examination of interdependencies, and application to widely differing classes of enterprises. These results are then used to suggest the implications of alternative government policies and strategies that might enhance the outcome of the divestiture effort (chapter 10).

The final chapter provides a summary of the book and then moves from ex-ante valuation to ex-post evaluation. Here we outline how the methodology developed earlier can be applied to the evaluation of actual historic divestitures to shed light on future decisions.

2   Basic Concepts

In this section we answer the three fundamental questions at the most general level in terms of three key values of the enterprise:

V_{sg}: social value under continued government operation,

V_{sp}: social value under private operation, and

V_{pp}: private value under private operation

and two parameters:

λ_g: shadow multiplier on government revenue

λ_p: shadow multiplier on private funds.

Together these five values in turn define three alternative sales prices:

Z_g: the minimum price acceptable to the government.

Z_p: the maximum price acceptable to the private buyer, and

Z: the actual price at which the sale is executed.

For example, the relationship between V_{sg}, V_{sp}, Z, λ_p, and λ_g determines whether or not the enterprise *should* be sold; adding V_{pp} determines whether or not the enterprise *can* be sold, and so forth.

A very broad range of divestiture issues are thus encapsulated in a few basic concepts. In this chapter we define these basic concepts and establish the fundamental relationships among them. Subsequent chapters extend the analysis by specifying the various V's in increasingly complex environments.

Our basic approach here is that of standard applied welfare economics or cost-benefit analysis. That is, we assume that the government wishes to maximize social welfare, which in turn is assumed to be an aggregation of the levels of welfare of all the different economic actors—consumers, producers, workers—in the economy. However, much of our framework is applicable even in cases where government rather than being a welfare maximizer simply responds to interest groups in a manner consistent with maintaining or reinforcing its hold on power. In fact, we believe that an understanding of this point is essential to an understanding of the forces that drive governments to undertake policies such as divestiture. We shall discuss this point in detail in chapter 9. In the meantime, we will work with the notion of a welfare-maximizing government. In their turn, private firms are assumed to pursue their own interest, namely the maximization of profits. Thus, in our development of the various notions of value of the enterprise, the private value will refer to the privately appropriable profits that the enterprise will generate, whereas the social values will refer to the aggregate welfare of all economic agents influenced by the decision to divest.

2.1   Private Value (V_{pp})

The private value of the company is simply what the company is worth to a private buyer. Generally, this is the present discounted value of the stream of expected net benefits accruing to the new owners. Ignoring possible nonmonetary benefits such as prestige and political power, this gives us the maximum willingness-to-pay of the private buyer:

$$V_{pp} \equiv Z_p \qquad\qquad\qquad (2.1)$$

That is, the maximum amount anyone would pay for a company is the net present value of its future earnings stream.

Two variants of V_{pp} are particularly important:

V_{ppa}: the private value as a stand-alone operation

V_{ppc}: the private value to a larger corporate group

A corporate group may be willing to pay more than the stand-alone value of the firm for a number of reasons, including the following:

1. There may be economies of scope associated with spreading some overhead over a larger base.

2. The company may realize reductions in transaction costs and risk through the merger, whether they be horizontal (i.e., with a competitor) or vertical (i.e., with a company either higher up or lower down the production chain). In other words, there may be scale effects and vertical integration effects.

3. The corporation may be able to utilize otherwise unmarketable assets of the firm, such as accrued or expected tax liabilities.

4. There may be positive effects through portfolio diversification.

5. The company may raise the profitability of its existing operations through the exercise of newly created monopoly, oligopoly, or monopsony power.

While some of these private synergies are also socially desirable, others are only transfers, and still others are clearly undesirable. We shall elaborate on these distinctions in chapter 7.

An understanding of the determinants of V_{ppa} and V_{ppc} is thus useful for the government for a number of reasons. First, it is not sufficient merely to know *what* the private sector is willing to pay; it is also necessary to have some idea *why* it is willing to pay such an amount. It is quite legitimate for government to refuse to sell to a company that will thereby acquire market power, to the detriment of consumers' interests. Thus, sale should not necessarily go to the highest bidder. For example, in the sale of the American cargo railroad Conrail, the Norfolk Southern railroad might have been willing to pay more than an independent buyer simply because of the resulting change in its competitive position. That fact would not have necessarily justified sale to Norfolk Southern. Second, even where non-competitive practices are precluded, existing private companies will often be willing to pay more than independent individuals, groups of individuals, or fiduciaries (for any of reasons 1 through 4), and this may conflict with the social goal of diversified ownership. Third, understanding private motivations helps government to structure terms and conditions to facilitate the sale. Fourth, as part of the bargaining strategy, it is useful for the government negotiator to have some independent idea of the private sector's demand price, or the maximum amount it is willing to pay. Finally, V_{pp} must be known as a precondition to establishing the social value under private operation, which in turn is a precondition to establishing the government's supply price, or the minimum it is willing to accept.

2.2 Value to Society under Private Operation (V_{sp})

The social value under private operation is the present value of expected net benefits accruing to society as a whole from the private operation of the enterprise. Under private operation the enterprise will have certain behavior, characterized by the output and price levels it chooses for its products. This behavior will influence not only the profits of the enterprise itself but also the welfare of consumers, the profits of other firms, the incomes of workers, tax revenues, and so on. The social value of the enterprise includes the welfare of all actors influenced by the enterprise. Thus, V_{sp} differs from V_{pp} because V_{sp} includes the welfare of actors not considered in the calculation of V_{pp}. The difference between social goals and private goals results in (1) a different *classification* of flows (some private costs—e.g., taxes—are not social costs; some private benefits—e.g., sales gained through predatory pricing or other noncompetitive behavior—are not social benefits), and (2) different *pricing* of flows (the private benefits from increasing output or reducing inputs is evaluated at market prices, which may differ from the corresponding benefits to society evaluated at shadow or accounting prices).[1]

In sum, the private valuation is concerned with returns to the *equity* shareholder evaluated at *market* prices, whereas the social valuation is concerned with returns to *all economic actors* evaluated at *shadow* prices.

2.3 Value to Society under Government Operation (V_{sg})

The value to society under public operation is the present value of expected net benefits accruing to society as a whole from the continued public operation of the enterprise. Thus, it is the social valuation of the alternative to divestiture—continued operation of the enterprise in the public sector. It differs from V_{sp} for two quite distinct sets of reasons:

1. For a given economic environment, private behavior will likely differ from public behavior. This may be because of intrinsic differences but also because private goals are different from public goals. The effects may be seen in terms of both static efficiency and dynamic entrepreneurship.

2. As part of the terms and conditions of the sale, the economic environment may change (e.g., tax rates, tariff protection or exemption, output pricing policies, financial structure, and credit availability).

The first set of factors is critical because it constitutes the single most important, though by no means the only, economic motivation for divestiture in the first place. The second set is critical analytically because ignoring it may obscure the true benefits or costs of divestiture. For example, in one LDC divestiture, a losing public enterprise was turned into a profitable private enterprise, in part because of increased efficiency but in part because of a five-year grant of effective prohibition of competing imports. To evaluate the desirability of such a divestiture, it would be necessary to compare performance after divestiture with performance as it would have been under continued government ownership but with the changed economic environment. Accordingly, it is useful to distinguish between two alternative values under continued public operation:

V_{sga}: value under continued operation "as is"

V_{sgr}: value under restructuring under conditions paralleling those of divestiture

These distinctions are the focus of chapter 10.

2.4   The Shadow Multiplier on Government Revenue (λ_g)

The parameter λ_g summarizes our answer to the question, Is money in government hands worth more than, less than, or the same as consumption? This is a fundamental question in shadow pricing that is discussed in the standard cost-benefit literature. Because this parameter is fundamental to our analysis, we devote a considerable part of chapter 3 to discussing it in some detail. However, a brief preview of the concept is essential at this point.

Suppose we can characterize the effects of the divestiture under discussion as changing the welfare of consumers by ΔC, the profits of private sector firms by $\Delta\Pi$, and the revenues of government by ΔG. The usual neoclassical expression for the total change in social welfare would be

$$\Delta W = \Delta C + \Delta\Pi + \Delta G.$$

This equation implies that (1) the "welfare" of firms can be represented by their profits; (2) the welfare generated by the government can be measured by the government's revenues; and (3) consumers, firms and government-generated welfare all have equal weight in the social welfare function.

A more general formulation would allow each component of welfare to have a different weight. These weights might derive either from distributional considerations (for example, a dollar to the rich might contribute less to social welfare than a dollar to the poor) or from efficiency considerations (for example, taxes or other distortions might make a dollar on government revenue displace more than a dollar of consumption). We could then write

$$\Delta W = \lambda_c\Delta C + \lambda_p\Delta\Pi + \lambda_g\Delta G,$$

where each of the λ terms is the weight attached to that particular component of welfare. We argue in chapter 3 why it is important to introduce such weights. All that we need note here is that, since our purpose in calculating ΔW is to *rank* alternative policies, we can, without loss of generality, *normalize* this last expression by setting any one of the weights equal to one. That is, we could choose one of the welfare components to be the *numeraire*, in terms of which we would measure the values of the other components. The choice of numeraire is arbitrary and makes no difference to the fundamental nature of the calculation. We choose consumption as the numeraire and accordingly set $\lambda_c = 1$.[2] Thus, λ_g is the value of \$1 of government revenue in terms of its consumption-equivalent. In other words, a \$1 increase in government revenue yields the same increase in social welfare as \$$\lambda_g$ of consumer welfare. Chapter 3 provides detailed theoretical and empirical evidence to support the assumption that $\lambda_g > 1$, although this assumption is not necessary for our analysis.

2.5   The Shadow Multiplier on Private Profits (λ_p)

The brief discussion in the previous section suggested that if consumption were used as the numeraire in the measurement of welfare, two parameters would be left to be determined: λ_g and λ_p. Just as λ_g measures the value of government revenue relative to consumption, λ_p measures the value of private profits or corporate funds in terms of consumption. Normally, the assumption in welfare economics is that $\lambda_p = 1$; that is, that there is no difference from the welfare point of view whether benefits accrue to consumers or producers. However, it can be argued that this assumption is valid only when the level of investment is optimal. If the level of investment is suboptimal, then private profits become more valuable than consumption benefits because they lead to greater investment. In this scenario, $\lambda_p > 1$.

We discuss this parameter in considerable detail in chapter 3. At this point we note only that, for much of the analysis, the relative values of λ_p and λ_g will be important. In other words, the results will vary depending on whether $\lambda_g > \lambda_p$ or the other way around. Although this is ultimately an empirical question, there is very little solid evidence that would allow us to conclude which way this inequality is likely to go. We therefore present results for both cases. However, we feel that there are theoretical grounds for preferring the assumption that $\lambda_g > \lambda_p$. These grounds are spelled out as we go along, partly in succeeding sections of this chapter and partly in chapter 3. However, this assumption is not central to our analysis, which would be equally valid in either case. In fact, we do expect that the opposite is likely to be true in some countries and might provide an explanation for certain observed phenomena.

2.6   The Fundamental Formula of Divestiture

We now have the tools that allow us to set forth the basic expression needed. for the analysis of the divestiture decision. If the government did not divest the enterprise, society would enjoy V_{sg}, the social value under continued government operation. For each potential buyer we must calculate V_{sp}, the social value under that buyer's operation. Note that this number could be different for different buyers, since their behavior might be different. If the sale price of the enterprise is Z, we can write the change in social welfare as a result of the sale to any particular buyer as

$$\Delta W = V_{sp} - V_{sg} + (\lambda_g - \lambda_p)Z. \tag{2.2}$$

We call this expression the *fundamental formula of divestiture*. Interpretation is straightforward: the first term gives welfare after the sale, the second term gives welfare before the sale, and the last term gives the welfare effect of the sale transaction itself.[3] The government's bottom-line decision-rule is to maximize ΔW. Answers to the basic questions follow directly.

2.7   Should the Enterprise Be Sold?

To maximize welfare, ΔW must be positive; otherwise the government should not sell. The selling rule is therefore:

Sell if $\Delta W = V_{sp} - V_{sg} + (\lambda_g - \lambda_p)Z > 0.$ $\qquad\qquad$ (2.3)

This may be rearranged to read:

Sell if $V_{sp} + (\lambda_g - \lambda_p)Z > V_{sg}.$ $\qquad\qquad$ (2.4)

This simply says that the government should sell if welfare under public ownership is less than that under private ownership plus any sale premium.

It might be thought that when λ_g is very high relative to λ_p, sale is more likely and that this explains the heightened contemporary interest in divestiture in LDCs, following fiscal and balance-of-payments crises. However, this conclusion would be premature, because λ_g and λ_p also enter into the calculation of V_{sp} and V_{sg}, most prominently as multipliers for tax revenue and government profits on the one hand and for firm profits on the other. Until we have specified the V's more fully in later chapters, no such conclusion is warranted.

If $\lambda_g > \lambda_p$,[4] the sell rule can be rewritten as:

Sell if $Z > \dfrac{V_{sg} - V_{sp}}{\lambda_g - \lambda_p}.$ $\qquad\qquad$ (2.5)

The right-hand side of this expression represents the government's supply price (Z_g) or the *minimum* that it should accept for the enterprise:

$$Z_g = \frac{V_{sg} - V_{sp}}{\lambda_g - \lambda_p}.$$ (2.6)

Note that whenever social welfare is higher under private operation than under public operation ($V_{sg} < V_{sp}$)[5] and $\lambda_g > \lambda_p$, this price will be negative, meaning that the government should be willing to *pay* the private sector to take over the enterprise. This might happen, for instance, if the enterprise is losing money under government operation but becomes viable under private operation without large deleterious welfare effects on consumers or workers. If the government is neutral between funds in public and private hands ($\lambda_g = \lambda_p$), then it should be willing to pay the private sector any arbitrarily large amount to take over the enterprise. If λ_g exceeds λ_p, the amount the government should be willing to pay becomes finite, but it should still be willing to pay the amount indicated by equation (2.6).

This rather strong result may seem surprising at first, but it is really quite intuitive. If the nation is economically better off with the enterprise in private hands, then the government should be willing to pay *something* to accomplish this improvement. If it is neutral between funds in private and public hands, then it should be willing to pay *anything*, because the payment is in this case only a transfer and is welfare neutral. This extreme result is unlikely (and its implausibility is one argument for assuming $\lambda_g > \lambda_p$), but the weaker result of a negative supply price remains.

If $\lambda_g < \lambda_p$, then, the higher the value of Z, the lower the change in welfare. Accordingly, the direction of the inequality in equation (2.5) is reversed,[6] and the sell rule becomes:

Sell if $Z < \dfrac{V_{sg} - V_{sp}}{\lambda_g - \lambda_p}.$ (2.7)

The government now has no minimum supply price, only a *maximum* supply price. It would not accept a price higher than that given by (2.7) because it would involve an excessive drain of funds from the private to the public sector. The implausibility of this solution is a further argument for assuming that $\lambda_g > \lambda_p$.

The main result of this section is (2.6), which gives us a formula for determining the minimum price at which government should be willing to sell. This is based on the assumption that $\lambda_g > \lambda_p$. The minimum supply price is of course not the price at which the sale should actually be executed, a topic to which we now turn.

2.8   At What Price Should It Be Sold?

The sale price Z should be chosen so as to maximize ΔW. Now (2.2) shows the net welfare effect of divestiture *for any given buyer*. We see from this expression that the sale price Z affects social welfare only through the factor $(\lambda_g - \lambda_p)$. Formally,

$$\frac{\partial \Delta W}{\partial Z} = (\lambda_g - \lambda_p), \tag{2.8}$$

which says that as Z rises, welfare rises at the rate $(\lambda_g - \lambda_p)$. There are now three cases. If $\lambda_g = \lambda_p$ (i.e., there is no premium on government revenues), then $\partial \Delta W / \partial Z = 0$, and the gain in welfare is unaffected by the sale price. This is the usual neoclassical type of result that treats the price paid as a pure transfer between the purchaser and the government and therefore accords no particular value to it. That is, the sale price does not matter, and any price (positive or negative) is just as good as any other. Anyone who believes that $\lambda_g = \lambda_p$ therefore has a very simple answer to the basic question of what price to charge: just flip a coin.

The second case is where $\lambda_g < \lambda_p$. In this case (2.8) would be negative, indicating that government would want to minimize the sale price. In principle, this means that government should pay the private sector an arbitrarily large amount to take over the enterprise. In fact, an assumption that $\lambda_g < \lambda_p$ implies that it would be optimal at the margin for government to simply transfer funds to private firms.

The third case is the one we regard as the most reasonable, specifically, where $\lambda_g > \lambda_p$. In this case (2.8) shows that $\partial \Delta W / \partial Z > 0$ and that the government should therefore attempt to obtain the highest possible sale price for the enterprise from any given buyer. This, however, is simply the maximum the private buyer would be willing to pay, so that

$$Z^* = Z_p = V_{pp}, \tag{2.9}$$

where * denotes the optimal value of the variable. It follows that the maximum welfare increment (ΔW^*) is

$$\Delta W^* = V_{sp} - V_{sg} + (\lambda_g - \lambda_p)V_{pp}. \tag{2.10}$$

It is, of course, exceedingly unlikely that this price will actually be obtained. Recall that Z_p reflects the price at which the buyer is indifferent between buying the enterprise or retaining his or her existing portfolio; at this price, the buyer would simply be trading one asset for another of equal value. The situation is symmetrical, of course, with Z_g representing the price at which society neither wins nor loses from the transaction. One asymmetry that does arise, however, is that whereas there is certainly only one seller in this transaction (the government), there is potentially more than one buyer. Competition between buyers could force the eventual buyer to pay close to his or her maximum willingness-to-pay. In most developing countries, as compared to developed economies, this may be less of a possibility because of the small size of the private sector.

In any case, the point is that Z_g and Z_p provide only boundaries for the actual sale price. If the former exceeds the latter, then no transaction can take place, but given the negative supply price, there is likely to be a considerable economic range for bargaining. Within this range, where will the price be set? For a given set of terms and conditions of sale, the answer is indeterminate in a small-number bargaining environment and depends upon the skill of the two bargaining parties.

In practice, of course, the terms and conditions of sale are anything but predetermined and are in fact the focus of negotiations. A case can be made for the bargaining sequence to be reversed, with the price first determined arbitrarily and the terms and conditions then negotiated to make this price acceptable to both parties. That is, while a negative price will generally be economically acceptable, it will never be politically acceptable. Under such circumstances a minimally acceptable political price becomes the starting point, and negotiations focus on terms and conditions that make it mutually acceptable. We return to this theme in chapter 10.

It is worth reemphasizing that all the expressions for ΔW and for its rate of change are derived with respect to a given buyer. Thus, we have demonstrated in this section that, for any given buyer, the government should seek to maximize the sale price. This is not the same as saying that government should choose the buyer with the highest bid, because the high bid may be associated with a low social valuation. We turn to this problem in the next section.

2.9   To Whom Should the Enterprise Be Sold?

As we mentioned, the previous section does not say "sell to the highest bidder." The Conrail example given earlier makes clear why this is non-sensical. Rather, it says, extract the highest possible sale price from the "best" bidder.[7] How then is the best bidder to be determined?

Once again, the fundamental equation (2.2) gives the starting point for an answer. Rank bidders according to their ΔW's, and focus on the highest.

Unfortunately, this often provides only a starting point for the selection because Z will remain subject to negotiation. If some bidders can be induced to raise their final bid (or adjust the terms of conditions of sale more favorably), then the rankings may change. Exactly how this process will work itself out depends on the bargaining or negotiating structure employed. However, (2.2) provides the basis for the iterative calculation. Further, as one step in the screening procedure, calculation of ΔW^* [equation (2.10)] allows identification of the bidders with the highest potential for striking the best deal for the country. Also, note that in the LDC context, having a plethora of qualified bidders should be considered a luxury for which some iterative indeterminacy is a small price to pay. Finally, note that the concept of ranking bidders by their ΔW's in order to choose among them is valid regardless of the relative magnitudes of λ_g and λ_p.

2.10   The Difference Principle

It is important to note that, in answering the basic questions, we have nowhere needed to know V_{sp} or V_{sg} individually but only their difference $(V_{sp} - V_{sg})$. This turns out to be immensely fortuitous, because otherwise this exercise would be of purely theoretical interest with no practical import whatsoever. Except under the most egregiously simplistic assumptions (e.g., the competitive equilibrium of chapter 4), the individual values are simply unknowable. We shall argue, however, that analytic tools are available that allow reasonable approximations to the difference. This point will be elaborated upon in concrete terms as we proceed. For the present note only that this *difference principle* simplifies our task considerably and constitutes our final basic concept.

2.11   Conclusion

This chapter has shown how the basic divestiture questions can all be answered if we can agree on two parameters (λ_g and λ_p) and can estimate one value (V_{pp}) and one difference in values ($V_{sp} - V_{sg}$). Accordingly, subsequent sections focus on methodologies for quantifying these values in increasingly complex environments.

3   Welfare Weights

3.1   Shadow Pricing

Privately relevant prices differ from publicly relevant prices, thereby adding considerable zest to cost-benefit games in general and to the divestiture game in particular. In most cases the differences are straightforward. If the world price of fertilizer is \$200, but the regulated internal price is \$100 (or \$400), and if at the margin the economy adjusts fertilizer supplies via imports or exports, then the privately relevant price is the domestic market price, the publicly relevant shadow price is the world market price, and 2.0 (or 0.5) is the shadow multiplier linking the two prices. More generally, if p_x is the market price of x, and λ_x is its shadow multiplier, then the shadow price is $\lambda_x p_x$.

Whereas the use of shadow multipliers for commodities is widely accepted, their application to such aggregate economic abstractions as investment and government revenue is less familiar outside the project evaluation and taxation literature. Because our analysis relies critically on such multipliers, in this chapter we summarize the essential features of this literature.

We begin with the framework of applied welfare economics and then consider both the theory and measurement of λ_g. We then briefly consider the composition of λ_p, which is not in the literature but which turns out to be largely a function of the shadow multiplier for investment (λ_i), which is a staple of the literature. We consider both the theory and measurement of λ_i. Finally, we provide order-of-magnitude estimates of our critical parameter, $(\lambda_g - \lambda_p)$.

3.2   The Basic Framework for Welfare Aggregation

All applied welfare economics faces the problem of specifying a social welfare function. We ask the questions, What is it that we are trying to achieve in our policy analysis? What objective can we use as our criterion for choosing between alternative policies? Unless we answer these questions, we cannot provide policy prescriptions.

One commonly accepted social welfare function is the *present discounted sum of society's consumption stream*, perhaps with allowance for differential weights for the consumption of different income classes. The main justification for this kind of welfare function is that individuals derive utility from consumption, so the consumption stream should be our focus. Although this idea is appealing theoretically, it is not very easy to implement in practical applications because it would require the construction of a general equilibrium model that calculates an entire future stream of consumption for every policy.

For practical applications, therefore, a partial equilibrium approach is often adopted. This sort of approach typically yields net benefits of three different types: consumption, profits, and government revenues. Although we are ultimately interested in measuring the consumption benefits, we cannot ignore the other categories of benefits because they serve as proxies for consumption benefits that are not directly captured in the model. For example, government revenues, when spent, may give rise to consumption of public goods and also future consumption based on government investments. Profits may also proxy for future consumption because of the private investment that they make possible. Thus we need to include these other categories of benefits in our measure of net welfare. The remaining question is, How should this aggregation be achieved?

To make the discussion more concrete, suppose we wish to evaluate the welfare effects of the imposition of an excise tax in a particular market. Figure 3.1 illustrates the pre- and posttax equilibria in the market. DD and SS represent the demand and and the supply curves, respectively. Prior to the imposition of the tax, the equilibrium quantity is Q_0 and the price is P_0. A per-unit tax is introduced, which shifts the supply curve up to $S'S'$. The tax-inclusive price rises to P_d, and the quantity traded in the market is Q_1. Sellers receive a price of only P_s per unit; the remainder of the tax-inclusive price is of course the tax revenue per unit.

We can identify three broad changes brought about by the imposition of the tax. First, consumers face an increase in the price, from P_0 to P_d. Second, sellers experience a decline in the price they receive, from P_0 to P_s. Third, government realizes tax revenue equal to the area $P_d A C P_s$.

How much worse off are consumers as a result of the price increase? This question is answered by asking, What would they have been willing to pay to avoid this price increase? This amount is known as the *equivalent*

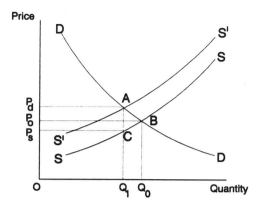

Figure 3.1
Effect of a commodity tax in a competitive market

variation of the price change. Under certain conditions, the equivalent variation can be approximated by the area P_dABP_0. This area is known as the *change in consumer surplus* and has a long history as the most common measure of consumer welfare change.[1] We also will use it as our measure. Thus the tax makes consumers worse off by the area P_dABP_0. We denote this change in consumer welfare by ΔC. Note that, because consumer welfare has declined, $\Delta C < 0$.

How about producers? Because they have experienced a decline in price, their profits will suffer. It can be shown that their profits (strictly, quasi-rents) will decline by an amount equal to the area P_0BCP_s. We denote this change in profits by $\Delta\Pi$. Again, because firms have suffered a fall in profits, $\Delta\Pi < 0$.

We have already identified the change in government revenue as given by the area P_dACP_s. We denote this change by ΔG. Because there has been an increase in revenue, $\Delta G > 0$.

We have identified three major effects of the tax: ΔC, $\Delta\Pi$, and ΔG. $\Delta\Pi$ is relevant to our welfare calculation, since profits form the basis for consumption by producers; also, profits have a bearing on investment, which results in future consumption increases. ΔG is important because when government uses its revenue for expenditure, it creates consumption benefits, either directly by providing public goods, for example, or indirectly through investments that result in future consumption benefits. Therefore, a natural measure of the welfare effects of the tax would be

$$\Delta W = \lambda_c\Delta C + \lambda_p\Delta\Pi + \lambda_g\Delta G, \tag{3.1}$$

where the λ terms are weights reflecting the relative contributions of each of the components to social welfare. In much of applied welfare economics, these weights are set equal to one, that is, each component is given the same weight.

Let us examine the implications of doing this. The change in welfare as a result of the tax is then simply

$$\Delta W = \Delta C + \Delta \Pi + \Delta G. \tag{3.2}$$

We see from the figure that ΔW then becomes a negative number, represented by the area ABC. This value is called the *excess burden* of the tax. If we were to adopt equation (3.2) as our measure of welfare change, the presence of this excess burden would mean that the tax was not justifiable, because it would result in a fall in welfare.

The fact that governments do impose taxes that create excess burdens indicates an inadequacy in this welfare concept. Indeed, the value to society of the government expenditures made possible by the tax must be greater than the cost as measured by $\Delta C + \Delta \Pi$. One way to capture this fact is to assign ΔG a weight greater than one. We call this weight λ_g the shadow price of government funds. If we assigned each of the components a different weight, we would get equation (3.1) as our measure of welfare change.[2]

As we mentioned in chapter 2, it is not necessary to provide three weights. Rather, one of the components can be taken as the numeraire, or yardstick against which the other components are valued. Two choices for numeraire appear in the cost-benefit literature. The UNIDO *Guidelines for Project Evaluation*[3] choose domestic consumption, whereas Squire and van der Tak use "public income," or government revenue, as the numeraire.[4] We follow the UNIDO approach, which agrees more closely with the standard approach in welfare economics. Squire and van der Tak themselves first calculate a value of public income relative to average consumption (the parameter they denote v) and then use this to normalize their calculations. Thus we set $\lambda_c = 1$, and our parameter λ_g becomes the same as Squire and van der Tak's v.

3.3 The Valuation of Public Income (λ_g)

3.3.1 Analytic Framework

We turn now to consider the magnitude of the parameter λ_g. Because consumption is our numeraire, λ_g measures the increase in social welfare measured in consumption units from an increase in government revenue of $1. For example, one might image that some external benefactor granted the government this dollar, and one could ask, What is the value to society of this grant? Obviously, the answer depends upon what the government does with the dollar. There are two broad categories of activities on which the government may "spend" the dollar it has received: it can reduce taxes and/or it can raise expenditures. Thus in order to find the value of λ_g, it is necessary to know something about the value of each of government's separate activities.

Suppose, for the sake of the discussion, that the government "spends" this dollar by reducing the tax rate on fuel enough to reduce its tax revenue by 30¢ and by increasing spending on education by 45¢ and on road construction by 25¢. Suppose λ_f, λ_e, and λ_r represent the marginal social value of reducing fuel taxes by $1, of increasing education expenditures by $1, and of increasing spending on road construction by $1, respectively. Then it can be shown (see the appendix for details) that the shadow price for government revenue will be

$$\lambda_g = 0.3\lambda_f + 0.45\lambda_e + 0.25\lambda_r.$$

Thus the shadow price of government funds is a weighted average of the shadow values of all of government's activities, with the weights being the share of each of those activities in the marginal dollar of government "spending."

As a practical matter, we are unlikely to know how the government plans to spend any revenue it receives as part of a divestiture. In fact, it is generally difficult to determine how money from one particular source is spent when spending is based on revenues from many different sources. For example, the government might announce that it will spend the proceeds from an enterprise sale on building a road from A to B. Can we therefore conclude that the relevant shadow value of the government's revenue is given by the value of the road? Not necessarily. If the road would have been built regardless of whether or not the particular enterprise had been sold, its value should not enter into the calculation. Rather, we need to determine which expenditures would not have been made or which taxes would have been higher in the absence of the enterprise sale. Obviously, this is a difficult job.

Thus, in practice, we need to make some assumptions about the marginal effects on taxation and spending patterns of a change in government revenue. Squire and van der Tak assume that any new or "uncommitted" funds will be spent on investment, on the theory that government capital spending is a residual category which rises and falls with the health of the government exchequer. But of course this assumption is arbitrary. Another assumption might be that the marginal changes will follow the government's *average* tax and expenditure pattern. This assumption would implicitly calculate the average value of government revenue and apply that at the margin. Any number of similar arbitrary assumptions could be made. This is obviously a serious problem, because the size of λ_g is important to the analysis, just as it is in the cost-benefit literature. We will not attempt here to estimate the size of this parameter, but we will discuss some of the extensive amount of theoretical and empirical work that has been done on this problem.

3.3.2 Theoretical Arguments

Let us consider first some of the theoretical arguments on the relative magnitude of λ_g. The conclusion from this discussion is that $\lambda_g > 1$. Let us examine why. The key point is that there are very few taxes that are not distorting. As we know from the theory of public finance and as was discussed earlier, taxes generally cause excess burdens; that is, they cause welfare losses that exceed the amount of tax revenue they collect.[5] Figure 3.1 showed the excess burden of a commodity tax. Commodity taxes create excess burdens because they distort consumption away from the efficient level. But other types of taxes also create excess burdens. For example, income taxes create excess burdens because they distort the choice between work and leisure. In particular, since leisure is untaxed, there is a tendency to work fewer hours because of income taxes. The so-called nondistorting lump-sum taxes that economists are so fond of are hard to find in reality.

There are a few taxes, however, that do not cause excess burdens. These are the taxes that are themselves welfare-improving, generally because they impose a price equal to the true marginal social cost of the activity in question. One example of such a tax is an effluent charge against environmental pollution. Such a tax reduces the level of an undesirable activity (pollution) and thereby collects revenue at the same time as it is improving social welfare. The optimal tariff of a large country on its export goods is another tax that may be welfare-improving. Here the distortionary effect of the tax is felt primarily by foreign buyers, whose welfare is not included in the domestic country's welfare function. However, it can be argued that the existence of such taxes does not create any problem for our analysis; they simply can be left out of consideration because it would be reasonable to suppose that if the government found itself with some extra revenue, it would certainly not "spend" this by reducing such welfare-improving taxes. Thus only those taxes that create excess burdens need be included in our calculations of λ_g. We see, therefore, that at least from the tax side of the picture there is strong reason to believe that λ_g is greater than one.

Let us consider now the value of government expenditures. Here it is difficult to create a theoretical argument for whether the value of an additional dollar of spending is greater or less than $1 of consumption. In fact, whether it is greater or less than one is an empirical matter. The benefits of government expenditures, however, are notoriously hard to measure. Expenditures on public goods, such as defense and police, and expenditures on activities that create strong positive externalities, such as transportation, communication, health, and even education are very difficult to value. Redistributive expenditures, by their very nature, are hard to evaluate in terms of some average level of consumption. We are forced, therefore, to consider a revealed preference type of argument. If government spends on such activities, it is revealing that it values such expenditures more highly than their cost. Obviously, such a statement is prone to criticism. Also, it clearly has greater validity in a democracy than in a dictatorship, to the extent that the spending patterns of a democratic government have the implicit approval of some sort of plurality of the population. The point remains that there is a sense in which government reveals that it values certain expenditures simply by undertaking them.

A fully optimizing government would select the levels of its activities optimally. If it did so, all the different shadow prices of taxing and spending activities would be equal to one another. To see this intuitively, consider the problem of a government that must select its different expenditure activity levels given that it has available to spend some fixed budget. It would be optimal for the government to select these levels in such a way that the marginal welfare contribution of the last dollar spent on each activity was the same. If this were not done, it would be welfare-improving for the government to reduce spending on an activity with a low marginal welfare contribution and to increase expenditure correspondingly on an activity with a high marginal welfare contribution. Similarly, it can be argued that government must set equal the marginal welfare cost of each revenue-raising activity; otherwise it could improve welfare while raising the same amount of revenue simply by increasing collections from one activity and reducing collections elsewhere. Finally, we may similarly argue that it must set the marginal welfare contribution of the expenditure activities equal to the marginal cost of the revenue-raising activities. In the ideal case, therefore, λ_g would simply be given by this common marginal valuation of government's various activities.[6] Clearly, in the case of an optimizing government, λ_g would be greater than unity. Suppose this optimal value of λ_g is 1.5. Then for a person to believe that λ_g is actually less than one would require a belief not only that government is not optimizing (a belief to which we would be sympathetic) but that the government's behavior is extremely suboptimal. The latter would be difficult to sustain in most cases.

3.3.3   Empirical Estimates

There are two broad classes of empirical evidence that shed light on the value of λ_g. Estimates have been made of the excess burden of various types of taxes, and there have been attempts to estimate the shadow price of uncommitted fiscal resources (Squire and van der Tak's v). All the empirical evidence that we have seen is in accord with the expectation that λ_g is greater than unity. We will review each type of evidence separately. Our review is not meant to be exhaustive, but it indicates the kinds of estimates that are available in the literature.

There have been a number of estimates of the shadow cost of taxes on labor income for the United States. Browning, using a partial equilibrium framework, calculated this cost to range between 1.09 and 1.16.[7] Rosen used explicit utility function estimates to calculate the same shadow price and came up with figures ranging between 1.014 and 1.14.[8] Browning later used a more complicated model than in his earlier work but retained a partial equilibrium approach and estimated the shadow cost to be in the

Table 3.1
Marginal excess burden from raising extra revenue from specific portions of the tax system

Uncompensated saving elasticity	0.0	0.4	0.0	0.4
Uncompensated labor supply elasticity	0.0	0.0	0.15	0.15
All taxes	0.170	0.206	0.274	0.332
Capital taxes at industry level	0.181	0.379	0.217	0.463
Labor taxes at industry level	0.121	0.112	0.234	0.230
Consumer sales taxes	0.256	0.251	0.384	0.388
Sales taxes on commodities other than alcohol, tobacco, and gasoline	0.035	0.026	0.119	0.115
Income taxes	0.163	0.179	0.282	0.314
Output taxes	0.147	0.163	0.248	0.279

Source: Ballard et al. 1985, table 4, p. 136.

region of 1.32 to 1.47, with a much wider range for less plausible parameter values.[9] Stuart adopted a general equilibrium framework, and his estimates were in the range 1.21 to 1.24.[10]

The most broad-based study of the welfare cost of taxation in the United States is the general equilibrium approach of Ballard, Shoven, and Whalley.[11] They used their model to estimate the welfare cost of each major tax category and of the tax system as a whole. As in all the other studies, the specific estimates were sensitive to the values of estimated parameters. Two parameters that are important in their model are the elasticities of saving and of labor supply. They presented their basic results for different values of these elasticities. Table 3.1 reproduces their table 4. Note that their numbers are of excess burden; to obtain our notion of shadow cost, we must add 1 to the chosen number in their table. Their summary result is that the implied shadow cost of government funds lies between 1.17 and 1.56.[12]

In summary, estimates of the welfare cost of raising tax revenue have ranged quite widely, from 1.01 to 1.56. The base case from Ballard et al. for all taxes lies somewhere in the middle of these estimates at 1.33 and may serve as a reasonable approximation for this parameter. However, these studies have been for the United States; other countries may have different experiences. Hansson and Stuart (for income taxes in Sweden) and Campbell (for commodity taxes in Canada) provide some evidence that the broad results for the United States may be generalized to other developed

Table 3.2
Estimates of the shadow price of government funds

Country	Source	Base value	Range
Colombia	Schohl (1979)	2.50	2.13–3.19
Côte d'Ivoire	Linn (1977)		1.76–2.50
Egypt	Page (1982)	1.20	0.92–4.74
Malaysia	Bruce (1976)	2.20	1.95–2.63
Morocco	Cleaver (1980)	3.65	
Pakistan	Squire et al. (1979)		1.20–1.25
Philippines	Bruce (1976)	3.48	2.96–4.09
Thailand	Bruce (1976)	2.19	1.35–2.01
Thailand	Ahmed (1983)	2.54	1.80–4.20
Turkey	Mashayekhi (1980)	3.37	2.25–24.3
9 Sahel countries*	Gray (1989)	2.34	

* The countries are Burkina Faso, Cape Verde, Chad, The Gambia, Guinea-Bissau, Mali, Mauritania, Niger, and Senegal.

countries.[13] And some evidence on the experience of less-developed countries is available through the estimates of the shadow price of government funds that the followers of Squire and van der Tak have calculated.

The results for some of the estimates of λ_g that have been made for LDCs are given in table 3.2. The lowest estimates here are for Egypt and Pakistan, at approximately 1.20. Most estimates are over 2, with several "best estimates" at over 3. We feel this evidence is overwhelmingly in favor of the assumption that our parameter λ_g is greater than unity, with a precise value to be determined for the particular country being considered. Perhaps more important is the question of the relative magnitudes of λ_g and λ_p, a question we consider in section 3.6.

3.4 The Valuation of Private Income (λ_p)

3.4.1 Analytic Framework

Just as a dollar of government revenue may be worth more or less than a dollar of private consumption, so also may a dollar of private after-tax profit vary. The value of a dollar used to purchase a public enterprise will depend on where that dollar comes from. A portion (Φ_i) will come at the expense of other private investment, a portion (Φ_g) will come at the expense of government, a portion (Φ_f) will come from foreign sources, and the balance will come from private consumption. That is, the social value of a dollar used to buy a public enterprise is

$$\lambda_p = \Phi_i \lambda_i + \Phi_g \lambda_g + \Phi_f \lambda_f + (1 - \Phi_i - \Phi_i - \Phi_f)$$

(where the last term is the share of private consumption valued at the numeraire value of 1).

The private income multiplier thus depends on the government income multiplier (discussed in the previous section), the private investment multiplier (to be discussed in section 3.5), and financing parameters (which will be discussed in the balance of this section). Most commonly, one might expect the bulk of this investment to come at the expense of other investment and therefore for λ_p to approach λ_i. However, this need not always be the case, and other possibilities need to be considered.

3.4.2 Public Financing

When might public financing of a portion of the purchase take place ($\Phi_g > 0$)? The most obvious and important case occurs when the government ultimately lends a portion of the purchase price. It is important to note, however, that this is by no means equivalent to the purchaser's borrowing from a public bank. If there is no additional injection of public funds, then the borrowing is at the expense of other private investment, and $\Phi_g = 0$.

A second category of public funding comes via the tax mechanism. Assume that shares are entirely purchased with corporate funds that would otherwise be distributed and taxed at the personal income tax rate t_p ($\Phi_g = t_p$). Or it is possible (although we know of no such cases) that purchasers of shares might be given explicit or implicit tax deductions.

Such cases are likely to be rare, however. Accordingly, unless there is strong evidence to the contrary, we will take the default value of Φ_g to be zero.

3.4.3   Consumption Financing

When might a portion of the purchase be at the expense of private consumption ($(1 - \Phi_i - \Phi_f - \Phi_g) > 0$)? The answer will depend in part on the impact of the purchase on the interest rate. We will generally follow the project evaluation literature in assuming that the divested firm is small relative to the capital market and that therefore the interest rate does not change. If this is not the case then it is possible to introduce elasticities of supply and demand for investable funds and thereby identify the shares of consumption and investment displaced. Note, however, that when the divestiture is large enough to move such a fundamental variable as the interest rate, the limitations of the extended partial equilibrium approach increase. We will focus on the small-project case but conclude with reference to the large-project context.

What if the purchase is by domestic consumers, for example, by sale to workers? Often, pension funds are forced to buy shares for this purpose. If the purchase is small relative to the capital market, then the interest rate will not change, there will be no net increase in savings, and the marginal investment will again be crowded out. If, on the other hand, workers are free to buy or not, then additional purchases here will mean only an inframarginal change in their portfolio, total domestic savings will not be changed, and once again investment alone will be displaced.

What if the employees are compelled to buy shares? To some extent they will compensate by reducing savings elsewhere, but they are also likely to adjust by reducing consumption. In the extreme case where they were previously saving nothing, then the entire increment will come from consumption, no investment will be crowded out, and $1 - \Phi_i - \Phi_g - \Phi_f = 1$. Nonetheless, in the small-project case, we would expect financing out of consumption commonly to be much closer to zero than to one. In the large-project case, the interest rate may rise, total investment will rise by less than the project increment, and a larger share of the project will be financed from consumption.

3.4.4   What Is Crowded Out?

If the bulk of the purchase generally comes at the expense of private investment, then it is critical to identify just which investment is crowded out. What if the bundle of entrepreneurship and capital used to purchase the public enterprise would otherwise have been used to build some very valuable high-yielding project? Alternatively, what if it would otherwise have been used for a project that was privately profitable but socially unproductive because it was built behind high tariff walls? Does this mean that λ_p is well above unity in the first case and well below in the second?

The answer is no in both cases, because what is ultimately crowded out is not the particular project foregone, but the marginal project. That is, there is a hierarchy of investment opportunities, and others will step up to take the better (privately) yielding projects, with the project ultimately crowded out at the lowest yielding margin.

3.4.5   Foreign Funding

Is a foreign capital inflow a net addition to domestic resources? For example, it has been argued in Pakistan that divestiture will attract repatriation of capital by expatriate nationals operating in the Gulf states. Does this not enhance the gains from divestiture? Again, the answer is, not necessarily. Total foreign inflows may ultimately be limited by foreign exchange constraints that restrict the ability to service debt and repatriate capital. Accordingly, even "untied" inflows can ultimately crowd out marginal inflows as the national macromanagers impose or strengthen exchange controls or as foreign sources become reluctant to lend. For reasons such as these, the standard project evaluation assumption is that foreign project funding ultimately crowds out domestic investment at the margin. To the extent that this is so, any foreign funding will be included in Φ_i.

There are, however, a number of quite realistic cases in which the standard assumption will not hold. One important case is that of open capital markets. Under the reasonable assumption that the project is small relative to international capital markets, the addition of the new investment opportunity will not alter the attractiveness of other domestic opportunities, and they will not be crowded out, but total inflows and investment will increase.

Note that this result can obtain even if the initial source of investment is domestic. With a small project and open capital markets, the government creates a new investment opportunity yielding more than the world rate of return. If a domestic investor takes advantage of this in the first round, the marginal project will not be crowded out but will be financed by an inflow of foreign funds, because it still lies above the preexisting world cutoff rate of return.

The possibility of open capital markets probably constitutes the strongest case for assuming a low value of λ_p. As a first approximation, foreign funds might be considered costless in the sense that $\lambda_f = 0$, because no domestic resources are diverted.[14] In the extreme case where the entire purchase is ultimately financed from abroad, and no other foreign inflows are thereby crowded out ($\Phi_f = 1$), there is no domestic diversion of funds ($\lambda_p = 0$).

However, it is commonly argued in the project evaluation literature that foreign exchange is *more* valuable than domestic consumption (for example, because distorted exchange markets mean that capital inflows allow additional imports that allow utilization of excess capacity and multiple expansion of output and consumption). In this case, λ_f would be *negative* because the foreign funding would not only not impose a burden on the economy but would confer a benefit. Note, however, that the circumstances that could create a negative λ_f would be incompatible with the most common case where Φ_f is nonzero (open capital markets), so that the possibility that $\Phi_f \lambda_f$ would be negative is unlikely.

Another special case is reverse capital flight. What if the buyer is a domestic entrepreneur who has previously informally exported resources abroad, who would otherwise never have brought the funds back, and where no other foreign inflows would thereby be crowded out? If the domain of our welfare function contains the buyer's consumption out of foreign income, then foreign sourcing is, as a first approximation, irrelevant, since what is foregone is other investment and Φ_f can be incorporated into Φ_i.[15] Analogous to National Income Accounting practice, this can be termed a *national* welfare function.[16] If on the other hand we select a *domestic* welfare function, then the buyer's foreign consumption is irrelevant, and we return to treating the inflow as part of Φ_f.

3.4.6   Bottom Line

In sum, λ_p varies with the way in which the project is ultimately financed (the Φ's) and the degree to which public funds and investment are worth more than consumption (the λ's). The former are project-specific variables, and the latter may generally be taken to be national parameters. Of particular importance is the degree of openness to international capital flows. At one extreme, with open capital markets, a case can be made that no domestic investment is crowded out at the margin, and λ_p will equal λ_f, which approaches zero. With closed capital markets on the other hand, the vast bulk of the purchase will come at the expense of other private investment, and λ_p will approach or equal λ_i. We now therefore consider the determinants of λ_i.

3.5   The Valuation of Investment (λ_i)

3.5.1   Capital Market Imperfections

Capital market imperfections drive a wedge between opportunities available to consumers and those available to investors. This generally makes a dollar of current investment more valuable than a dollar of current consumption ($\lambda_i > 1$). We first briefly explain why this occurs, then examine the various estimation methodologies for and empirical magnitudes of λ_i.

Assume that consumers are indifferent between a marginal dollar's worth of consumption today and $(1 + i)$ dollars' worth next year.[17] Then i is the consumption rate of interest used to discount future consumption into current consumption equivalents. Assume further that a marginal dollar invested by an enterprise today will yield a cash return of $(1 + r)$ next year. Then r is the marginal return to capital.

In a perfectly competitive economy, i has to equal r because the decisions of households and enterprises are linked by a frictionless capital market for investable funds. Consumers adjust between consumption and savings (future consumption) according to this common rate, and investors select all projects yielding more than this common rate. If r were to exceed i, then investment would yield greater satisfaction than current consumption, investment would rise (driving r down), and current consumption would fall (driving i up). This process would continue until balance was restored ($i = r$), with no further opportunities for gain by reallocating between present and future consumption.

Under these circumstances, a dollar of investment today will yield $(1+r)$ dollars next year. This is equivalent to $(1+r)/(1+i)$ of present consumption or the present value of a dollar of investment relative to a dollar of consumption. That is, for the simple two-period case,

$$\lambda_i = \frac{(1+r)}{(1+i)}.$$

But since i equals r, investment is neither more nor less worthwhile than consumption, and λ_i equals unity.

Now we introduce a single pair of market imperfections: public goods exist and lump-sum taxes are not feasible.[18] For example, we need a police force that must be paid for—at least in part—by a tax on income from capital. If the tax is at rate t, then i will exceed r by this amount. For example, if the sum of corporate and personal income taxes absorbs two-thirds of corporate profits, then an i of 5 percent would mean an r of 15 percent. Under these circumstances, \$1 of investment this year will yield \$1.15 next year, which is valued as equivalent to $1.15/1.05 = 1.095$ of consumption this year. Current investment is thus worth more than current consumption, and λ_i exceeds unity (in this case, 1.095) when capital markets are imperfect.

3.5.2   Standard Methodology

Additional complications associated with moving to the multiperiod case are dealt with in a surprisingly standardized fashion in the literature.[19] Assume that out of next year's return r, a fraction s (the marginal propensity to save) is reinvested, and the balance is consumed. Next year's return will then no longer be simply $(1+r)$ but

$$1 + (1-s)r + \lambda_i sr.$$

Assume further that the investment is a perpetuity yielding a stream of r per year forever but with principal never returned. Or, equivalently but more realistically, assume that any return of principal is immediately reinvested at the rate r. Then the designated flow (less one) will occur forever, and its net present value gives λ_i:

$$\lambda_i = \sum_{t=1}^{\infty} \frac{(1-s) + \lambda_i sr}{(1+i)^t}. \tag{3.3}$$

Using the standard formula for calculating the present value of an infinite series with a constant return and discount rate gives us

$$\lambda_i = \frac{(1 - s) + \lambda_i sr}{i}.$$

Solving algebraically for λ_i yields the standard formula

$$\lambda_i = \frac{(1 - s)r}{i - sr}. \tag{3.4}$$

3.5.3 Alternative Methodologies

More recently, two modifications of the standard method have been proposed that incorporate alternative assumptions about reinvestment.[20] Bradford[21] suggests using

$$\lambda_i = \frac{(1 - s_1)\dfrac{(1 + r)}{(1 + i)}}{1 - s_1\dfrac{(1 + r)}{(1 + i)}}.$$

This formula follows from the assumption that the entire amount $(1 + r)$ is returned each year (not just r, as in the standard formulation), of which a fraction s_1 is reinvested and $(1 - s_1)$ is consumed. This is fine, so long as it is kept in mind that s_1 is the marginal propensity to consume out of liquid funds, including both a return *of* principal and a return *to* principal. This is quite distinct from the usual s that is the marginal propensity to consume out of income and does not apply to a simple conversion of wealth from one form to another. Since people presumably consume little or nothing extra when wealth is simply converted from an illiquid to a liquid form, s_1 will be far higher than s. The danger comes from forgetting this distinction and plugging a conventional magnitude for s into Bradford's formula. For example, Bradford himself illustrates his method using values of s in the range of 0.10 to 0.30. This amounts to assuming that if we buy a $100 time deposit at 10 percent this year, our consumption will increase by between $77 and $99 next year, whereas conventional wisdom would put the increment at $7 to $9. With such a huge leakage into consumption after only one year, Bradford naturally gets extremely low values for λ_i. To avoid such misunderstandings, we prefer to stay with the standard formulation.

Lind begins with Bradford's analysis and makes two modifications.[22] The first is the one just given and brings him implicitly to the standard formula. The second begins from the realistic observation that investments typically are illiquid and, in the extreme case, might yield no cash flow whatsoever until N years after the project begins. In the meantime, all the principal and interest would be compounded internally with no leakage into consumption until year N. This naturally would lead to a considerably higher value for λ_i as compared with the standard formula. For example, if $r = 0.10$, $i = 0.02$, and $s = 0.20$, then λ_i equals 1.10 for Bradford, 2.67 under the standard formula, but 3.04 if there is no cash flow until year 15.

Lind himself does not go so far as to propose a single payout; instead he assumes that each project generates an annuity (A) with equal payments of principal (depreciation) plus return over the project's life. The depreciation (D) is entirely reinvested, whereas the return is reinvested at rate s, together generating additional annuities of duration N, and so forth. He concludes that the present value of this stream yields

$$v = Ax(1 - z)\frac{1}{1 - Axz},$$

where

$$A = \frac{r}{1 - (1 + r)^{-N}},$$

$$z = \frac{D + (A - D)s}{A},$$

$$D = \frac{1}{N} \qquad \text{(for straight-line depreciation case)},$$

$x =$ annuity present value operator.[23]

Compared with the standard model, this expression generally yields somewhat higher values of v over a conventional range of parameters. As can be seen from table 3.3 these differences are generally of moderate magnitude (5 percent to 25 percent) until one gets to the extreme values in the lower right-hand corner.

How should this procedure be evaluated? First, note that it is a step toward a realistic cash flow. Second, note that further steps are possible, because most projects would have a few years' lag before throwing off any cash flow but then would jump to a very high rate (via some form of accelerated depreciation) before tailing off. Some such adjustments would move v values back toward the standard formulation. In many cases the differences are not that great in the first place, because computational costs are significant and because the standard formula is much simpler to interpret, so in the balance of our exposition we will continue to use the

Table 3.3
Comparative values of shadow multiplier for investment (for all $i = 0.05$; $N = 15$)

Marg. prop. save	Marginal return on investment						
	0.00	0.05	0.10	0.15	0.20	0.25	0.30
Bradford formula							
0.00	0.95	1.00	1.05	1.10	1.14	1.19	1.24
0.05	0.95	1.00	1.05	1.10	1.15	1.20	1.25
0.10	0.95	1.00	1.05	1.11	1.16	1.22	1.27
0.15	0.94	1.00	1.06	1.11	1.17	1.23	1.29
0.20	0.94	1.00	1.06	1.12	1.19	1.25	1.32
0.25	0.94	1.00	1.06	1.13	1.20	1.27	1.34
0.30	0.93	1.00	1.07	1.14	1.22	1.30	1.38
Standard formula							
0.00	0.00	1.00	2.00	3.00	4.00	5.00	6.00
0.05	0.00	1.00	2.11	3.35	4.75	6.33	8.14
0.10	0.00	1.00	2.25	3.86	6.00	9.00	13.50
0.15	0.00	1.00	2.43	4.64	8.50	17.00	51.00
0.20	0.00	1.00	2.67	6.00	16.00	ERR	−24.00
0.25	0.00	1.00	3.00	9.00	ERR	−15.00	−9.00
0.30	0.00	1.00	3.50	21.00	−14.00	−7.00	−5.30
Lind formula							
0.00	ERR	1.00	2.18	3.51	4.96	6.48	8.06
0.05	ERR	1.00	2.32	4.05	6.26	9.11	12.80
0.10	ERR	1.00	2.51	4.88	8.86	16.60	37.40
0.15	ERR	1.00	2.76	6.32	16.40	202.00	−32.00
0.20	ERR	1.00	3.10	9.48	506.00	−17.00	−10.00
0.25	ERR	1.00	3.60	21.80	−15.00	−7.80	−5.90
0.30	ERR	1.00	4.43	−44.00	−7.10	−4.80	−3.90

standard formula as a reasonable economy-wide average. In many specific practical instances, however, some variant of the Lind modification might prove superior.

Given a theoretical structure, the next problem is to insert some numbers. At first glance, the problem may appear daunting. A glance at table 3.3 shows that for apparently reasonable values of the parameters, λ_i can vary from 1.00 to infinity, and for lower values of i, the value of λ_i explodes even more quickly. Much of this ambiguity is illusory, however, because some ranges of values are ruled out by theory and others by empirical evidence. We treat these deletions sequentially.

3.5.4   Extension: Taxes

The standard formulation cries out for a theoretical modification. It is internally inconsistent in that whereas taxes are the principal reason that λ_i differs from unity, they are ignored when we actually calculate λ_i. This is easily remedied by modifying the numerator of equation (3.3). Savings and reinvestment are now out of after-tax income, whereas the taxed share is valued at λ_g. If we let t represent the total corporate and personal tax rate on income from capital, the annual flows become

$$(1 - t)(1 - s)r + \lambda_i(1 - t)sr + \lambda_g tr.$$

The associated multiplier becomes

$$\lambda_i = \frac{(1 - s)(1 - t)r + \lambda_g tr}{i - (1 - t)sr}.$$

However, since taxes are the only relevant distortion,

$$i = (1 - t)r.$$

If we substitute and simplify, the multiplier then reduces to

$$\lambda_i = 1 + \lambda_g \frac{t}{(1 - t)} \frac{1}{(1 - s)}. \tag{3.5}$$

This formulation makes it clear that marginal investment will be worth more than consumption ($\lambda_i > 1$) as long as taxes on income from capital exist.[24] Further, the magnitude of λ_i will be greater: the larger the distorting tax $[t/(1 - t)]$, the less the leakage into consumption $[1/(1 - s)]$ and the more valuable the use to which the government puts the collected tax dollar $[\lambda_g]$. We examine what this equation indicates for empirical magnitudes in the next section.

3.6 Synthesis: Comparison of λ_g and λ_p

3.6.1 Implications of the Previous Discussion

In the previous sections we have argued that both λ_g and λ_p are greater than unity, with values of between 2 and 3 emerging as reasonable parameters. This suggests the importance of allowing for the presence of both these parameters, something that is not always done in cost-benefit analysis. Obviously we cannot be more specific about their respective values without reference to a particular country. However, for some of our analysis, the *relative* magnitude makes a significant difference; that is, it is important to know whether λ_g is greater or less than λ_p.

Here, neither theory nor informed empiricism suggests an unambiguous answer. It appears that the comparison between the parameters can indeed go either way. We examine several different approaches to the analysis in turn.

First, let us look at the implications of equation (3.5). If we assume that all the private funds for the divestiture come at the expense of investment, λ_p will be equal to λ_i. Thus equation (3.5) might shed some light on the relative values of λ_g and λ_p. To get a sense for what the relative values of λ_g and λ_p might be, we have constructed table 3.4. For two different values of s, the table shows values of λ_p as a function of values of t and λ_g. We can see from the table that $\lambda_g > \lambda_p$ for low values of t and high values of λ_g, that is, for cells in the top right-hand corner of each panel of the table. The inequality is reversed in the bottom left-hand corner.

Table 3.4 indicates that whether λ_g is greater or smaller than λ_p depends upon the tax rate t. What then is a reasonable estimate of t? A common argument runs as follows: the personal tax rate is 30 percent, the corporate rate is 30 to 40 percent, and the two together put t well above 50 percent. In our view, this is an exaggeration, and the effective rate is considerably lower. In the first place, a considerable portion of capital is provided in the form of debt, and this is taxed only once.

Second, much of the debt is held by pension funds and retirement plans and is, therefore, effectively taxed at well below even the personal tax rate. Third, returns to equity are typically favored by special treatment of capital gains and favorable depreciation rules. Fourth, in many countries, a considerable portion of economic activity (although a smaller share of investment) occurs in either the informal or black sectors of the economy and hence is untaxed. Fifth, many countries subsidize investment via special privileges (e.g., tax holidays) or by lending at less than the market rate,

Table 3.4
Values of λ_p $(= \lambda_i)$

$s = 0.2$

λ_g						
t	1.00	1.25	1.50	2.00	2.50	3.00
0.1	1.14	1.17	1.21	1.28	1.35	1.42
0.2	1.31	1.39	1.47	1.63	1.78	1.94
0.3	1.54	1.67	1.80	2.07	2.34	2.61
0.4	1.83	2.04	2.25	2.67	3.08	3.50
0.5	2.25	2.56	2.88	3.50	4.13	4.75

$s = 0.3$

λ_g						
t	1.00	1.25	1.50	2.00	2.50	3.00
0.1	1.16	1.20	1.24	1.32	1.40	1.48
0.2	1.36	1.45	1.54	1.71	1.89	2.07
0.3	1.61	1.77	1.92	2.22	2.53	2.84
0.4	1.95	2.19	2.43	2.90	3.38	3.86
0.5	2.42	2.79	3.14	3.86	4.57	5.29

thereby creating an effective negative tax rate on a portion of investment. On the other hand, all these circumstances that create lower effective rates need to be set against the disadvantageous impact of inflation. Exactly how this comes out is highly country- and time-specific, but for the United States, Stiglitz concludes that the corporate tax itself applies in effect only to *excess* profits.[25] If so, then t is well below 50 percent. In most other countries some combination of favorable treatment of income from capital, higher debt-equity ratios, and tax avoidance is likely to keep t even lower. From table 3.4 we see that λ_p tends always to be greater than λ_g for high values of t. Thus lower effective values of t look more promising for the outcome $\lambda_g > \lambda_p$.

Note that this table takes the values of λ_g as exogenously given. We could examine the implications of certain rules of public investment decisions on the value of λ_g. We begin by noting that, symmetric to equation (3.4), we may write a formula for λ_g as follows:

$$\lambda_g = \frac{(1 - s_g)r_g}{i - s_g r_g}. \tag{3.6}$$

What is an appropriate value for r_g (rate of return on government projects)? A long-standing debate in the project evaluation literature is whether government should discount its projects at i or at r_p (rate of return on private projects). In the former case, $r_g = i$; in the latter, $r_g = r_p$. Stiglitz argues that the correct answer depends upon just which market distortions are being considered.[26] And although the correct discount rate can lie outside the boundaries set by i and r, Stiglitz argues that for the most common distortions (including taxation of capital returns), it lies within. This would then imply that

$i < r_g < r_p.$

If so, then at the lower bound, $\lambda_g = 1$, because the rate of return on investment is the same as the rate at which future income is discounted; therefore, a dollar of savings and investment yields a future return equal to a dollar of consumption today. At the upper bound, equation (3.5) reduces to a function of s_g and t, so that

$$1 < \lambda_g < \frac{(1 - s_g)}{(1 - t - s_g)}. \tag{3.7}$$

Let ϕ be the (0 to 1) parameter reflecting where r_g fits on the scale between i and r_p. Then

$$\lambda_g = (1 - \phi) + \phi \frac{(1 - s_g)}{(1 - t - s_g)}, \tag{3.8}$$

$$\lambda_p = 1 + \left[(1 - \phi) + \phi \frac{(1 - s_g)}{(1 - t - s_g)} \right] \frac{t}{(1 - t)(1 - s_p)}. \tag{3.9}$$

The last two expressions give λ_g and λ_p in terms of only the tax and savings rates and the government investment decision parameter. We can therefore proceed to a sensitivity analysis of empirical magnitudes. Table 3.5 displays the results. It provides further indication that λ_g and λ_p are of similar magnitude. Here, however, for all realistic values of t, we find $\lambda_p > \lambda_g$. Note that this is true when the savings rates in the two sectors are assumed to be the same. Whether or not this is true is of course an empirical matter.

3.6.2 The Optimizing Government

As an alternative approach to examining the relative magnitudes of λ_g and λ_p, consider the behavior of an optimizing government. The simple partial equilibrium approach to this analysis would be to examine the optimal

Table 3.5
Multipliers of private and public income: sensitivity analysis

Private multipliers (λ_p)

	s = 0.2					s = 0.3				
	φ					φ				
t	0.00	0.25	0.50	0.75	1.00	0.00	0.25	0.50	0.75	1.00
0.1	1.14	1.14	1.15	1.15	1.16	1.16	1.17	1.17	1.18	1.19
0.2	1.31	1.34	1.36	1.39	1.42	1.36	1.39	1.43	1.46	1.50
0.3	1.54	1.62	1.70	1.78	1.86	1.61	1.73	1.84	1.96	2.07
0.4	1.83	2.04	2.25	2.46	2.67	1.95	2.27	2.59	2.90	3.22
0.5	2.25	2.77	3.29	3.81	4.33	2.43	3.32	4.21	5.11	6.00
0.6	2.88	4.28	5.69	7.09	8.50	3.14	6.36	9.57	12.79	16.00
0.7	3.92	9.02	14.12	19.23	24.33	4.33	******	******	******	******
0.8	6.00	******	******	******	******	6.71	−4.71	******	******	******
0.9	12.25	******	******	******	******	13.86	−0.61	******	******	******
1.0	ERR	ERR	ERR	ERR	ERR	ERR	ERR	ERR	ERR	ERR

Table 3.5 (*continued*)

Public multiplies (λ_g)

0.1	1.00	1.04	1.07	1.11	1.14	1.00	1.04	1.08	1.13	1.17
0.2	1.00	1.08	1.17	1.25	1.33	1.00	1.10	1.20	1.30	1.40
0.3	1.00	1.15	1.30	1.45	1.60	1.00	1.19	1.38	1.56	1.75
0.4	1.00	1.25	1.50	1.75	2.00	1.00	1.33	1.67	2.00	2.33
0.5	1.00	1.42	1.83	2.25	2.67	1.00	1.63	2.25	2.88	3.50
0.6	1.00	1.75	2.50	3.25	4.00	1.00	2.50	4.00	5.50	7.00
0.7	1.00	2.75	4.50	6.25	8.00	1.00	**********	**********	**********	**********
0.8	1.00	**********	**********	**********	**********	1.00	−1.00	−3.00	5.00	−7.00
0.9	1.00	−1.25	−3.50	−5.75	−8.00	1.00	−0.13	−1.25	−2.38	−3.50
1.0	1.00	−0.25	−1.50	−2.75	−4.00	1.00	0.17	−0.67	−1.50	−2.33

Public less private multipliers ($\lambda_g - \lambda_p$)

0.1	−0.14	−0.11	−0.08	−0.05	−0.02	−0.16	−0.12	−0.09	−0.05	−0.02
0.2	−0.31	−0.26	−0.20	−0.14	−0.08	−0.36	−0.29	−0.23	−0.16	−0.10
0.3	−0.54	−0.47	−0.40	−0.33	−0.26	−0.61	−0.54	−0.47	−0.39	−0.32
0.4	−0.83	−0.79	−0.75	−0.71	−0.67	−0.95	−0.94	−0.92	−0.90	−0.89
0.5	−1.25	−1.35	−1.46	−1.56	−1.67	−1.43	−1.70	−1.96	−2.23	−2.50
0.6	−1.88	−2.53	−3.19	−3.84	−4.50	−2.14	−3.86	−5.57	−7.29	−9.00
0.7	−2.92	−6.27	−9.62	−13	−16	−3.33	**********	**********	**********	**********
0.8	−5.00	**********	**********	**********	**********	−5.71	3.71	13.14	22.57	32.00
0.9	−11.3	11.81	34.88	57.94	81.00	−12.9	0.48	13.82	27.16	40.50
1.0	ERR	ERR	ERR	ERR	ERR	ERR	ERR	ERR	ERR	ERR

levels of commodity taxes. In the standard market model, represented by figure 3.1, a tax drives a wedge between the demand price (P_d) and the supply price (P_s). Tax revenue is given by the area $P_d ACP_s$, the loss in consumer surplus by the area $P_d ABP_0$, and the loss in producer surplus or profit by $P_0 BCP_s$. Using our usual notation of equation (3.3), we know that the change in welfare as a result of the tax is given by

$$\Delta W = \Delta C + \lambda_p \Delta \Pi + \lambda_g \Delta G. \tag{3.10}$$

Obviously, each of the components of ΔW is a function of the (commodity) tax rate t. The optimum tax rate would be the one that maximized ΔW. Our strategy here will be to write ΔC, $\Delta \Pi$, and ΔG in terms of t, to find the optimal t, and then to study the implications of this for the relative values of λ_p and λ_g.

The analysis of the effect of a tax on a commodity market is discussed in most microeconomics textbooks. If P_0 and Q_0 represent the price and quantity, respectively, that would prevail in the absence of any tax, the new demand price, supply price, and quantity are given by

$$P_d = P_0(1 + t)(\varepsilon_s / \varepsilon_s + \varepsilon_d), \tag{3.11}$$

$$P_s = P_0(1 + t) - \varepsilon_d / (\varepsilon_s + \varepsilon_d), \tag{3.12}$$

$$Q_1 = Q_0(1 + t) - \varepsilon_d \varepsilon_s / (\varepsilon_s + \varepsilon_d), \tag{3.13}$$

where ε_s and ε_d are the elasticities of supply and demand in the market, respectively. Without loss of generality, the base price and quantity, P_0 and Q_0, can be normalized to unity.

Equations (3.11)–(3.13) can then be used to derive expressions for ΔC, $\Delta \Pi$, and ΔG. They may be written as follows:

$$\Delta C \simeq -\left(\frac{\varepsilon_s}{\varepsilon_s + \varepsilon_d}\right) t$$

$$\Delta \Pi \simeq -\left(\frac{\varepsilon_d}{\varepsilon_s + \varepsilon_d}\right) t,$$

$$\Delta G = \left\{1 - \left[\frac{\varepsilon_d(1 + \varepsilon_s)}{\varepsilon_s + \varepsilon_d}\right] t\right\} t.$$

Thus from (3.10) we have

$$\Delta W = -\left(\frac{\varepsilon_s}{\varepsilon_s + \varepsilon_d}\right) t - \lambda_p \left(\frac{\varepsilon_d}{\varepsilon_s + \varepsilon_d}\right) t + \lambda_g \left\{1 - \left[\frac{\varepsilon_d(1 + \varepsilon_s)}{\varepsilon_s + \varepsilon_d}\right] t\right\} t.$$

Maximizing ΔW with respect to the tax rate t yields the following expression for the optimal tax rate, t^*:

$$t^* = \frac{(\lambda_g - 1)\varepsilon_s + (\lambda_g - \lambda_p)\varepsilon_d}{2\lambda_g \varepsilon_d (1 + \varepsilon_s)}. \tag{3.14}$$

Note that if $\lambda_g = \lambda_p = 1$, this expression reduces to $t^* = 0$, which is the standard neoclassical result that taxes create excess burdens, and should optimally be set to zero.

If we do observe taxes in practice, then we may infer that $t^* > 0$, and this means that the numerator in (3.14) is positive. Thus

$$(\lambda_g - 1)\varepsilon_s + (\lambda_g - \lambda_p)\varepsilon_d > 0,$$

or simplifying,

$$\lambda_g > \left(\frac{\varepsilon_d}{\varepsilon_s + \varepsilon_d}\right)\lambda_p + \frac{\varepsilon_s}{\varepsilon_s + \varepsilon_d}. \tag{3.15}$$

Certainly condition (3.15) would be satisfied if $\lambda_g > \lambda_p$; however, it is also consistent with situations where $\lambda_g < \lambda_p$, where, for example, ε_d is small relative to ε_s. Thus this expression suggests that if we observe commodity taxation, either $\lambda_g > \lambda_p$ or there is an upper bound on λ_p. Equation (3.15) can also be rewritten as

$$\lambda_p < \left(\frac{\varepsilon_s + \varepsilon_d}{\varepsilon_d}\right)\lambda_g - \frac{\varepsilon_s}{\varepsilon_d}. \tag{3.16}$$

We know of no studies that would help us assign specific numerical values to equation (3.16), but if we consider a base case to be one where $\varepsilon_d = \varepsilon_s = 1$, (3.16) implies that

$$\lambda_p < 2\lambda_g - 1.$$

So if $\lambda_g = 2$, we must have $\lambda_p < 3$, and if $\lambda_g = 3$, we must have $\lambda_p < 5$. Note that these are merely upper bounds; it could well be that $\lambda_p < \lambda_g$.

A second approach to the behavior of an optimizing government would be to analyze the imposition of a tax on capital income, the tax that distorts investment and hence "creates" the problem of $\lambda_p > 1$. Could it be that observing such a tax implies something about the relative magnitudes of λ_p and λ_g? We shall show a simple model that suggests that optimality requires that $\lambda_g > \lambda_p$.

The model is highly simplified to allow us to capture the essential points. Consider equilibrium in the capital market. The demand for capital is a function of the net rental price of capital r. The supply price of capital is i. For simplicity, we assume that i is exogenously given, a function of tastes, monetary policy, and international capital flows. There is a wedge between r and i because of capital taxes. If t is the effective corporate tax rate, then

$$r(1 - t) = i$$

is the condition equilibrating supply and demand in the capital market.

If ε_k represents the elasticity of demand for capital, the equilibrium price and quantity in this market can therefore be characterized by the equations

$$r = \frac{i}{1 - t}$$

$$K = K_0(1 - t)^{\varepsilon_k},$$

where K_0 represents the equilibrium quantity of capital in the absence of taxes, which can be normalized to unity without loss of generality.

As before, we can show that the presence of the tax causes a loss in profits,

$$\Delta\Pi = \frac{i}{(\varepsilon_k - 1)}[(1 - t)^{\varepsilon_k - 1} - 1],$$

and a gain in tax revenue,

$$\Delta G = it(1 - t)^{\varepsilon_k - 1}.$$

Thus the change in welfare due to the tax is

$$\Delta W = \lambda_g it(1 - t)^{\varepsilon_k - 1} + \lambda_p \frac{i}{(\varepsilon_k - 1)}[(1 - t)^{\varepsilon_k - 1} - 1].$$

Optimizing with respect to t yields

$$\frac{\partial \Delta W}{\partial t} = \lambda_g i(1 - t)^{\varepsilon_k} - \lambda_p i(1 - t)^{\varepsilon_k - 2} = 0,$$

which simplifies to

$$\lambda_g(1 - t)^2 = \lambda_p. \tag{3.17}$$

Equation (3.17) shows that as long as $t > 0$, $\lambda_g > \lambda_p$.

The intuitive reason for this is simple, as can be seen in figure 3.2. Taxing capital lowers profits by the area $rABi$, whereas it raises revenue by $rACi$, a smaller area. More important, raising the tax would lower profits by an

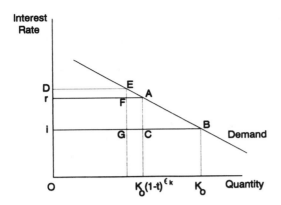

Figure 3.2
The optimal capital tax

area such as $DEAr$ while raising tax revenue by $DEFr - ACGF$, which is obviously smaller. Since on the margin (that is, at the optimal tax), the net gain in welfare is zero, it must be true that the weight attached to the smaller area (λ_g) must be bigger than the weight attached to the bigger area (λ_p).

We have therefore shown that if capital taxation is desirable, it must be the case that $\lambda_g > \lambda_p$. Further, this is also consistent with optimal commodity taxation.

3.6.3   Conclusion

On the whole, this section is rather inconclusive. We have argued that we need to allow in our calculations for the possibility that private profits and government funds are worth more to society, dollar for dollar, than consumption. Further, we have argued that the values of λ_g and λ_p are likely to be quite close to one another. However, we are unable to make any definitive statement about which of these two parameters is in fact larger. This is actually an empirical question that must be settled for specific countries by careful empirical analysis. We believe that there are likely to be cases where $\lambda_g > \lambda_p$ and also cases where the opposite is true.

We conclude the chapter by pointing out again one rather surprising conclusion that would arise if $\lambda_p > \lambda_g$. As we mentioned in chapter 2, this inequality would imply that in a divestiture, government would typically be willing to pay arbitrarily large amounts to the private sector to take over public enterprises. Not only would we be unable to place a floor on what would be an acceptable price for the enterprise, a *ceiling* would, in fact, emerge on the acceptable price. The fact that we do not observe such phenomena in reality suggests that either $\lambda_g > \lambda_p$ or that political forces exist that behave as if this last inequality were true. On balance, therefore, it seems prudent to take as our base case the one where $\lambda_g > \lambda_p$.

Appendix: Development of the Formula for λ_g

The basic approach adopted here is a variant of a model presented by Bell and Devarajan.[27] Suppose there are X commodities, whose availability levels in the economy can be represented by a vector $\mathbf{x}$. In addition, suppose that the government undertakes A different expenditure activities, whose levels are represented by a vector $\mathbf{a}$, and raises revenues to finance these activities using B different revenue-raising activities, whose levels will be captured in a vector $\mathbf{b}$. Now suppose there exists a social welfare function

$$W = W(\mathbf{x}, \mathbf{a}, \mathbf{b}),$$

where we would expect that W_x, $W_a > 0$ and $W_b < 0$. The effects of any new government policy, such as a divestiture, might be summarized by changes in the vectors $\mathbf{x}$, $\mathbf{a}$, and $\mathbf{b}$, that is, by a vector $[dx, da, db]$. Then, by totally differentiating the welfare function, we may write the net welfare effect of the policy as

$$dW = \sum_{i=1}^{X} W_{x_i} dx_i + \sum_{j=1}^{A} W_{a_j} da_j + \sum_{k=1}^{B} W_{b_k} db_k. \tag{3.18}$$

The partial derivatives W_{x_i}, W_{a_j}, and W_{b_k} are thus the *shadow prices* of commodities and government's expenditure and revenue-raising activities, respectively. If we use the symbol * to represent a shadow value, we could write the net benefit of the policy as

$$dW = \sum_{i=1}^{X} p_i^* dx_i + \sum_{j=1}^{A} p_j^* da_j + \sum_{k=1}^{B} p_k^* db_k. \tag{3.19}$$

Note that as a consequence of the assumption that revenue-raising activities cause a *fall* in social welfare, the shadow prices of these activities, p_k^*, would be expected to be negative. Equation (3.19) has the characteristics of a usual net-benefit calculation, where the net benefit of a policy or project is expressed as the weighted sum of all the changes the policy induces, the weights being the shadow prices. However, while we are used to identifying the shadow prices of goods as being distinct from one another, traditional approaches do not generally identify separately the government's various activities. Thus we are more liable to see a given policy identified by a vector such as $[dx, dG]$ rather than $[dx, da, db]$, where dG represents the net change in government's fiscal position. The net benefit of the project would then be expressed as

$$dW = \sum_{i=1}^{X} p_i^* \, dx_i + p_g^* \, dG. \tag{3.20}$$

In terms of the literature on cost-benefit analysis, dG represents the net change in investable funds in the hands of the government, or what Squire and van der Tak call simply *public income*. Correspondingly, p_g^* represents the shadow price of government revenue. This is the parameter we are calling λ_g.

Let us turn to a discussion of what precisely is λ_g. Let us represent by p_j and p_k the prices of the government's expenditure and revenue-raising activities. Then the policy's fiscal effect on the government may be written as

$$dG = -\sum_{j=1}^{A} p_j \, da_j + \sum_{k=1}^{B} p_k \, db_k. \tag{3.21}$$

Here the expenditure activities are preceded by a negative sign, indicating that they cause a decline in government's revenue position. In what follows we assume for convenience without any loss of generality that the units in which the government's activities a_j and b_k are measured are normalized so that the respective prices are unity. Thus equation (3.21) becomes

$$dG = -\sum_{j=1}^{A} da_j + \sum_{k=1}^{B} db_k. \tag{3.22}$$

Now from (3.19) and (3.20) and using the symbol λ_g for p_g^*, we have

$$\lambda_g \, dG = \sum_{j=1}^{A} p_j^* \, da_j + \sum_{k=1}^{B} p_k^* \, db_k. \tag{3.23}$$

Thus

$$\lambda_g = \sum_{j=1}^{A} p_j^* \frac{da_j}{dG} + \sum_{k=1}^{B} p_k^* \frac{db_k}{dG}. \tag{3.24}$$

In other words, the shadow price of government revenue is a weighted average of the shadow prices of all the government's expenditure and revenue-raising activities, with weights equal to the share of each activity's contribution to the net fiscal effect of the policy. This is the equation underlying the example in the text.

We note here a few points about equation (3.24). First, it may be useful to remember that we would expect the shadow prices of the revenue-raising activities, p_k^*, to be negative, because an increase in any such activity is likely to cause a fall in social welfare. Second, note that for the case of a fully optimizing government that chooses the levels of all its expenditure and revenue-raising activities in order to maximize social welfare, it will be true that the absolute values of all the shadow prices will be equal. In other words,

$$p_j^* = -p_k^* \qquad \text{for all } j \text{ and } k.$$

In this case the weights in equation (3.24) will no longer be important, and λ_g will simply be equal to the common value for all the individual shadow prices. Third, a special case of this last statement is that if all the p_j^* and p_k^* are equal to unity, then $\lambda_g = 1$ also. Finally, the formula is meant to use as weights the proportions of each revenue-raising and expenditure activity in the *marginal* dollar of government revenue. Thus if the divestiture proceeds are earmarked for specific purposes that would not be undertaken in the absence of divestiture, it is the shadow value of these announced uses of the funds that should be used in the calculation.

4

Competitive Equilibrium: No Sale

In this chapter we identify the various values of the firm in the simplest possible environment of stable competitive equilibrium; that is, we assume private operation is identical to public operation, all prices reflect social scarcity, the world does not change, and so forth (for details, see table 4.1). This is not a question of direct practical import, but it is nonetheless critical, because if there is no agreement on values in the simplest case, then there is little hope of agreement on more relevant values.

We first establish the general result at the theoretical level (section 4.1). This is a relatively easy task under the simple assumptions used here. The bulk of the section however, is devoted to the much more difficult task of converting generic α's and β's into real numbers for real companies in real countries.

We begin the empirical discussion by considering an actual (though disguised) public enterprise case as described by its profit and loss statement and balance sheet (see tables 4.2 and 4.3 in section 4.3). Under the simplifying assumptions of table 4.1, we then ask two bottom-line questions. First, as a private buyer, what is the *maximum* you would be willing to pay (Z_p) for the enterprise? Second, as the government minister in charge of selling the enterprise, what is the *minimum* you would be willing to accept (Z_g)? If you agree that the answers are

$$Z_g = Z_p = 100,$$

because

$$V_{ppa} = V_{ppc} = 100,$$

$$V_{sg} = 14048, \text{ and}$$

$$V_{sp} = 14018,$$

then please proceed directly to chapter 5. Otherwise, we invite you to consider the process that generated these numbers.

Table 4.1
Assumptions for corporation A

---

1. Conceptual simplifications (to be relaxed in later chapters)

A. Private operation next year will be identical to public operation this year. (chapter 5)

B. All prices correctly reflect social scarcity and do not change over time. (chapter 6)

C. Taxes are neutral (identical rates across income classes—interest, dividends, capital gains, wages, etc.—across individuals, across companies, for both positive and negative income, for both public and private enterprises, etc.). (chapter 7)

2. Exogenous parameters

A. The opportunity cost of capital is 10 percent ($r = 0.10$).

B. The scrap value of the fixed capital at the end of period T is zero.

C. Public goods exist and lump-sum transfers are not feasible, so distortion-creating taxes are required, making the shadow price of government revenue greater than 1 ($\lambda_g = 1.3$).

D. The marginal direct tax rate is 33 percent ($t = 0.3333$). There are no indirect taxes.

E. There are no taxes on income from capital, nor other distortions in capital markets, making $\lambda_p = 1$.

3. Computation simplifications

A. Flows occur only once in each period (e.g., in the middle) or are evenly distributed so as to have the same effect.

B. $T = 1$. That is, the enterprise will operate for one more year and then die.

C. Scrap value is zero.

D. Physical deterioration follows a one-hoss shay pattern (i.e., zero until scrapped).

The starting point of our analysis is the *base state* of affairs given by the current public operation of the firm as reflected in its financial statements. Valuation is accomplished by making a series of adjustments to this base state: the private buyer adjusts for such factors as improved efficiency and synergies, whereas the public seller adjusts for elements such as controlled prices and the opportunity cost of labor. A systematic quantitative description of existing conditions is thus central to any analysis and is the second topic of this section. It is accomplished by converting from the private logic of the profit and loss statement and balance sheet to the economic or public logic of national income and wealth accounting (section 4.2).

Sections 4.3 and 4.4 then combine the general formulas with the specific data to generate the explicit value that answer the basic questions. The implications are then summarized in section 4.5.

4.1 General Results

4.1.1 A Trivial Case ($\lambda_g = \lambda_p$)

If the premium on government revenue is the same as that on private profit ($\lambda_g = \lambda_p$), then we have a trivial case, because if public behavior is the same as private behavior and all prices are the same, then divestiture cannot change the wealth of society but only its distribution. But if $\lambda_g = \lambda_p$, then distribution doesn't matter either, so the government should be completely indifferent as to whether the enterprise is in public or private hands (i.e., $V_{sg} = V_{sp}$). Further, given no change in wealth and distributional neutrality, the government would be happy to accept Z_p (whatever that might be) for the enterprise. However, it would be equally happy to accept any other price for the enterprise or, indeed, to *pay* the private sector any amount of subsidy to take the enterprise. The intuition is obvious and algebra confirms the results:

$$Z_g = \frac{V_{sg} - V_{sp}}{\lambda_g - \lambda_p} = \frac{0}{0} = \text{undefined.} \tag{4.1}$$

In summary, if conduct doesn't change, and government revenue doesn't matter, then nothing matters, and we need not bother calculating V_{sg}, V_{sp}, or anything else.

4.1.2 Revenue Motive ($\lambda_g \neq \lambda_p$)

In reality, government revenue does matter, and one of the major motives for divestiture is to relax a fiscal constraint. We therefore introduce a revenue concern by assuming public goods exist, lump-sum taxes are not feasible, and, therefore, $\lambda_g > 1$. Likewise, in reality, private profit also matters if there are any distortions in capital markets. We therefore assume that income from capital is taxed, so that $\lambda_p > 1$.

Now a bit more calculation is required. We establish the general result under two assumptions: first, that only an operating capital good is being sold (that is, there are no debts, working capital or nonoperating assets) and second, that the capital good yields a stable stream of profits (quasi-rents, or Π) in perpetuity. These assumptions are made only to simplify the initial exposition, and both are relaxed later in this section, with no loss of generality.

Under these assumptions, the private buyer's calculation of his or her maximum willingness to pay is simply

$$Z_g = V_{pp} = \frac{\Pi - X^d}{r}, \tag{4.2}$$

where X^d is the direct tax paid.[1]

The value to society of this outcome differs only in the values attached to Π and X^d:

$$V_{sp} = \frac{\lambda_p \Pi + (\lambda_g - \lambda_p) X^d}{r}. \tag{4.3}$$

In the event of continued public operation, the government revenue premium applies to the entire stream of quasi-rents:

$$V_{sp} = \frac{\lambda_g \Pi}{r}. \tag{4.4}$$

From equation (2.6)

$$Z_g = \frac{V_{sg} - V_{sp}}{\lambda_g - \lambda_p}.$$

By substitution,

$$Z_g = \frac{\dfrac{\lambda_g \Pi}{r} - \dfrac{\lambda_p \Pi + (\lambda_g - \lambda_p) X^d}{r}}{\lambda_g - \lambda_p}. \tag{4.5}$$

Rearranging gives

$$Z_g = \frac{\Pi - X^d}{r}, \tag{4.6}$$

which is precisely V_{pp}. The general result is, therefore, that in the absence of behavioral changes or price distortions,

$$Z_g = Z_p = V_{pp}. \tag{4.7}$$

That is, the *minimum* price at which the government is willing to sell is just equal to the *maximum* price that the private sector is willing to pay.

Intuitively, this result may be explained as follows. The government is relinquishing a portion (not all, because of taxes) of its claim on future earnings. To make itself whole, it must receive at least the present value of that claim today. It is important to note that the values of λ_g and λ_p do not matter, because they enter symmetrically on both the future and present value sides.[2] Stripped of λ_g and λ_p (which are the only differences between public and private valuations), the resulting public calculation is precisely the same as the private calculation except that benefits and costs are reversed (the buyer gives up cash now for a future claim). The public minimum thus becomes the private maximum.

This equivalence is all that can be established at the general level. To determine actual values requires data, whose extraction from enterprise-level accounts we now consider.

4.2 Base Flows and Stocks

4.2.1 Production and Distribution Flows

The profit and loss statement provides considerable information on the base state of the enterprise. However, the data become more accessible for economic analysis if mapped into a production and distribution table along the lines suggested by national income accounting methodology. No information is lost or added in this conversion; it is merely rearranged.[3] Nonetheless, we find it useful to make this rearrangement at the outset for two reasons. First, it is simply handy to have the data directly in the economic categories that we will use for analysis. Second, it increases the accuracy of the results. All too often, when faced with complex profit and loss statements, economists implicitly make one set of mappings when calculating value-added, for instance, another for profit, and a third for

Table 4.2
Profit and loss statement for corporation A (1/1/90 through 12/31/91)

Sales			17,667
— Cost of sales			— 13,950
Initial inventory (finished products)		147	
Manufacturing costs		14,474	
Wages and salaries	1,294		
Materials	10,761		
Depreciation	2,419		
Ending inventory (finished products)		671	
= Sales profit			= 3,717
— Administrative and selling expenses			— 611
Wages and salaries		337	
Purchases of advertising, etc.		250	
Rent		24	
= Operating income			= 3,106
+ Nonoperating income			+ 272
Rental income (from land)		112	
Interest and dividends received		160	
— Nonoperating expenses			— 1,124
Interest payment		1,029	
Amortization of start-up expenses		95	
= Net profit for the period			= 2,254
Income tax		751	
Dividends		694	
Retained earnings		809	

Table 4.3
Balance sheet for corporation A

	12/31/90			12/31/91		
Assets						
Current assets			4,811			8,076
Cash		58			123	
Demand deposits		190			380	
Time deposits		60			40	
Marketable securities		58			1,556	
Inventory: inputs		1,518			1,746	
Inventory: outputs		147			671	
Accounts receivable		2,780			3,560	
Fixed assets			12,865			11,279
Tangible		8,786			7,292	
Land	709			1,121		
Capital goods	8,077			6,171		
(Depreciation reserve)	(7,356)			(9,775)		
Intangibles		72			75	
Deferred account						
(Start-up expenses)		4,007			3,912	
Total assets			17,676			19,355
Liabilities						
Current liabilities			1,980			1,765
Accounts payable		1,680			1,372	
Short-term debt		300			393	
Fixed liabilities (long-term debt)			9,893			9,893
Equity			5,803			7,697
Paid-in capital		5,122			5,122	
Appropriated surplus		69			321	
Net profit for the period		612			2,254	
Income tax reserve	200			751		
Dividends reserve	160			694		
Retained earnings	252			809		
Total liabilities and equity			17,676			19,355

domestic savings. This problem is avoided by making a single initial mapping under the discipline of the following rule: map all accounting entries into one and only one economic category. Results for corporation A are given in table 4.4.

4.2.2 Wealth Statement

Unfortunately, the accountant's balance sheet is considerably less useful to the economist than its profit and loss statement. Most obviously, the net worth category is a residual that bears no particular relation to the V_{ppa} that we are seeking. This is because the balance sheet is not intended to show values but only costs not yet posted to the profit and loss statement.[4]

Nonetheless, the balance sheet remains useful for two reasons. First, in pursuit of V_{ppa}, it does provide some entries that are directly relevant (e.g., cash on hand on the assert side and long-term debt on the liability side). Second, a time-series of balance sheets provides the basis for a meaningful flow of funds statement, which in turn is of central importance in ex-post evaluation.

Accordingly, we first rearrange the balance sheet into economically relevant categories in a wealth statement at accountants' values in table 4.5. No information is added to or dropped from the balance sheet, and valuation remains at book value. The table is therefore of use only as a starting point for flow of funds (table 4.5, column 2) and as one input into a wealth statement at economist's values (table 4.6).

On the asset side, a fundamental distinction is made between an operating asset (owned and used by the enterprise to produce something of value) and a nonoperating asset (owned by the firm but held for speculative purposes or rented to other firms to produce value through *their* production processes). Within operating assets a further distinction is made between fixed and variable assets, reflecting those that cannot readily be varied within a single period (e.g., capital goods, land) and those that can (e.g., inventories, cash). On the liabilities side, the fundamental distinction is between equity and debt, with the latter further subdivided into interest-bearing debt and non-interest-bearing debt. The latter category (tax and dividend reserves, accounts payable, etc.) is sometimes ignored but is often significant.

4.2.3 Flow of Funds

For ex-post evaluation a time-series of uses and sources of funds is indispensable. We calculate it using a simple and straightforward methodology

Table 4.4
Production and distribution flows for corporation A (at current market prices)[1]

Generation of surplus	Notes	
Production (at market cost)	2	18,191
— Indirect taxes (plus subsidies)	3	0
= Production (at factor cost)	4	18,191
— Intermediate inputs	5	11,011
= Gross value added (at factor cost)		7,180
— Employee compensation (return to labor)	6	1,631
— Rental expenses (return to other factors)	7	24
= Return to operating assets		5,525
+ Nonoperating return	8	272
= Total return to capital		5,797
Distribution of surplus		
Total return to capital		5,797
— Interest payments (return to debt holders)	9	1,029
— Direct taxes (return to government)	10	751
= Return to equity holders		4,017
— Dividends	11	694
= Gross domestic savings (by enterprise)		3,323
— Depreciation and amortization	12	2,514
= Retained earnings	13	809

Notes: 1. This is simply a rearrangement of the profit and loss statement (P&L). No information is lost or added. All entries on the P&L are explicitly mapped into some category below. Although we are working with a very simplified P&L in this example, the same exercise can be carried out to reduce the most complex P&L into the basic flows described here.

2. Residual (no. 4 + no. 3).

3. Assumed equal to zero.

4. Sales + ending inventory — initial inventory.

5. Materials from manufacturing cost plus purchases of advertising, etc., from administrative and spelling expenses.

6. Wages and salaries from manufacturing costs and from administrative and selling expenses.

7. Rent.

8. Rental income, plus interest and dividends.

9. Interest payments.

10. Income tax.

11. Dividends.

12. Depreciation allowance plus amortization allowance.

13. Residual (equals retained earnings).

Table 4.5
Wealth statement and fund flows (at accountants' values) for corporation A

	Wealth 12/31/90	+Fund flows 1–12/91	+Value adjustments 1–12/91	=Wealth 12/31/91
Assets				
Fixed operating assets				
Capital goods	8,077[1]	513	−2,419[2]	6,171[1]
Land	0[2]	0	0	0[3]
Intangibles	4,079[4]	3	−95[5]	3,987[4]
Variable operating assets				
Inventories	1,665[1]	752	0	2,417[1]
Financial	3,028[6]	1,035	0	4,063[6]
Nonoperating assets	827[7]	1,890	0	2,717[7]
Total	17,676	4,193	−2,514	19,355
Liabilities				
Debt				
Interest bearing	10,193[8]	93	0	10,286[8]
Zero interest	2,040[9]	777	0	2,817[9]
Equity	5,443[10]	3,323[2]	−2,514[11]	6,252[10]
Total	17,676	4,193	−2,514	19,355

Notes: 1. Directly from balance sheet.

2. From profit and loss or, in this case, from change in depreciation reserve.

3. Land must be split between operating and nonoperating. In this case, we have arbitrarily assigned it all to the latter category.

4. Intangibles plus deferred account.

5. Amortization from profit and loss.

6. Cash plus demand deposits plus accounts receivable.

7. Land plus marketable securities plus time deposits.

8. Short-term plus long-term.

9. Accounts payable plus income tax reserve plus dividend reserve. This category is "zero interest" in the sense that the amount entered on the balance sheet is all that is owed by the firm. This is distinct from the "interest bearing" category, where the firm is liable for the balance sheet amount plus interest. There may of course be an implicit interest built into accounts payable. In some tax systems income tax reserves carry an interest charge under certain circumstances, and these would be then listed as interest bearing. We know of no case where corporations pay interest on dividends from the time of declaration to the time of distribution. However, it is common for them to be payable to the holder of record at the time of distribution rather than at the time of declaration. If so, then they would be part of equity rather than part of debt.

10. Paid-in capital plus appropriated surplus plus retained earnings.

11. From total value adjustments on asset side.

12. This is a residual item in this calculation, but as a check it should be equal to gross domestic savings from the production and distribution flow.

Retained earnings	728
+ depreciation and amortization	2,514
= gross domestic savings	3,242

Table 4.6
Private wealth statement (at economists' values) for corporation A, 12/31/90

Assets	Notes		12,635
Fixed operating	1	3,439	
Working capital	2	6,480	
Nonoperating	2	2,717	
Liabilities and net worth			12,635
Net worth	3	100	
Debt: interest bearing	4	9,974	
Debt: zero interest	5	2,561	

Notes: 1. Net present value of future quasi-rents, less taxes, from text ($V_{pp}^\pi = 3,783/1.1$).

2. Unchanged from accountants' values in table 4.5.

3. Residual, but equal to V_{ppa} from text.

4. Equals the face value from table 4.5 (10,286) less the tax savings that follow from interest deductibility. [$(0.33)(1,028.6)/1.1 = 312$]. The real cost of the debt is therefore only 9,974.

5. Differs from table 4.5 in that real economic cost of zero-interest debt is not its face value (since it does not have to be repaid until next year) but that amount discounted by the opportunity cost. The present value of this debt is, therefore, not 2,817 as at accountants' values but only $2,817/1.1 = 2,561$.

based on the following accounting relationship that holds for any line item on the balance sheet:[5]

Beginning stock

+ real flows

+ value adjustments

= ending stock.

That is, the balance sheet entries change for two very different reasons. First, there are flows of funds representing real movements of assets or liabilities into and out of the firm. Second, there are value adjustments in which existing assets or liabilities are arbitrarily assigned new values, but nothing actually enters or leaves the firm.[6] For example, the initial book value of capital goods is increased by fixed capital formation (real flow) and reduced by depreciation (a value adjustment) to yield the ending book value. Other value adjustments include amortization, revaluation of fixed assets, and adjustments to loans denominated in foreign currencies after a devaluation.

Computationally, initial and ending stocks are found on the balance sheet (columns 1 + 4 of table 4.5), value adjustments are identified on the profit and loss statement (column 3), and fund flows are simply the residual (column 2). Flows on the asset side are deemed uses, whereas flows on the liability side are deemed sources. Note that this procedure means that negative signs will occur: for example, sale of a capital good is a negative use, and repayment of debt is a negative source.

4.2.4   Profit

Profit is the bottom line of the profit and loss statement, but it will vary with where that line is drawn. In this book our fundamental measure of profit is as a quasi-rent—that is, the return to fixed factors, or production revenues less variable costs, or

Return to operating assets	
(from production and distribution flows: table 4.4)	5,525
— opportunity cost of working capital	
(exogenous interest rate) × (variable operating	
assets from the wealth statement: table 4.5)	
= 0.1 (6,480)	648
= profit	4,877

In terms of supply-and-demand diagrams, this is given by the (horizontal) quantity times the (vertical) gap between the price and the short-run variable cost curve. When we use "profit" (or Π) without further modification, it will always be in this sense. Occasionally we will refer to quasi-rent as public profit to distinguish it from the traditional private profit.

4.3   Private Values (V_{pp})

4.3.1   General

The present value of a net benefit stream is given by the standard relationship

$$NPV = \sum_{t=0}^{\infty} \frac{B_t - C_t}{(1 + r)^t}.$$

The problem is to identify correctly the benefits and costs from the perspectives of different actors. We first illustrate the method with a simple calculation from the private perspective, then generalize the method, and finally apply it from the public perspective.

4.3.2 V_{ppa}: Obvious Method

What would a private buyer offer on a stand-alone basis for the enterprise described in tables 4.1 and 4.2, under the simplifying assumptions of table 4.3?

One obvious method of calculation is the following:

1. 1991 current receipts:		+ 4,017
Dividends	694	
Retained earnings	809	
Amortization allowance	95	
Depreciation allowance	2,419	
2. Plus liquidation of assets in 1991:[7]		+ 9,197
Current assets	8,076	
Land	1,121	
3. Less outstanding obligations in 1991:		− 13,103
Current liabilities	1,765	
Fixed liabilities	9,893	
Tax reserve[8]	751	
Dividend reserve[9]	694	
4. Equals net 1991 cash flow		= 110

Discounting to 1990, we have

$$V_{ppa} = \frac{110}{1.1} = 100 = Z_p.$$

That is, the owner of the enterprise will receive a net cash flow of 110 in 1991, equivalent to 100 in 1990, which is, therefore, the maximum a private buyer would be willing to pay on a stand-alone basis.

4.3.3 Synergies: Taxes

In general, V_{ppa} is not the final willingness to pay because interdependence with preexisting operations must also be taken into account. Under present assumptions the only such consideration is taxation. Since the buyer will be paying with after-tax dollars but receiving pretax dollars, it might be thought that because he or she will actually be netting considerably less than 100, the buyer will be willing to pay considerably less than 100. In fact, given our assumption of tax neutrality, we will show that $V_{ppc} = V_{ppa} = 100$, because both numerator and denominator must be adjusted symmetrically.

For the single-period case,

$$V_{ppc} = \frac{(B_t - C_t) - D_t x^{dd} - (B_t - C_t - D_t - V_{ppc})x^{dc}}{1 + r(1 - x^{dr})}, \tag{4.8}$$

where D represents dividends and the new superscripts reflect different tax rates on different forms of income. That is, net benefits next year are reduced by taxes on dividends (x^{dd}) and again by taxes on capital gains (x^{dc}),[10] whereas the opportunity cost is also reduced by taxation (x^{dr}). If tax rates are neutral, then $x^{dd} = x^{dc} = x^{dr} = x$, and we have

$$V_{ppc} = \frac{(B_t - C_t) - x(B_t - C_t - V_{ppc})}{1 + r(1 - x)}, \tag{4.9}$$

which says that it doesn't matter whether quasi-rents are arbitrarily classified as depreciation, dividends, or retained earnings. Further rearrangement yields

$$V_{ppc} = \frac{(B_t - C_t)(1 - x)}{(1 + r)(1 - x)} = \frac{B_t - C_t}{1 + r}. \tag{4.10}$$

That is, V_{ppc} equals V_{ppa} in this case. This simply says that if taxes are truly neutral, they can be ignored.

Taxes, of course, are not neutral. If dividends and interest are taxed at 33 percent but capital gains at half that, then substituting values for corporation A into equation (4.8) gives

$$V_{ppc} = \frac{110 - 694(0.3333) - (110 - 694 - V_{ppc})0.1667}{1 + 0.1(1 - 0.3333)}$$

$$V_{ppc} = -26.67,$$

which says that a buyer would have to be *paid* to take over the company, because taxes on (positive) retained earnings are only half compensated for by tax rebates on (negative) capital gains. Of course, direct tax rebates are uncommon, but the same thing is accomplished if the buyer's positive capital gains are set against the negative capital gains of the enterprise being sold, and this is the previous implicit assumption.

The validity of the foregoing assumption will, of course, vary with the level and composition of the buyer's profit. This means that the effective marginal tax rates will vary with the buyer (requiring buyer subscripts in the notation). Further, even the original corporate tax rate included in V_{ppa} may change (e.g., if the buyer can revalue assets at the sale price) and thus increase the depreciation allowance.

In summary, in this case $V_{ppa} = V_{ppc}$, but only because taxes are neutral. Asymmetric taxes on income create synergies that alter willingness to pay relative to the stand-alone value. That is, an enterprise will throw off a stream of earnings whose present value (V_{ppa}) is to a considerable extent (though by no means entirely) independent of the buyer, but the value of that stream will vary with the circumstances of the individual buyer (V_{ppc}). This is covered in detail in chapter 7.

4.3.4   Depreciation and Amortization

In the foregoing calculation one item requires elaboration, namely, the treatment of depreciation and amortization allowances as benefits rather than costs. After all, is it not the case that depreciation is a real cost and that public enterprise profits are overstated because insufficient depreciation is deducted, rather than that they are understated because any depreciation is deducted?

The answer lies in the distinction between single- and multiple-period analyses. Capital is a cost that must be charged once in each analysis but not twice. In accountants' profit and loss analysis, or economists' production function analysis, or any other single-period analysis, depreciation is charged to reflect the cost of holding assets. In project evaluation, on the other hand, the cost of capital is charged as the initial investment in period zero, and depreciation is not charged in subsequent periods, because to do so would be to double-count capital costs and, therefore, to reject profitable projects. The same is true of divestiture valuation. The present value reflects our willingness to pay for the assets, or the cost of capital; charging again for this cost via depreciation would be double-counting.

Consider a company with one year left to run, zero expected profits after a depreciation charge of 110, and no residual breakup value. If depreciation were a real cost, then this company would be worthless on a stand-alone basis. In fact, it is worth $110/1.1 = 100$. Note that the problem is not the use of accountants' historically based depreciation instead of economists' future-oriented depreciation based on the change in value. In the foregoing example the value of the company is 100 at the beginning of the period and zero at the end, making economists' depreciation 100. Deducting this as a cost again yields the incorrect answer of zero present value for an enterprise worth 100. Deducting either form of depreciation is thus simply wrong in multiperiod analysis, however valid it may be in single-period calculations.

The foregoing assumes that the enterprise has a discrete and known remaining life span T. In fact, one cannot know in advance when an enterprise will become obsolete and be shut down or, indeed, whether it will be shut down at all. In such circumstances, a prudent investor will set aside a certain sum each year to replace the existing assets when they do become obsolete. If the funds thus accumulated are just sufficient to replace the obsolete assets with new ones yielding the same amount, and if this process continues indefinitely, then the firm will live forever, creating a perpetuity. The present value of such a firm is simply the net annual benefits after depreciation, over the interest rate. Treating depreciation as a cost in this sense of a replacement reserve can thus be defended as a practical alternative to the unknowable T and a realistic reflection of an enterprise as an ongoing entity.

Two objections may be raised to this approach. The first is quantitative. The correct annual replacement reserve contribution will bear no necessary relationship to either the economists' or the accountants' notion of depreciation. Instead it will depend upon the period T until replacement, the interest rate earned in the meantime, and the acquisition cost of assets yielding an equivalent stream. It is, therefore, far more uncertain than the earlier method because it implicitly requires knowing not only T but other unknowables as well. The second assumption is that the funds can and should be reinvested in the present activity, instead of elsewhere.

Nonetheless, in a perfect world the two methods are equivalent if handled correctly. Consider the firm at the beginning of this subsection with a present worth of 100. Treating depreciation allowance directly as a benefit simply says I'm going to get 110 back next year, and at 10 percent that is worth 100 today. On the other hand, treating it as a cost says we are going to have 110 of surplus next year, but we are going to reinvest some of it to yield a perpetual income stream. If capital yields 10 percent and lasts forever, then buying 100 of capital goods next year will yield a perpetual stream of 10. Alternatively, if capital lasts four years but still yields 10 percent, then the return stream will be 31.548. These three alternative and equivalent ways of treating depreciation are summarized in the tables.

	Period						
	NPV	1	2	3	4	5	6
Direct credit method	100	110	0	0	0	0	0
Indirect credit 1	100	10	10	10	10	10	10...
Indirect credit 2	100	31.55	31.55	31.55	31.55	0	0...

All three streams have the same net present value of 100. The essential point is that the depreciation allowance confers a net benefit. This benefit can be credited in a number of different ways, but it must be credited. In this book we follow the simplest method of crediting it when earned. The alternative, of crediting it in terms of reinvestment returns, is equivalent but much more cumbersome.

One final argument for not crediting depreciation is that capital goods do not wear out all at one time T but sporadically. Some capital goods with a short life span must be replaced well before period T if the enterpise is to be kept running. It can be argued that the depreciation allowance covers these costs and ensures that returns continue until T but conveys no further benefits after time T. If so, then we must not credit depreciation at all.

What this argument really says is that there is some current return on past investment (the depreciation allowance), but we will use it to cover future investment costs. Because the current benefit and the future cost more or less cancel one another, we ignore both. while this is not an unreasonable argument, in this book we prefer to enter explicitly both current depreciation benefits and future replacement costs. In some particular case it may make sense to assume that the present values of the two streams happen to be precisely equivalent, but we prefer not to prejudge the issue.

4.3.5 V_{pp}: Standard Method

We have just seen that there are many equivalent ways of dealing with depreciation, and the same is true of any other element of the calculation. In this subsection we propose a standarized method and use it to generate the same result as in section 4.4.2.

Three distinctions are fundamental. First, we wish to distinguish between net returns to fixed capital (Π) and returns to other assets and liabilities in the portfolio that constitutes the firm. We will refer to these latter flows as financial ($B^f - C^f$) to stress their portfolio-choice nature and distinguish them from the production flows summarized in Π. This will be a central distinction both for shadow pricing purposes and also for reasons of calculation methodology. Accordingly, we will use the following (and similar) bifurcations:

$$V_{pp} = V_{pp}^{\pi} + V_{pp}^{f},$$

where the superscripts refer to the respective valuations of the returns to fixed capital (V^{π}) and to the financial portfolio (V^{f}).

Second, within the return to fixed capital we wish to distinguish between those accruing between now and some arbitrary time τ and those accruing from τ to the expected end of the project's life T. Year T thus corresponds to the standard project evaluation terminal year. Year τ, however, represents some arbitrary time horizon, beyond which our estimation procedures change. These procedures become cruder and more arbitrary after time τ both because the future is less knowable and because—given the discount rate—it is much less important to know it. Third, we want to specifically identify any fixed capital formation (F_t) required to maintain the flows of quasi-rents specified previously (including a negative scrap value). Our standard present value formula then becomes

$$\text{NPV} = \sum_{t=0}^{\tau} \frac{\Pi_t}{(1 + r)^t} + \sum_{t=\tau+1}^{T} \frac{\Pi_t}{(1 + r)^t} - \sum_{t=0}^{T} \frac{F_t}{(1 + r)^t} + \sum_{t=0}^{T} \frac{B^f - C^f}{(1 + r)^t}.$$

(4.11)

The first three terms of the equation constitute V_{pp}^{π}, whereas the last represents V_{pp}^{f}. Using data from the earlier example, the four terms are evaluated as follows:

1. Calculate the return to fixed capital in each period from now to τ. This is simply quasi-rents after taxes for 1987, or

Operating surplus	5,525[11]
— opportunity cost of working capital 0.10 (6480)	648
= total return to fixed capital	4,877
— taxes on operations[12]	1,094
= after-tax return	3,783

2. Calculate the return to fixed capital in years following year τ. In this case, zero.

3. Calculate additional fixed capital formation requirements and scrap value, in this case, zero.

4. Calculate the net value of all other enterprise assets and liabilities. In 1990 values, this is

Working capital[13]	6,480
+ nonoperating assets	2,717
= total assets	+ 9,197
debt: interest bearing	− 9,974
+ debt: zero interest[14]	− 2,561
= total liabilities	− 12,535
Net	− 3,339

Substituting these values into equation (4.11) and assuming $r = 10$ percent gives

$$V_{ppa} = \frac{3783}{1.1} + 0 - 0 - 3339 = 100 = Z_{p'}$$

as before, or

$$V_{ppa} = V_{pp}^{\pi} + V_{pp}^{f} = 3439 - 3339 = 100.$$

4.3.6   Private Wealth Statement (at Economists' Values)

One advantage of the standard method is its straightforward interpretation in terms of the private wealth statement at economists' values (table 4.6). The correct valuation of fixed assets is given by V_{pp}^{π}, whereas V_{ppa} gives the net worth.

Under present assumptions working capital and nonoperating assets can be read directly from table 4.5, but the debt entries differ. The accountant enters the non-interest-bearing debt at its face value, a practice that would be correct only if payment were made immediately. In the present instance these are not due until next year, allowing the company to earn a return in the meantime (or avoid borrowing), making their economic value equal to the accountants' cost discounted by one plus the interest rate. This particular example is in part a contrived result of our assumptions (on the timing of dividend and tax reserve payouts), but it will generally hold for accounts payable.

Turning to interest-bearing debt, first consider a debt of 100 at a non-concessionary rate of 10 percent. The amount that must be paid back next year is 110, and discounting yields a net present value of 100. Compounding and discounting cancel, so the face value is correct. On the other hand, consider a loan at a concessionary interest rate of 5 percent when the market rate is 10 percent. This is valued by the accountant at 100 but by the economist at $100(1.05/1.1) = 95.5$. In the present example the loan is not at a concessionary rate, but it is subsidized by the standard tax deduction allowed for interest payments. Accordingly, the accountants' value must be modified as follows:

$$\text{Economists' value} = (\text{accountants' value})\left(1 - \frac{rx}{1 + r}\right)$$

$$= 10{,}286\left(1 - \frac{0.0333}{1.1}\right) = 9{,}974.$$

In sum, accountants' values are generally not equal to economists' values, even as we move beyond fixed capital and net worth.

4.4   Sale Prices and Public Values

We now calculate V_{sg} and V_{sp} in two steps, treating the productive and financial elements of equation (3.11) separately, for convenience. First, we consider only the return to fixed capital component. We have already seen that

$$Z_p^\pi = V_{pp}^\pi = \frac{\Pi - X^d}{1 + r} = \frac{4{,}877 - 1{,}094}{1.1} = 3{,}439.$$

V_{sp}^π will differ from V_{pp}^π for two reasons: first, because taxes are not a public cost but a distribution; and second, because of the extra weight attached to revenue flowing to the government, making[15]

$$V_{sp}^\pi = \frac{\lambda_p\Pi + (\lambda_g - \lambda_p)X^d}{1 + r} = \frac{4{,}877 + 0.3(1{,}094)}{1.1} = 4{,}732.0.$$

If, on the other hand, the enterprise is govenment owned, then the entire surplus accrues to the government, making

$$V_{sg}^\pi = \frac{\lambda_g\Pi}{1 + r} = \frac{1.3(4{,}877)}{1.1} = 5{,}763.7.$$

The minimum government sales price is then

$$Z_g^\pi = \frac{V_{sg}^\pi - V_{sp}^\pi}{\lambda_g - 1} = \frac{5{,}763.7 - 4{,}732.0}{0.3} = 3{,}439.$$

This confirms the general result of equation (4.7) that under current assumptions the government's minimum price for the fixed capital equals the private maximum:

$$Z_g^\pi = Z_p^\pi = 3{,}439.$$

Before commenting on this result, we need to show that it continues to hold as we take other assets and liabilities into account. We have already seen that for the firm as a whole

$$V_{pp} = 100.$$

This is the value to the equity shareholder, but V_{sp} will be considerably larger, because it includes returns to *all* economic actors. It thus amounts to the total public wealth represented by the firm.

As with V_{sp}^π, this differs from the private wealth in treating taxes as benefits and in the adjustment for government revenue. The details are given in table 4.7, with the major changes summarized as follows:

Private wealth		12,635
+ operating taxes (discounted)		995
= public wealth at market prices		13,630
+ external effects $(\lambda_g - \lambda_p)(T_t/(1 + r)^t)$		
1986 tax reserve	0.3(711/1.1)	194
1987 tax flow	0.3(711/1.1)	194
− public wealth at shadow prices (V_{sp}) =		14,018

Note that the external effects are contributions to the creation of wealth elsewhere (externalities, or general equilibrium effects). For example, as a result of government tax revenues here, taxes will be reduced (or not imposed) elsewhere, increasing the wealth of participants in that other market by 388. They therefore are entered as an external effect on the production (asset) side of the public wealth statement and as a distribution to society on the liability side.

If the enterprise were to remain in government hands under current assumptions, the value to society would differ in only one respect, namely, that the equity share would also accrue to government:

$$V_{sg} = V_{sp} + (\lambda_g - 1)V_{pp} = 14{,}018 + 0.3(100) = 14{,}048.$$

Calculation of Z_g follows directly:

$$Z_g = \frac{14{,}048 - 14{,}018}{0.3} = 100.$$

Table 4.7
Public wealth statement (at shadow values) for corporation A, 12/31/90

	V_{sp}	V_{sg}
Assets (NPV of benefits)		
Fixed operating	4,434[1]	4,434
Working capital	6,480[2]	6,480
Nonoperating	2,712[2]	2,717
External effects	388[5]	418[7]
Total	14,018	14,048
Liabilities and net worth (distribution of benefits)		
Debt holders		
Interest bearing		
Paid by firm	9,974[2]	9,974
Government subsidy	312[3]	312
Non-interest-bearing	2,561[2]	2,561
Private equity holders	100[2]	0
Government	683[4]	783[6]
Society	388[5]	418[7]
Total	14,018	14,048

Notes: 1. Quasi-rents, discounted: 4,877/1.1.

2. Unchanged from private wealth at enconomists' values, under current assumptions.

3. Subsidy due to interest deductibility (10,286/3)/1.1.

4. Taxes less subsidies (1,094 − 343)/1.1.

5. External effects (see text):

$0.3(711)/1.1 + 0.3(711)/1.1$.

6. V_{sp} value plus return to equity holder.

7. V_{sp} value plus $(\lambda_g - \lambda_p)$ times return to equity holder (0.3 × 100 + 30).

Once again, we have the important results that underlie the assumptions of this chapter:

$$Z_g = Z_p = V_{pp} = 100.$$

4.5 Implications

This chapter has several important implications. First, at the technical level note that under present assumptions Z_g can be set without calculating V_{sg}, V_{sp}, or even λ_g or λ_p but knowing only V_{pp}.

In later chapters matters will not be so simple, but it will remain true that quantification requirements are less onerous than they appear initially because what matters is the *difference* $(V_{sp} - V_{sg})$. Since many variables enter V_{sp} and V_{sg} symmetrically, they will cancel and can be ignored. This is the first example of the *difference principle* enunciated in chapter 2.

At a more policy-oriented level, a second implication is that there can be no *pure* revenue motive for the sale of public enterprises. With behavioral changes or price distortions, revenue effects occur as second-order effects, but without them the government and private sector can exchange only streams of equal value.[16] The pattern of revenue can be altered (liquidity effect), but its level (wealth effect) is unchanged.

The third implication is that under these conditions, no sale is likely to occur. If there are any transaction costs (e.g., the cost of typing up a contract and walking across the street to sign it), then Z_p will fall and Z_g will rise, leaving no mutually acceptable Z.

The fourth and final implication is that sale is socially desirable only if the maximum willingness to pay is extracted from the private sector. If there is some uncertainty as to just what this number is (as there always will be) and if the bidding process is less than perfectly competitive (as it generally will be), then the chances of extracting this maximum are substantially less than 100 percent. It follows that a prudent minister will never sell, because he has nothing to gain. The best he can do is break even (if $Z = Z_p = Z_g$), whereas there is a serious possibility both of making the country worse off (if $Z < Z_p$) and of opening himself to political charges of giving away the national patrimony.

In short, in this chapter a zero-sum game is being played that, given information asymmetries, the government is likely to lose. No sale is likely to transpire under these conditions. If, however, enterprise conduct changes and/or there are price distortions, then there is potential for a positive-sum game. We now turn to this possibility.

**Allocative versus
Cost Efficiency:
the Fundamental
Trade-off**

The economics of divestiture become interesting only when enterprise conduct is altered as a result of sale. In chapter 4 we argued that if divestiture did not cause conduct to change, it was unlikely that any sale could be made. The maximum price any private buyer would offer would be equal to the minimum price government would be willing to accept. The presence of any transactions cost of the sale itself would then drive a wedge between these two prices and make the sale impossible. Thus we need to allow for behavioral changes in order to make the analysis meaningful.

What kind of behavioral changes might we expect? Proponents of divestiture argue that private management will improve static operating efficiency and dynamic entrepreneurial innovation. On the other hand, opponents say that private motivation leads to exploitation of consumers, workers, and/or the environment. Taking both these viewpoints into consideration, there is a potential trade-off between the possibility that private objectives will be less desirable socially and the possibility that the private sector will pursue these objective more efficiently. This may be called the *fundamental trade-off of divestiture.*

In this chapter we focus on the most common manifestation of the trade-off, namely, the possibility that divestiture increases cost-efficiency through better management but reduces allocative efficiency through exploitation of market power.[1] We choose this particular characterization not because we believe it to be universally true but because it seems to capture some of the major implications of divestiture as seen from the opposing sides of the debate. We begin by extending our simple model of chapter 2, and then we apply it to different market structures. In competitive output markets (section 5.3) there is no trade-off because market power cannot be exercised, divestiture is unambiguously desirable socially, and the only interesting question is how the fruits of this positive-sum game are to be divided. In monopolistic and oligopolistic markets (sections 5.3, 5.4, and 5.5) the trade-offs are fundamental, and the focus is on quantification. Finally, in section 5.6 we consider some extensions to allow for more complicated cases, including intermediate goods and quality changes.

5.1 The Basic Methodology

Our task is to analyze in greater detail the summary variables discussed in chapter 2. We first introduce some notation and then present our analytic framework. In the interest of simplicity, we assume here that the enterprise produces a single product; this assumption can easily be changed to allow for multiple products without substantially changing any of the results of our analysis.

We use the following notation:

q_p, q_g: levels of output under private and government operation,

P_p, P_g: corresponding output prices,

c_p, c_g: average costs of production,

Π_p, Π_g: annual profits of the firm,

S_p, S_g: annual consumer surplus accruing to domestic consumers,

X: annual corporate tax payments after divestiture.

We may now write some key relationships. First, firm profits (before taxes) may be written as quantity produced times the difference between price and average cost:

$$\Pi_g = (P_g - c_g)q_g, \tag{5.1}$$

$$\Pi_p = (P_p - c_p)q_p. \tag{5.2}$$

Equations (5.1) and (5.2) should, in principle, be computed for each year in the future. If we index by t the value of a variable in year t, then we can represent the private value of the enterprise as

$$V_{pp} = \sum_{t=0}^{\infty} \rho^t[\Pi_p(t) - X(t)], \tag{5.3}$$

where ρ represents the discount factor.[2]

Note that this relationship is true for the enterprise as an independent firm; we are ignoring here in this simple version any synergies that the acquiring private firm may have with this enterprise.[3] Under this assumption equation (5.3) represents the maximum willingness to pay for the operating assets of the enterprise, which may be denoted Z_p.[4]

Next consider the *social* value of the enterprise under the alternative regimes of government and private ownership. The essential point here is that, in our measure of social value, we must include not only the returns to the enterprise but also those to other agents in the economy. These can include consumers, other firms, owners of factors of production (including labor), and government. Properly speaking, all these elements should be included in our welfare measure. In order to keep matters as simple as possible, let us consider at this time only three agents—the enterprise, consumers, and the government. In section 5.4 we extend the analysis to include owners of factors of production, and in section 5.5 to include other firms.

With this simplification we first need to specify how we will measure the welfare of the different agents. For firms we will use economic profit as the measure of their welfare. For consumers we will adopt the welfare economics approach and choose consumer surplus as a measure of their welfare.[5] The social value of the enterprise can then be taken to be the sum of producer and consumer surplus plus government revenue receipts, with the producer surplus valued at λ_p and the government revenue valued at the shadow value λ_g.

Keeping our various simplfications in mind, we may write the social values for any given year (say, year t) as

$$V_{sg}(t) = S_g(t) + \lambda_g \Pi_g(t), \tag{5.4}$$

and

$$V_{sp}(t) = S_p(t) + \lambda_p \{\Pi_p(t) - X(t)\} + \lambda_g X(t). \tag{5.5}$$

Equation (5.4) is straightforward. It sets the level of welfare under public operation equal to the sum of consumer surplus and enterprise profits, with the latter evaluated at λ_g. Equation (5.5) shows the social value under private operation as the sum of consumer surplus plus the net profits of the firm, valued at λ_p, plus government tax revenues, valued at λ_g. Note that in (5.4) we did not make any separate allowance for the tax payments of the enterprise, because the profits accrue to the government (including the public enterprise) anyway.

In fact, $V_{sg}(t)$ and $V_{sp}(t)$ are only flows for year t. The true social values are the present discounted values of the streams of these flows. Thus we may write

$$V_{sg} = \sum_{t=0}^{\infty} \rho^t [S_g(t) + \lambda_g \Pi_g(t)] \tag{5.6}$$

$$V_{sp} = \sum_{t=0}^{\infty} \rho^t[S_p(t) + \lambda_p\Pi_p(t) + (\lambda_g - \lambda_p)X(t)]. \tag{5.7}$$

Equations (5.6) and (5.7) may be used to find the *change* in welfare as a result of divestiture, defined in equation (2.2) as

$$\Delta W = V_{sp} - V_{sg} + (\lambda_g - \lambda_p)Z.$$

Substituting (5.6) and (5.7) into this equation we can write, after some manipulation,

$$\Delta W = \sum_{t=0}^{\infty} \rho^t\{S_p(t) - S_g(t) + \lambda_g[\Pi_p(t) - \Pi_g(t)]\}$$

$$- (\lambda_g - \lambda_p)\left\{\sum_{t=0}^{\infty} \rho^t[\Pi_p(t) - X(t)] - Z\right\}. \tag{5.8}$$

But from (5.3) we know that

$$V_{pp} = \sum_{t=0}^{\infty} \rho^t[\Pi_p(t) - X(t)],$$

and we also know that $V_{pp} = Z_p$, the maximum willingness to pay of the buyer. Thus (5.8) can be rewritten as

$$\Delta W = \sum_{t=0}^{\infty} \rho^t[\Delta S(t) + \lambda_g\Delta\Pi(t)] - (\lambda_g - \lambda_p)(Z_p - Z), \tag{5.9}$$

where $\Delta S(t)$ and $\Delta\Pi(t)$ represent the change for year t in consumer surplus and in net pretax profits, respectively.

The basic analytic equations for the divestiture decision are (5.3) and (5.9). Equation (5.3) provides the simplest estimate of the willingness to pay of a potential buyer. Although adjustments are needed to allow for asset values (see chapter 4) and for synergies of the enterprise with the buyer's other operations (see chapter 7), (5.3) provides the basic framework for estimating V_{pp}. Equation (5.9) provides an estimate of how much society will gain from selling the enterprise to a particular buyer. Again, complications will be added later, but equation (5.9) illustrates the virtue of our differencing procedure. The *gain* in welfare will be much easier to estimate than the *levels* of welfare. For example, as we will see in our illustrative numerical examples, the gain in consumer surplus $(S_p - S_g)$ is quite easy to estimate, even though the individual elements of this difference are nearly unknowable. Equation (5.9) provides us the key information for the divestiture decision. We need $\Delta W > 0$ to consider divestiture, and we can choose among alternative bids by choosing the one that yields the highest ΔW.

Finally, we note here a simplification of (5.9) that is of some interest. As we argued in chapter 2, government ought to attempt to maximize the sale price Z from the chosen buyer as long as $\lambda_g > \lambda_p$. Thus government's target price is $Z = Z_p$. If indeed government *does* receive this price, then (5.9) simplifies to

$$\Delta W^* = \sum_{t=0}^{\infty} \rho^t [\Delta S(t) + \lambda_g \Delta \Pi(t)]. \tag{5.10}$$

Equation (5.10) is a remarkable result. It says that as long as government obtains the maximum price the buyer is willing to pay, the gain in welfare from divestiture can be written as the present value of the sum of the change in consumer surplus plus the change in company profits, with the latter evaluated at λ_g. Thus we get quite a simple formula for the net gain from divestiture. Of course, estimation of future variables is always problematic, and some simplifying assumptions will be necessary. For example, if we assume that $\Delta S(t)$ and $\Delta \Pi(t)$ are constant over time and accrue in perpetuity, then (5.10) reduces to

$$\Delta W^* = \frac{1}{r} (\Delta S + \lambda_g \Delta \Pi),$$

where r is the discount rate. Alternatively, if we assume that ΔS and $\Delta \Pi$ will grow at a constant rate g, then (5.10) becomes

$$\Delta W^* = \frac{1}{r - g} [\Delta S(0) + \lambda_g \Delta \Pi(0)].$$

Obviously, some judgment in the face of an uncertain future is necessary here and will at least partially depend upon the particular circumstances under consideration.

We will illustrate the use of our methodology by taking the data for the illustrative company of chapter 4 and then calculating the values of Z_p and ΔW under different scenarios of behavioral changes and market structure. This process will reveal exactly what information is needed to make the best divestiture decision.

5.2   Perfect Competition

5.2.1   Analytics

The simplest case to analyze is that of an enterprise operating in a perfectly competitive market. The price at which the output is sold is then given by the market, so divestiture has no effect on consumer surplus. One special case of this is that in which the sales are exports, so that the consumer surplus does not even enter into the measure of aggregate domestic welfare. Assume that $Z = Z_p$, because adjustments can always be made later according to equation (5.9). Then (5.10) gives us our measure of ΔW. For this case then, since $\Delta S = 0$ and if we suppress the time index for simplicity,

$$\Delta W^* = \sum_{t=0}^{\infty} \rho^t \lambda_g (\Pi_p - \Pi_g). \tag{5.11}$$

Using (5.1) and (5.2), we may write

$$\Delta W^* = \sum_{t=0}^{\infty} \rho^t \{\lambda_g [(P_p - c_p) q_p - (P_g - c_g) q_g]\}.$$

Let $P = P_g = P_p$ be the given market price. Then it is possible to write

$$\Delta W^* = \sum_{t=0}^{\infty} \rho^t \{\lambda_g [(c_g - c_p) q_g + (P - c_p)(q_p - q_g)]\}, \tag{5.12}$$

where the first term within the brackets represents the cost saving in producing the original quantity q_t, and the second term gives the net value of any increase in production.

The simplest way to picture this relationship is shown in figure 5.1. Here the public enterprise produces at a constant average cost of c_g up to some level of "capacity," q_g. When the firm is divested, average cost falls to c_p, and the firm also manages to increase capacity utilization, so that output rises to q_p. The shaded area then represents the net gain, to be valued at λ_g.

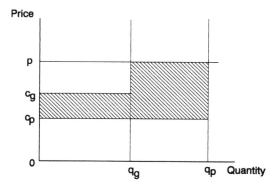

Figure 5.1
Increase in profits under competition (constant cost case)

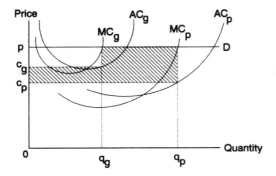

Figure 5.2
Increase in profits under competition (U-shaped cost case)

The identical net result is obtained in the somewhat more complicated picture in figure 5.2, where the cost curves are U-shaped. Here, divestiture has the effect of causing the firm's average and marginal cost curves to shift downward, raising the optimal level of output from q_g to q_p.

The net result is the same, however, with the shaded area representing the net gain. Note that in this case, if our behavioral assumption is correct (i.e., that divestiture will lead to improved efficiency), then ΔW is always positive, and divestiture will always be desirable. To determine the best sale price, we must return to (5.3) and note that

$$Z_p = \sum_{t=0}^{\infty} \rho^t[\Pi_p - X] = \sum_{t=0}^{\infty} \rho^t[(p - C_p)q_p - X]. \tag{5.13}$$

Thus, in this case, in order to find Z_p we need estimates only of the extent to which cost will be reduced and output increased.

5.2.2   An Example

As an example, consider corporation A, the enterprise whose data were presented in chapter 4. Suppose that, once divested, the enterprise could raise its output by 10 percent while using the same level of intermediate inputs and labor. That is, assume an all-around 10 percent improvement in efficiency. The production and distribution flows now look like the data in table 5.2. In this case the willingness-to-pay calculation is as in table 5.1.

Thus, the amount a private buyer is willing to pay for an enterprise is higher if the buyer feels that efficiency gains in the enterprise are feasible. In fact, if bidding is competitive, the amount a potential buyer bids for the enterprise may be an indication of just how much the buyer expects to

Table 5.1
Willingness to pay with perfect competition and efficiency gains

1991 operating surplus	7,344
− Opportunity cost of working capital	−618
= Total return to fixed capital (quasi-rents)	6,726
− Taxes on operating return[1]	1,710
= After-tax return	5,016
Discounted to 1986 ($= Z_p^\pi$)	4,560
+ Financial value (Z_p^f from chapter 4)[2]	−3,339
− Transaction costs	0
= Maximum willingness to pay (Z_p)	1,221

Notes: 1. Obtained by applying the tax rate of 33 percent to taxable operating income = quasi-rents (6,726) minus depreciation (1,595). Depreciation is applied at a rate of 0.157 (arbitrarily chosen to represent the true rate of deterioration) on the fixed operating assets of (6,171 + 3,987). See table 4.5.

2. This is unaltered by divestiture.

improve efficiency. Unfortunately, the bid is also affected by synergies the enterprise may have with the buyer's other activities, so it is impossible to choose a bid solely on its size.

How much better off is society as a result of divestiture and the realization of efficiency gains? The answer was provided in equation (5.10): the change in pretax profits multiplied by the shadow value of government revenue. Assuming that without divestiture the base year results would be repeated, the pretax profits are given by 1990 production minus costs (intermediate inputs, labor, rentals, and the opportunity cost of working capital). We therefore have the following calculation:

	Before divestiture	After divestiture
Production	18,191	20,010
− Intermediate inputs	11,011	11,011
− Labor costs	1,631	1,631
− Rentals	24	24
− Opportunity cost of working capital	648	618
= Gross pretax profits	4,877	6,726
− Taxes on operations	1,094	1,710
= Net after-tax profits	3,783	5,016

Table 5.2
Production and distribution flows (at current market prices) for corporation A

Competitive case	1990 (Before divestiture)	1991 (After divestiture)
Generation of surplus		
Production (at market cost)	18,191	20,010
— Indirect taxes (plus subsidies)	0	0
= Production (at factor cost)	18,191	20,010
— Intermediate inputs	11,011	11,011
= Gross value added (at factor cost)	7,180	8,999
— Employee compensation (return to labor)	1,631	1,631
— Rental expenses (return to other factors)	24	24
= Return to operating assets	5,525	7,344
+ Nonoperating return	272	272
= Total return to capital	5,797	7,616
Distribution of surplus		
Total return to capital	5,797	7,616
— Interest payments (return to debt holders)	1,029	1,029
— Direct taxes (return to government)	751	1,358
= Return to equity holders	4,017	5,229
— Dividends	694	694
= Gross domestic savings (by enterprise)	3,323	4,535
— Depreciation and amortization	2,514	2,514
= Retained earnings	809	2,021

The change in gross profits is, therefore, $6,726 - 4,877 = \$1,849$. If λ_g, the shadow value of geovernment revenue, is 1.3, then $\Delta W^* = (1.3 \times 1,849)/1.1 = 2,185$.

Alternatively, V_{sp} is the net private return plus taxes on operations, evaluated at λ_g, and discounted:

$$V_{sp} = \frac{5,016 + 1,710 \times 1.3}{1.1} = 6,581.$$

V_{sg} is the gross return to public operation evaluated at λ_p and discounted:

$$V_{sg} = \frac{4,877 \times 1.3}{1.1} = 5,764.$$

Therefore,

$$V_{sg} - V_{sp} = 5,764 - 6,581 = -817,$$

$$Z_g = \frac{-817}{(1.3 - 1)} = -2,724.$$

Since $Z_p = 1,221$, there is plenty of room to strike a deal. In the unlikely event that $Z = Z_p$,

$$\Delta W^* = 817 + 1,221(1.3 - 1) = 2,185,$$

as before.

If government is evaluating more than one bid, this figure (ΔW^*) becomes the criterion for selecting the winner—the one yielding the highest gain in social welfare.

5.3   Monopoly

5.3.1   Analytics

If the enterprise occupies a monopoly position, the divestiture decision is not so easy. There is now the possibility that the divested firm will attempt to exploit its monopoly power. Government may consider the imposition of regulation, but this will lower the willingness to pay of private buyers. We consider this problem in greater detail in chapter 9 and ignore the possibility of regulation for the time being. In that case, it may well be that in equation (5.12) there will be a welfare loss for consumers against which may be weighed the gain in profits from increased efficiency and altered profit-maximizing behavior. The possible trade-off can easily be seen in figure 5.3. For simplicity in the diagram it is assumed that the public enterprise sets $P_g = c_g$ (which is regarded as welfare-maximizing pricing); therefore, $\Pi_g = 0$.[6] The private enterprise is more efficient ($c_p < c_g$), but it curtails output ($q_p < q_g$) in order to raise prices ($P_p > P_g$). The area $P_p ABP_g$ represents the loss to consumers ($S_p - S_g$) in (5.9), whereas the area $P_p ACc_p$ represents the gain in profits. In this example if the divested enterprise is expected to curtail output and raise price considerably, it may be in the social interest neither to divest nor to introduce regulation. If, however, the enterprise cuts costs *and* lowers prices, then this divestiture will be unambiguously desirable from the social point of view.

The sale price of the enterprise can be determined by application of equation (5.13). Once again, therefore, we need estimates of the cost savings and of the new price and quantity figures. In order to derive these last estimates, it is possible to use the standard formulas for monopoly behavior.

An illustration may give us some greater insight into the relative importance of the different variables. Suppose that, initially, the public enterprise is setting price equal to the (constant) marginal cost. Without loss of generality, we normalize this initial price to unity. Suppose also that a point estimate of the elasticity of demand at the initial quantity is given by ε. A linear approximation of the demand curve, of the form

$$p = \alpha - \beta q,$$

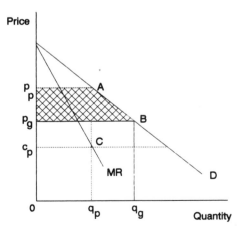

Figure 5.3
Change in profits and social welfare under monopoly

must then satisfy, because of the price normalization,

$$1 = \alpha - \beta q_g,$$

and $\varepsilon = 1/\beta q_g$, where q_g is the initial level of production. Thus the parameters of the linear approximation to demand will be given by

$$\alpha = 1 + \frac{1}{\varepsilon} \quad \text{and} \quad \beta = \frac{1}{\varepsilon q_g}. \tag{5.14}$$

Now suppose that if the enterprise is divested, the (constant) average cost will be given by c. If there is an improvement in efficiency, we must have $c < 1$; then, for a linear demand curve, it is straightforward to find the price and quantity that would be set by a profit-maximizing monopolist. We would have

$$p_p = \frac{\alpha + c}{2} \tag{5.15}$$

and

$$q_p = \frac{\alpha - c}{2\beta}. \tag{5.16}$$

Since α and β can be estimated from initial conditions according to (5.14), an estimate of the cost improvement that is likely to be effected by the buyer is all that is needed to estimate the new price and quantity. Note that our methodology does not in any way depend upon the monopolist's adopting this particular pricing strategy. We need to estimate what the private firm will do after divestiture, and our exercise here is to illustrate how one particular behavioral strategy can be modeled and incorporated into our methodology. Naturally, other strategies are possible, and they could just as easily yield price and quantity estimates that could then be incorporated into our formulas.

To return to our example, the willingness to pay of the buyer and the welfare gain from divestiture remain to be calculated. The profits for the monopolist are given by

$$\Pi_p = \frac{(\alpha - c)^2}{4\beta},$$

so V_{pp} may easily be calculated. The welfare gain has two components. The change in gross pretax profits is given by $\Pi_p - \Pi_g$, where Π_g represents the public enterprise's initial level of profits. From figure 5.3 it can be seen that the change in consumer surplus is given by

$$\Delta S = \Delta p \left(q_p + \frac{q_g - q_p}{2} \right). \tag{5.17}$$

Since q_p and p_p can be estimated, so can ΔS. Note that our assumption of a linear demand curve is less restrictive than it may seem, because all we are really interested in is ΔS. As long as the demand curve is approximately linear in this region, our calculation will be reasonably accurate. We do not need the demand curve to be linear at prices higher than P_p.

Finally, it is possible to calculate the improvement in social welfare as a consequence of divestiture. Once again, this will depend upon the sale price. Equation (5.9) remains the general formula for ΔW. If government receives the maximum willingness to pay, this reduces as before to

$$\Delta W^* = \sum_{t=0}^{\infty} \rho^t [\lambda_g (\Pi_p - \Pi_g) + \Delta S]. \tag{5.18}$$

Whether or not the enterprise should be divested depends upon whether or not $\Delta W > 0$. The way we have outlined the model here, we would expect the first term in (5.18) to be positive and the second term to be negative—that is, firm profits would rise, but consumers could well be made worse off if the enterprise behaved as a profit-maximizing monopolist. The relative magnitude of the two effects will determine which way the trade-off pushes the decision. For example, in the simplest case, with $c = 1$ (no cost reduction) and $\lambda_g = 1$, it may be shown that

$$\Pi_p = \frac{q_g}{4\varepsilon} \quad \text{and} \quad \Delta S = \frac{-3q_g}{8\varepsilon}.$$

Thus, as we would expect in the linear case, the fall in consumer welfare is 1.5 times the rise in prifits. In this case, the enterprise should not be divested. If $\lambda_g = 1.5$, however, ΔW would become zero, and for $\lambda_g > 1.5$, $\Delta W > 0$. In that case, the enterprise should be divested. Thus if government revenues are needed badly enough (i.e., if λ_g is high enough), divestiture may be justified even if no cost reductions are expected to result.

If c is indeed less than 1 (i.e., there is a cost reduction from divestiture), then λ_g need not be that high to justify divestiture. In fact, it is entirely possible for $\Delta W^* > 0$ even with $\lambda_g = 1$ if c is sufficiently low.

5.3.2 An Example

To flesh out the argument, consider again the example of the previous section: corporation A with the same efficiency gain parameters as in our analysis of the competitive case. The difference here is that the firm may exploit its monopoly position and may, in fact, curtail output in order to raise the price. In order to predict what the firm might do, we must have some information on demand conditions.

One simple piece of information that may be available or may be estimated is the elasticity of demand for the product. Suppose for the commodity in question that $\varepsilon = 1.1$, then, using equation (5.14), it is possible to make an estimate of a linear approximation to demand. In the case of our example, given $q_g = 18,191$, we have the demand curve given by

$$p = 1.909 - \frac{q}{20,010}.$$

That is, we estimate that $\alpha = 1.909$ and $\beta = 1/20,010$.

Next, in order to use this demand curve to predict what the firm is likely to do, we need an estimate of the per unit cost. We make the following estimates for the components of unit cost:

Intermediate inputs	0.5503[7]
+ labor	0.0815[8]
+ rental	0.0012[9]
+ opportunity cost of working capital	0.0309[10]
= total per unit cost	0.6639.

This is our estimate of c.

Thus, we have estimates of all the key parameters, a, b, and c. Using these in equations (5.15) and (5.16), we can estimate the price and quantity that the monopolist will set:

$P_p = 1.2865$

$q_p = 12,458,$

so that the value of total production is given by

$P_p q_p = 16,028.$

It is now possible to construct the table of production and distribution flows for the enterprise; see table 5.3. It is then possible to estimate the maximum willingness to pay of the buyer:

Table 5.3
Production and distribution flows (at current market prices) for corporation A

Monopoly case

	1990 (Before sale)	1991 (After sale)
Generation of surplus		
Production (at market cost)	18,191	16,028
— Indirect taxes (plus subsidies)	0	0
= Production (at factor cost)	18,191	16,028
— Intermediate inputs	11,011	6,856
= Gross value added (at factor cost)	7,180	9,172
— Employee compensation (return to labor)	1,631	1,015
— Rental expenses (return to other factors)	24	15
= Return to operating assets	5,525	8,142
+ Nonoperating return	272	272
= Total return to capital	5,797	8,414
Distribution of surplus		
Total return to capital	5,797	8,414
— Interest payments (return to debt holders)	1,029	1,029
— Direct taxes (return to government)	751	1,624
= Return to equity holders	4,017	5,761
— Dividends	694	694
= Gross domestic savings (by enterprise)	3,323	5,067
— Depreciation and amortization	2,514	2,514
= Retained earnings	809	2,553

Willingness to pay with monopoly and efficiency gains

1991 operating surplus	8,142
− Opportunity cost of working captial	− 385
= Total return to fixed capital (quasi-rents)	7,757
− Taxes on operations[11]	2,054
= After-tax return	5,703
Discounted to 1990 (= Z_p^π)	5,184
+ Financial value (Z_p^f from chapter 3)	−3,339
− Transaction costs	
= Maximum willingness to pay	1,846

The last number gives the government a target price that it should attempt to achieve in negotiations with the buyer. Naturally, the maximum willingness to pay calculated here (1,846) is higher than in the competitive case (1,221). Suppose, in fact, that the government is attempting to divest this enterprise and has received two proposals.

One bidder has demanded as a condition of sale to be granted protection from foreign competition so that it can enjoy the benefits of a domestic monopoly. The other bidder has placed no such precondition, so it will face competition from imports. As we can see, the monopolist has a higher profit potential. Let us suppose each firm bids its maximum—that is, the monopolist firm bids 1,845, whereas the competitive firm bids 1,221. Which proposal should the government accept?

To answer this question, we must complete our calculations for the monopoly case. Specifically, we must estimate how much better off society will be under the monopoly divestiture. If government receives the full price for the enterprise, we know ΔW is given by equation (5.10):

$$\Delta W^* = \sum_{t=0}^{\infty} \rho^t [\Delta S + \lambda_g(\Pi_p - \Pi_g)].$$

To estimate ΔS, we use the usual measure of consumer surplus to estimate the shaded area of figure 5.3. This is found to be

$$\Delta S = -\{0.2865[12,450 + 0.5(18,191 - 12,458)]\}$$

$$= -4,390.$$

This is an estimate of how much worse off consumers will be under the monopoly regime.

Against this loss to society must be weighed the gain in efficiency and profits, which we obtain from the following calculation:

	Before divestiture	After divestiture
Production	18,191	16,028
— Intermediate inputs	11,011	6,856
— Labor costs	1,631	1,015
— Rentals	24	15
— Opportunity cost of working capital	648	385
= Gross pretax profits	4,877	7,757

Thus the gain in profits will be $7,757 - 4,877 = 2,880$. If $\lambda_g = 1.3$, we may write our estimate of the discounted net gain in social welfare as

$$\Delta W^* = \frac{-4,390 + 1.3(2,880)}{1.1}$$

$$= -588.$$

In this case, therefore, society will actually be worse off under divestiture than under continued public operation, so divestiture would be unadvisable. If there is a choice between this option and the competitive one, it is clear that the competitive option should be exercise. One final point is that there may be a third option: divest the enterprise to the monopolist but also introduce regulation. We consider this option in chapter 10.

5.4   Monopsony and Returns to Owners of Inputs

Thus far, our analysis of divestiture has ignored its impact on the owners of inputs. This neglect is justifiable if the enterprise is "small" relative to the input markets—that is, if it does not influence input prices in any substantive way and if the enterprise is truly paying the competitive market price. In fact, however, public enterprises are frequently likely to be "large" in input markets. This may be true in a local labor market and may be even more significant in cases where the enterprise is the only buyer of particular inputs, for example, of raw materials, such as tobacco in a cigarette monopoly, bauxite in aluminum, or sugar. If this is true, and if the enterprise also faces an upward-sloping supply curve of the particular input, input owners will be earning some rents from the enterprise. The impact of divestiture on these input owners must then be considered.

In addition to the case of upward-sloping input supply curves, we may also find situations where the public enterprise simply pays more than the market price. This may happen for political reasons and is most likely to happen for labor, but it could well also happen for, say, an agricultural raw material. In either event, if the enterprise pays more than the market price, the owners of inputs will once again enjoy rents. This situation is unlikely to continue after divestiture. It is frequently argued that one of the main benefits of divestiture is the greater eifficiency of resource use that results. Particularly with respect to labor, private owners will find ways to trim down the labor force to cut wages if at all possible. Workers as a class are thus likely to be worse off. Similarly, for other inputs, the private owners of the enterprise will attempt to use any available monopsony power by curtailing use and cutting the price they pay. The consequences for input owners must be then considered.

To be more precise, let us reexamine our basic model of section 5.2 and see what modifications are necessary. The calculation of V_{pp}, the private value of the enterprise, is unaltered. Thus (5.3) stands unchanged. The calculations for V_{sp} and V_{sg}, however, need to be adjusted. Let us represent by M the net welfare (or rents) of input owners. M is equal to the total revenues of input owners minus their opportunity costs and may be represented in a diagram (see figure 5.4) as the area above the input supply curve L^s and below the price, up to the level of input use. This is the shaded area in figure 5.4. In panel (a) we show a case with a rising input supply curve and in panel (b), a case where the public enterprise is simply paying a price w_g higher than the market price w_p but limiting use to L_g. The key point here is that if the enterprise is small in the input market (thereby facing a perfectly elastic supply curve at the market price) and if it pays this price, then no rents are enjoyed by input owners.

In the event that the input owners do enjoy rents, the definitions of V_{sg} and V_{sp} in equations (5.6) and (5.7) will be modified by the addition of a term in the welfare of input owners, M. Suppose that this welfare receives a weight of λ_m in the social welfare aggregate. Then

$$V_{sg} = \sum_{t=0}^{\infty} \rho^t [S_g(t) + \lambda_g \Pi_g(t) + \lambda_m M_g(t)], \tag{5.19}$$

$$V_{sp} = \sum_{t=0}^{\infty} \rho^t [S_p(t) + \lambda_p \Pi_p(t) + (\lambda_g - \lambda_p) X(t) + \lambda_m M_p(t)]. \tag{5.20}$$

Thus, after simplification, the modified version of (5.9) becomes

$$\Delta W = \sum_{t=0}^{\infty} \rho^t [\Delta S(t) + \lambda_g \Delta \Pi(t) + \lambda_m \Delta M(t)] - (\lambda_g - \lambda_p)(Z_p - Z). \tag{5.21}$$

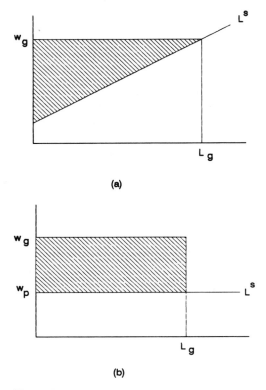

(a)

(b)

Figure 5.4
Rents to owners of inputs

The only change is the introduction of the term $\lambda_m \Delta M(t)$, the change in welfare due to the change in rents enjoyed by input owners.

Actually estimating ΔM involves a process similar to the estimation of ΔS in the monopoly case. We may write

$$M_g = w_g L_g - \int_0^{L_g} L^s \, dL, \tag{5.22}$$

and

$$M_p = w_p L_p - \int_0^{L_p} L^s \, dL. \tag{5.23}$$

Once again, differencing simplifies the calculations, so that

$$\Delta M = w_p L_p - w_g L_g - \int_{L_g}^{L_p} L^s \, dL. \tag{5.24}$$

This is the shaded area in panel (a) of figure 5.5. The measure of ΔM is then analogous to the estimation of ΔS in equation (5.17):

$$\Delta M = \Delta w \left(L_p + \frac{L_g - L_p}{2} \right). \tag{5.25}$$

Thus estimation of ΔM requires information on the elasticity of input supply in order to generate estimates of w_p and L_p.

However, because there is somewhat of a presumption that the public enterprise was initially not optimizing its choice of inputs, there is some question whether the initial input price-quantity combination even lies on the supply curve. For example, in the case of labor, the enterprise may set the wage too high and then ration jobs.

Although we consider rationing situations in the next chapter, we note here a way of crudely approximating equation (5.24) that applies in a wide variety of situations (including rationing) and that requires considerably less information. This approximation involves approximating the integral in (5.24) as

$$\int_{L_g}^{L_p} L^s \, dL = w_p (L_p - L_g).$$

In that case, (5.24) becomes

$$\Delta M = (w_p - w_g) L_g. \tag{5.26}$$

This approximation would measure ΔM in panel (a) of figure 5.5 as the shaded area plus the small triangle enclosed by the dotted line. Thus it would overstate the (absolute value of the) loss by approximately $(\Delta w \Delta L / 2)$ and would correspondingly understate ΔW^*. Despite its presence, this is a second-order—and hence relatively small—error. If L_g were less than L_p, (5.26) would understate the true loss by a similar small magnitude. Note from figure 5.4 (b) that (5.26) is exact in the case where the enterprise has no monopsony power but simply sets w_g too high. In panel (b) of figure 5.6 we also consider the case where the initial price-quantity combination is off the input supply curve. Once again, the true ΔM, the second shaded area, is overestimated by the small triangle enclosed by the dotted lines.

Before we can apply our equations to actually estimating ΔW, we need to decide the value of λ_m. In principle, this parameter can take on any value, depending upon the distributional goals of the government and the identities of the input owners. If, for example, the inputs are natural resources, the input owner may be government, in which case $\lambda_m = \lambda_g$, or

Case (a)

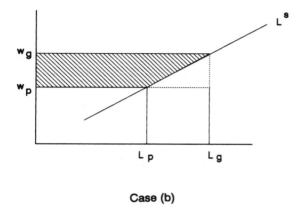

Case (b)

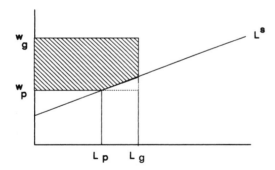

Figure 5.5
Change in input rents

it may be one or more firms, in which case $\lambda_m = \lambda_p$. If, on the other hand, the input in question is labor, then perhaps the most appropriate assumption is $\lambda_m = \lambda_c = 1$.

To illustrate the application of (5.26), let us assume the input in which we are interested is labor, so that $\lambda_m = 1$, and then consider our previous numerical example of the competitive case. Recall that, in that example, the enterprise increased output by 10 percent while holding labor costs constant. If this is achieved simply by using the existing labor more efficiently, then no further adjustment in our measure of ΔW is necessary, because $(w_p - w_g)$ in (5.26) is zero. If, however, this is achieved by increasing employment by 10 percent while cutting wages by the same proportion, then workers are worse off. Here $w_p = 0.9w_g$, so

$$\Delta M = -0.1w_g L_g.$$

Since we know $w_g L_g$ is the total wage bill prior to divestiture, we know $w_g L_g = 11,011$, and so $\Delta M = -1,101$. This figure is then used to modify the estimate of ΔW. We had previously calculated this for the competitive case, under the assumption that $\lambda_g = 1.3$, to be 2,391. Thus the new estimate is $\Delta W = 2,391 - 1,101 = 1,290$.[12]

5.5 Oligopoly and Returns to Other Firms

If the enterprise operates in an oligopolistic market, it becomes necessary to consider the impact of divestiture not only on consumers, the enterprise, and government but also on other firms in the industry. Let a prime (') indicate the value of a variable for other firms in the industry. Thus Π' represents the profits of other firms, with subscripts g and p indicating the value of the variable before and after divestiture. If we suppress time subscripts on the right-hand side for simplicity, we may express the welfare levels before and after divestiture as[13]

$$V_{sg} = \sum_{t=0}^{\infty} \rho^t [S_g + \lambda_g(\Pi_g + X_g') + \lambda_p(\Pi_g' - X_g')] \tag{5.27}$$

$$V_{sp} = \sum_{t=0}^{\infty} \rho^t [S_p + \lambda_p(\Pi_p - X) + \lambda_p(\Pi_p' - X_p') + \lambda_g(X + X_p')]. \tag{5.28}$$

Taking the difference between (5.28) and (5.27), after some manipulation and using the definition of ΔW given in (2.3), we get the net benefit from divestiture:

$$\Delta W = \sum_{t=0}^{\infty} \rho^t [\Delta S + \lambda_g \Delta \Pi + \lambda_p \Delta \Pi' + (\lambda_g - \lambda_p) \Delta X'] - (\lambda_g - \lambda_p)(Z_p - Z).$$

$$(5.29)$$

Equation (5.29) replaces (5.9) in the case of oligopoly. Note that it differs from (5.9) only in the last two terms within the square brackets, which may be interpreted as adjustments to the basic equation to allow for oligopoly. Thus equation (5.29) suggests that if the industry is oligopolistic, we need to add two terms to our measure of the change in welfare. The first represents the change in the profits of the rest of the industry, evaluated at λ_p, whereas the second is the change in tax collections from the rest of the industry, with this change being weighted by the term $(\lambda_g - \lambda_p)$, the excess of the shadow value of government revenue over the shadow value of private funds. As can be seen from this expression, the analysis of the oligopoly case is considerably more complicated; however, it is also clear that a systematic application of our valuation procedure will still yield the required estimates of willingness to pay and net social gain. It is worth remembering that ΔS in (5.29) refers to the change in consumer surplus in the whole market, not just the output produced by the divested enterprise.

The major problem is to decide on a model of oligopoly that is appropriate for the particular industry under consideration, because predictions of the outcome of divestiture depend very much on the behavioral assumptions that are made. We are not going to attempt to choose the "best" model, since there is no single best model. Rather, the appropriate model depends upon the particular circumstances, including the institutional environment and the degree of competition. It seems reasonable to suppose, however, that the equilibrium outcome in any oligopoly will tend to lie somewhere between the competitive and monopoly cases; thus it is possible to set bounds on the likely outcomes. This is particularly true for estimates of the private value of the enterprise, V_{pp}. If V_{pp}^c, V_{pp}^m, and V_{pp}^o represent the private value of the enterprise under competition, monopoly, and oligopoly, respectively, we may write

$$V_{pp}^o = \varphi V_{pp}^c + (1 - \varphi) V_{pp}^m,$$

where φ is the degree of competition in the industry ($\varphi = 1$ for perfect competition, and $\varphi = 0$ for monopoly).

It is the calculation of ΔW that is considerably more problematic. What happens to the profits of other firms depends very much on the nature of the competition that emerges in the industry, and there is a wide range of types of competition. For example, in a divestiture involving a large telecommunications enterprise, for instance, the dominant-firm model may be the most useful if the public enterprise that is being divested is initially in a near-monopoly situation. It is interesting to note that public enterprises that are in a dominant position have been known to behave in quite opposite ways. In general, we want a public enterprise to use its dominant position to force the industry close to the competitive situation. If this were done, then divestiture would have the undesirable effect of moving us away from this relatively good situation. Whether public enterprises actually do this in practice, however, is another matter. While some examples of the appropriate behavior can be found, public enterprises can on occasion be observed using their dominant position actually to enforce a cartel.[14] In this case, divestiture might encourage rivalry and a market outcome closer to the competitive one.

On particularly interesting case is one where the public enterprise being divested is a large multiplant monopoly that could be split up into several smaller firms that would then compete with each other. This case is particularly likely to arise in situations where the divestiture basically involves the denationalization of previously private but nationalized firms, such as the jute and textile industries in Bangladesh. Or the situation may be that the enterprise is simply large enough to be broken into several smaller firms. This would be true of large holding-company-type enterprises, such as India's steel and fertilizer companies or Britain's National Bus, which is currently being sold off in about 70 different pieces. In cases such as these, the industry structure may be endogenous to the divestiture decision, so the government may create the optimal level of competition for the industry. Thus a market structure that optimizes the trade-off between competition and scale economies may be achievable.

5.6 Intermediate Goods and Quality Changes

The discussion so far has made no mention of the particular type of good that is produced by the public enterprise being considered for divestiture. Implicitly, the good is a final good, as we have been speaking of consumer surplus as if it accrues to final consumers. But, of course, most public sector companies do not produce final consumer goods; rather, they produce intermediate goods that are used by downstream firms as inputs into their production processes. The meaning of consumer surplus in this context needs to be examined. This section performs such an examination. We also briefly discuss the problem of quality changes that divestiture may bring about.

Our discussion will show that the concept of consumer surplus is just as valid for an intermediate-good industry as for a final-good industry, as long as the appropriately defined demand curve is used in the calculations. We begin by noting that, whereas the demand curve faced by a final-good-producing industry is the demand curve of final consumers, the demand curve faced by an intermediate-good producer is a derived demand from other firms. This creates an apparent difference in significance between the two demand curves. The notion of willingness to pay that underlies the welfare basis of consumer surplus is not as relevant for a downstream firm that is buying this good, not for any reason of final consumption but only as an input into production. Nevertheless, we will see that the "consumer surplus" in this industry captures the welfare effects in the downstream industry.

Suppose for the sake of discussion that the particular enterprise we are discussing is an irrigation project that supplies water to a large number of small farmers. The farmers need the water only to irrigate their crops, which are then sold in the competitive food market. Their demand for water depends upon the demand for food. That is the sense in which the demand curve for water is a derived demand: it is derived from the demand for food. Figure 5.6 represents the relationship between the two markets. Panel (a) represents the water market and panel (b), the food market. In the initial (predivestiture) situation the equilibrium price and quantity in the water market are given by p_w^0 and W_0, whereas the corresponding levels in the food market are given by p_f^0 and F_0. In panel (a), the derived demand for water in the initial situation is shown as $D_w(p_f^0)$. This derived demand obviously depends upon conditions in the food market. Specifically, this curve is drawn on the assumption that the price of food is p_f^0. Technically, this is what is called an *unconditional demand curve* for water. If the price of food had been higher, the unconditional demand curve for water would lie farther to the right. Panel (b) characterizes the food market by a demand curve for food, D_f, and the supply curve for food, $S_f(p_w^0)$. The supply curve is itself a function of conditions in the water market; specifically, it is drawn on the assumption that the price of water is p_w^0. Had the price of water been higher, costs of production in the food industry would have been higher, and so the supply curve for food would be higher.

Now suppose the effect of divestiture is to raise the price of water, perhaps because of the exercise of market power by the now-private irrigation company. We ignore any efficiency improvements for the sake of clarifying the welfare notion here. Suppose the price of water rises to p_w^1. This shifts the supply curve of food up to, say, $S_f(p_w^1)$. The equilibrium

(a) Water Market

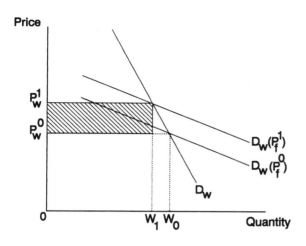

(b) Food Market

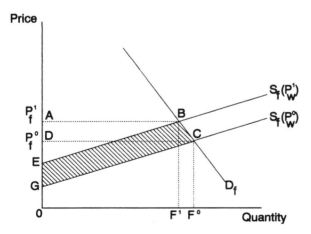

Figure 5.6
Derived demand

price of food rises to p_f^1, and this causes the unconditional demand curve for water to rise to $D_w(p_f^1)$. So the amount of water used in the final equilibrium, after allowing for adjustments in the food market that took place, is W_1.

What is the change in welfare in the food market? This is the appropriate question to ask if we want to find out the welfare effects on the consumers of water. The direct consumers are the farmers, and their profits matter, whereas the indirect consumers of water are the consumers of food, whose consumer surplus also matters. The sum of changes in consumer and producer surplus in the food market is given by the shaded area in panel (b). The fall in consumer surplus is given by area $ABCD$, and the change in producer surplus is the difference $ABE - DCG$. Putting these together yields the net loss of $EBCG$, the area shaded. It can be shown that this area is equal to the shaded area in panel (a). The proof is somewhat technical and may be skipped. We present it here for the interested reader.[15]

Suppose we represent the profits (strictly, quasi-rents) in the food industry by Π_f. We may write

$$\Pi_f = Fp_f - Wp_w - \sum_{i=1}^{n} x_i p_i,$$

where the last term refers to the cost of the other inputs used in the production of food. Consider what happens to Π_f when the price of water changes. If we assume that the prices of all other inputs are unaffected by this change, we may use the envelope theorem to obtain

$$\frac{\partial \Pi_f}{\partial p_w} = F \frac{dp_f}{dp_w} - W.$$

This expression gives us the rate at which quasi-rents in the food industry are changing. In order to determine the total change in quasi-rents for a discrete change in the price of water from p_w^0 to p_w^1, we integrate both sides of the equation with respect to p_w, which yields

$$\int_{p_w^1}^{p_w^1} \frac{\partial \Pi_f}{\partial p_w} dp_w = \int_{p_w^0}^{p_w^1} F \frac{dp_f}{dp_w} dp_w - \int_{p_w^0}^{p_w^1} W dp_w.$$

This equation can be expressed as follows:

$$\Delta \Pi_f = -\Delta S_f + \Delta S_w,$$

where S refers to the consumer surplus in the relevant market. Thus

$$\Delta S_w = \Delta \Pi_f + \Delta S_f.$$

In other words, the change in consumer surplus in the water market is equal to the sum of the changes in producer and consumer surplus in the food market.

This result can be generalized to the case where there are many downstream users and several layers. The consumer surplus in the intermediate-good market captures the welfare effect all the way downstream, as long as the relevant demand curve in the intermediate-good market incorporates the general equilibrium effects of price changes in that market.

This general equilibrium demand curve is marked D_w in the diagram. This curve reflects the demand for water, taking into account the effects of changing the price of water on the price of food. Note that it is less elastic than the conventional unconditional demand curves. As long as we calculate the change in consumer surplus under this kind of demand curve, the consumer surplus concept captures for an intermediate good the welfare effects on all downstream users of the good.

Although the preceding discussion has implicitly assumed that the downstream industry is perfectly competitive, the general result that consumer surplus in an upstream industry captures all welfare effects downstream does not depend on that assumption. The proof of the equivalence of areas in the two markets does not depend on the competitive assumption. Thus we may use the same sort of measures whether the enterprise is selling to competitive or to monopoly firms.[16]

Implicitly, the preceding discussion on welfare effects has followed conventional welfare economics in that the welfare weights attached to consumer and producer surplus are the same, equal to unity. In translating these concepts to our measures of the welfare effects of divestiture, we need to allow for the fact that λ_p may be greater than one. Thus the consumer surplus in the intermediate-good industry ought to receive a welfare weight greater than one, because it includes the welfare effects on consumers and producers downstream. In the particular case of water supply to agriculture, it might be argued that the downstream producers (the farmers) are more like what we think of as households than firms and, therefore, that the entire consumer surplus in the water market should receive a weight of one.

But clearly there are many other industries in which this is not true. Obvious examples are steel and cement. In such cases we need to have a sense of the proportion of the total surplus in the downstream industry that accrues to producers as opposed to consumers. In other words, what is the ratio $\Delta\Pi_f/(\Delta\Pi_f + \Delta S_f)$, using our previous notation? Let us call this ratio

ζ. Then the appropriate weight to attach to the upstream consumer surplus (ΔS_w) would be

$$\lambda_w = \zeta \lambda_p + (1 - \zeta).$$

This expression awards a weight of λ_p to the producer surplus downstream and a weight of one to the consumer surplus. More complicated cases arise when some of the downstream users are households and others are firms, as with electricity and telephones, for example. Here we need to know the proportion of demand that comes from the different sources and weight accordingly.

Finally, we need to consider the problem of capturing welfare effects of quality changes or of new product introductions. It is widely believed that one of the possible effects of divestiture is to improve the quality of goods, to improve the quality of service, and to encourage the introduction of a more varied array of goods. The measurement of the welfare effects of quality improvements is, however, a particularly difficult problem,[17] and little headway has been made in the literature on solving it.[18] In principle, one could use a Lancaster-type of attributes approach, in which it is assumed that consumers do not consume goods for themselves but rather for the attributes they possess.[19] Thus the consumer's utility function depends not on the quantities of goods, as in the conventional analysis, but on the quantities of the different attributes. As an example, it may be argued that utility is a function not of the quantities of hamburgers and salad but of the nutritive content, taste, and the like. New products can then be incorporated into the analysis by simply thinking of them as new combinations of existing attributes. Although this theory has some attractive properties, it is not very easy to implement empirically. There is therefore a tendency to try to capture quality improvements as though they were cost reductions. This may be particularly feasible in the category of intermediate goods (which account for most public sector output), since a quality improvement in, say, a machine can be translated into a reduction in the cost of production in the downstream industry. Thus we may be able to make meaningful calculations of the welfare effects of quality improvements (or, for that matter, of new product introductions) by looking at the effects on costs of production downstream.

5.7 Conclusion

This chapter looked at the fundamental trade-off of the divestiture decision, that the divested firm may be more efficient but that it may also tend to behave more in the private than in the public interest when exercising its market power. Successive sections looked at this trade-off at rising levels of complexity. The underlying premise was that markets generally clear and that we can take market prices as indicative of social value. In the next chapter we examine how the analysis must be modified if markets do not clear. More generally, we examine cases under which market prices cannot be used as indicators of social value.

Shadow Pricing of Inputs and Outputs

Thus far we have assumed that prices paid by the enterprise for its inputs and prices paid by the public for the enterprise outputs are market clearing and, further, that the private evaluation of these prices by the input suppliers and output purchasers coincides with the social evaluation.[1] These assumptions generally do not hold in reality, so in this chapter we modify our framework to incorporate rationing and differences between private and social evaluation of prices. In section 6.1 we analyze nonprice rationing of inputs and outputs, in section 6.2 we incorporate indirect taxes on the firm's inputs/outputs, and in section 6.3 we turn to shadow prices proper.

The common thread in this discussion is that the public enterprise and/or divested firm operate(s) off the relevant demand or supply curves. In the case of rationing, all actors perceive the correct curves, but they cannot reach some points on these curves. In the case of indirect taxes the government drives a wedge between curves as perceived by buyers and sellers. In the case of shadow prices proper, the actors optimize along curves that, from a social perspective, are incorrect. Thus, in the last case, buyers are on their private demand curves, and sellers are on their private supply curves. However, they are off the social demand and supply curves, respectively.

6.1 Nonprice Rationing

6.1.1 Direct Welfare Costs of Rationing

Public enterprises are often thought to pay higher wages to unskilled workers as compared with their counterparts in the private sector or to offer more job security and less job pressure than private firms. These advantages lead to a labor supply for the public enterprise that is larger than its labor demand at the lower end of skill requirements. In such cases it may use nonprice rationing for jobs.[2] On the output side, public firms often set artificially low prices for political reasons. At the same time they face capacity constraints or governmental desires to place a cap on public enterprise deficits. Again, the firm may use nonprice rationing methods.

Rationing of Outputs

In the case of nonprice rationing of outputs the consumer surplus measure $S(p)$ no longer gives a proper description of consumer benefits because at price p the consumers can no longer buy all the quantities they want. Rather, consumer benefits are now determined by the price, by the quantity available (q), and by the rationing method (R^o), where the superscript o indicates output rationing. For simplicity we consider only the monopoly case. If we designate $S(p)$ as consumer surplus under pure price rationing and $S(p, q, R^o)$ as consumer surplus under mixed price-quantity rationing, then it is well known that $S(p_0) \geqslant S(p_0, q, R^o)$ for all mixed rationing schemes and all prices p_0. This relationship says that under consumer sovereignty, price is the ideal rationing device. Each consumer is assumed to know best which quantity to buy at a given price. Any outside restriction on quantity and any additional nonprice rationing mechanism can make consumers only worse off. This result holds for each individual and therefore in the aggregate. Normally we can assume that unconstrained private enterprises depend on price rationing, whereas public and regulated private enterprises often resort to some form of nonprice rationing.[3]

Rationing methods can vary substantially. For example, the enterprise can designate priority groups that are served first, or it can established maximum consumption levels per customer, or it can make customers wait in line. For simplicity, all cases can be collapsed into a single continuum in terms of their effects on consumer surplus. The extreme cases are rationing in the order of willingness to pay and rationing in the reverse order of willingness to pay.

In the first extreme case, if the public enterprise rations consumers according to their willingness to pay, then

$$S(p_g, q_g, R_g^o) = S(p(q_g)) + q_g[p(q_g) - p_g], \tag{6.1}$$

where the subscript g indicates rationing under public ownership and $p(q)$ is the demand function. Equation (6.1) says that total consumer surplus under rationing by willingness to pay is equal to the consumer surplus at the price $p(q_g)$ that would have rationed the available supply q_g plus the money saved by the consumers due to the actual lower price p_g. $S(p_g, q_q, R_g^o)$ is given by the sum of the two shaded areas in figure 6.1. Thus under

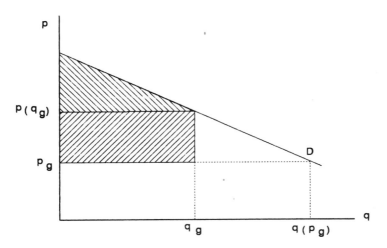

Figure 6.1
Consumer surplus under alternative rationing schemes: the linear case

rationing by willingness to pay, those consumers who actually receive the service are better off by the full price reduction compared with the price that would have rationed the service at the level. Simultaneously, the firm is worse off by the same amount.

In the other extreme, if the enterprise rations consumers in the reverse order of their willingness to pay, then

$$S(p_g, q_g, R_g^o) = S(p_g) - S(p(q\Delta)) - [p(q\Delta) - p_g]q\Delta, \tag{6.2}$$

where $q\Delta = q(p_g) - q_g$. Therefore, $q\Delta$ is the difference between the quantity demand at p_g and the quantity supplied by the enterprise. As can be seen in figure 6.2, the first difference in equation (6.2), $S(p_g) - S(p(q\Delta))$, is the area $ACDE$. From this we subtract the rectangle $ABDE$ (the last term in (6.2)) to arrive at the remaining consumer surplus of area BCD. This is quite small compared with the area between line segment AF and the demand curve that would have been the consumer surplus under rationing according to willingness to pay.

Another way of looking at the difference between the two types of rationing is in terms of consumer surplus lost compared with the full supply of the quantity demanded at price p_g. In case of rationing in the order of willingness to pay, this surplus loss is equal to the small triangle GFC in figure 6.2. However, with rationing contrary to willingness to pay, the consumer surplus loss becomes the large unshaded area below the demand

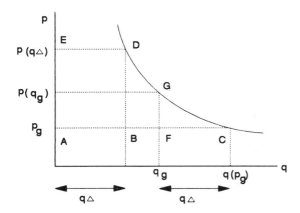

Figure 6.2
Consumer surplus under alternative rationing schemes: the nonlinear case

curve and above the line segment AB. Note that this includes the entire area above ED and below the demand curve.

Equation (6.2) is not intuitively obvious; hence it is good to know that for a linear demand curve it becomes

$$S(p_g, q_g, R_g^o) = S(p(q_g)).\tag{6.2a}$$

In this case consumers in total do not benefit from the lower price at all; total consumer surplus is simply equivalent to the upper shaded area in figure 6.1.[4] The reason is that under linear demand the area between $p(q_g)$ and the demand curve is the same as the area between P_g and the demand curve measured from D to $[q(p_g) - q_g]$ on the q-axis. Note that the lower shaded area in this case represents a deadweight welfare loss because the enterprise does not get this amount either. Also note that low-demand (and often low-income) customers benefit from this approach, whereas high-demand (and often high-income) customers suffer. Perverse as the second extreme type of rationing may look, it is not totally unrealistic. For example, rationing through queues may approximate this type if low-demand customers have a low value of leisure time, and high-demand customers value their time considerably more highly.[5]

Any real rationing scheme will lie somewhere between the two extremes. Using the linear demand function as a first-order approximation to an arbitrary demand curve, we can then write

$$S(p_g, q_g, R_g^o) = S(p(q_g)) - \mu^o q_g[p_g - p(q_g)],\tag{6.3}$$

where $0 \leqslant \mu^o \leqslant 1$ is a function of the rationing rule. In particular, we have $\mu^o = 0$ for rationing contrary to willingness to pay and $\mu_g^o = 1$ for rationing according to willingness to pay. Normally, we can expect the public enterprise to use rationing methods that differ from those of the divested firm. Hence we have to differentiate between μ_g^o for the publicly held firm and μ_p^o for the divested firm.

Now we can apply equation (6.3) to our divestiture valuation. In order to keep the formulas simple, we look at the one-period case only and thus leave out the discounting and summation over time. We further focus on ΔW^*, assuming unrealistically that the price Z paid for the enterprise equals Z_p, the private willingness to pay. Considering (6.3) and assuming nonprice rationing before and after divestiture, we get

$$\Delta W^* = \lambda_g \Delta \Pi + \Delta S(p(q_g)) + \mu_g^o q_g[p_g - p(q_g)] - \mu_p^o q_p[p_p - p(q_p)]. \quad (6.4)$$

Looking at the differences between surplus under rationing for the linear and nonlinear cases, it may be worth approximating consumer surplus changes by simpler formulas. One such approach is given by Turvey.[6] The Turvey approximation to a consumer surplus change ΔS resulting from a price change Δp is $\Delta S = \Delta p(q + \Delta q/2)$. This approximation is exact for linear demand curves, but it overestimates a surplus increase (decrease) for a convex (concave) demand curve and underestimates a surplus increase (decrease) for a concave (convex) demand curve.[7] Approximations are usually defined for changes that occur *on* the demand curve, whereas rationing occurs *off* the demand curve. If we know only observable prices and quantities, then we cannot approximate the demand curve. Hence we have to assume in addition that we know the approximate amount of rationing. We can then apply the Turvey approximations to expression (6.4) to obtain

$$\Delta W^* = \lambda_g \Delta \Pi + \tfrac{1}{2}[p(q_g) - p(q_p)][q_g + q_p]$$

$$+ \mu_g^o q_g[p_g - p(q_g)] - \mu_p^o q_p[p_p - p(q_p)]. \quad (6.5)$$

Note that λ_p does not appear in this equation. The reason is that for ΔW^*, we have assumed that $Z = V_{pp} = \Pi_p$. Thus the two terms involving λ_p (i.e., Z and Π_p) cancel each other.

Assuming rationing according to willingness to pay under both regimes, then we have[8]

$$\Delta W^* = \lambda_g \Delta \Pi + \tfrac{1}{2}[q_p - q_g][(p(q_g) + p(q_p)] + q_g p_g - q_p p_p. \quad (6.5a)$$

Figure 6.3 illustrates equation (6.5a). Here we assume that divestiture results in an average cost reduction from c_g to c_p, whereas the price remains

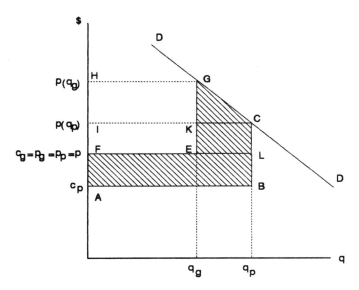

Figure 6.3
Approximation to welfare change under rationing

unchanged at $p = p_g = p_p$ and output is increased from q_g to q_p. For the case of $\lambda_g = 1$, the approximate welfare change is exact and is given by the shaded area $ABCGEF$.

For rationing contrary to willingness to pay, equation (6.5) becomes[9]

$$\Delta W^* = \lambda_g \Delta \Pi + \tfrac{1}{2}[q_g + q_p][p(q_g) - p(q_p)]. \tag{6.5b}$$

Compared with equation (6.5a), we are thus adding the difference between two rectangles, as illustrated by the difference between $GHIK$ and $ELCK$ in figure 6.3. This difference may be either positive or negative, depending on the amount of rationing before and after divestiture.

Now we are in a position to calculate the change in welfare for the numerical example introduced in chapter 5. In order to concentrate on the rationing aspect, let us assume that in spite of divestiture the output price remains unchanged (at 1.0), for instance, because it is regulated. However, as in our numerical example for the competitive case in chapter 5, private output goes up, and thus the amount of nonprice rationing is reduced. Then in equation (6.4) we have $p_p = p_g = p = 1.0$. As before, divestiture is taken to lead to an improvement of total factor productivity and to an increase in output of 10 percent. This output can easily be accommodated in the market, because at the regulated price there is excess demand. The reason for the inability to supply more is the capacity constraint of the plant that has been divested. As in the monopoly example of chapter 5, we assume a downward-sloping demand curve with an estimated elasticity of $\varepsilon = 1.1$ at the price p. In order to illustrate rationing, we now assume that demand $q(p)$ at that price is estimated to be 20 percent larger than the firm's supply q_g. In this case the linear approximation to the demand curve is $p = \alpha - \beta q(p)$. As in chapter 5 the assumption $p = 1$ leads to estimates for the parameter α and β of

$$\alpha = 1 + \frac{1}{\varepsilon} \quad \text{and} \quad \beta = \frac{1}{\varepsilon q(1)}.$$

Since $q(1) = (18{,}191)(1.20) = 21{,}829$, we get

$$p = 1.909 - \frac{q}{(21{,}829)(1.1)} = 1.909 - \frac{q}{24{,}012},$$

and

$$p(q_g) = 1.1514.$$

As a result, the flows turn out to be the same as in the competitive case of section 5.2. The relevant corporate cash flows are provided in table 5.3. All that changes is the economic story behind the accounting numbers. From table 5.3, output after divestiture is $q_p = 20{,}010$. The market clearing price after divestiture, $p(q_p)$, then becomes

$$p(q_p) = 1.909 - \frac{20{,}010}{24{,}012} = 1.0757.$$

As before, the change in profits is given by

$$\Delta \Pi = \Pi_p - \Pi_g = 6{,}726 - 4{,}877 = 1{,}849.$$

The assumption of $\lambda_g = 1.3$ then implies $\lambda_g \Delta\Pi = 2{,}404.$[10] For the case of rationing in the order of willingness-to-pay and a discount rate of 10 percent, approximation (6.5a) yields a present value of

$$\Delta W^* = \frac{2{,}404 + [20{,}010 - 18{,}191]\left[\dfrac{1.0757 + 1.1514}{2} - 1\right]}{1.1}$$

$$= \frac{[2{,}404 + 207]}{1.1} = 2{,}373.$$

Under this approximation next year's improvement in consumer surplus due to greater output under divestiture is thus estimated to be 207 monetary units.[11]

Let us now turn to rationing in the reverse order of willingness to pay under both private and government operation. For this case approximation (6.5b) becomes

$$\Delta W^* = \frac{2,404 + \dfrac{(18,191 + 20,010)(20,010 - 18,191)}{(2)(24,012)}}{1.1}$$

$$= \frac{(2,404 + 1,447)}{1.1} = 3,501.^{12}$$

Note that the type of rationing makes an enormous difference. In our example, next year's consumer welfare improves by a factor of seven from 207 to 1,447 when both public and private sectors ration in reverse order of willingness to pay instead of rationing in the right order. Asymmetric rationing changes the differential. If the public sector rations by willingness to pay but the private sector rations in reverse order, ΔW^* falls to only 995. If the converse occurs, ΔW^* rises to 4,879.

Rationing of Inputs

The case where the public enterprise pays above-market wages but employs only a limited amount of labor is quite symmetrical in terms of welfare effects to the case where it charges a low output price and applies nonprice rationing methods for its services. This symmetry between outputs and inputs appeared in section 5.4, where we introduced input rents into our welfare calculation. Thus with labor queuing for attractive jobs, the rents (M) will depend on the wage rate (w), on the amount of labor hired (L), and on the input rationing method (R^i): $M = M(w, L, R^i)$. Now formulas symmetrical to the case of output rationing can be developed.

If the public enterprise awards labor contracts in the order of the reservation wages of workers, then

$$M(w_g, L_g, R_g^i) = M(w(L_g)) + L_g[w_g - w(L_g)]. \tag{6.6}$$

The labor rents from (6.6) are given by the two shaded areas in figure 6.4.

If the public enterprise awards labor contracts in the reverse order of reservation wages, then

$$M(w_g, L_g, R_g^i) = M(w_g) - M(w(L^\Delta)) - [w_g - w(L^\Delta)]L^\Delta, \tag{6.7}$$

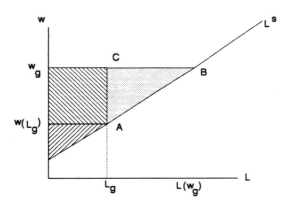

Figure 6.4
Job rationing in the order of reservation wages

where $L^{\Delta} = L(w_g) - L_g$. In this case the labor rents are represented by the shaded area in figure 6.5. Again, we can see the difference in the surplus loss due to rationing of jobs. Rationing in the order of reservation wages results in a surplus loss given by the dotted area ABC in figure 6.4, whereas rationing in the reverse order creates a surplus loss equal to the dotted area $ABCD$ in figure 6.5.

For a linear labor supply curve, equation (6.7) becomes

$$M(w_g, L_g, R_g^i) = M(w(L_g)). \tag{6.7a}$$

Hence by characterizing queuing methods along a scale $0 \leqslant \gamma^i \leqslant 1$, we can write

$$M(w_g, L_g, R_g^i) = M(w(L_g)) + \gamma^i L_g[w_g - w(L_g)]. \tag{6.8}$$

Noting that a public enterprise uses different methods of hiring than a private firm, we differentiate between γ_g^i and γ_p^i. We then arrive at

$$\Delta W^* = \lambda_g \Delta \Pi + \Delta S(p(q)) + \Delta M(w(L))$$

$$+ \gamma_p^i L_p[w_p - w(L_p)] - \gamma_g^i L_g[w_g - w(L_g)], \tag{6.9}$$

which corresponds to equation (6.4). The Turvey approximation to this expression is

$$\Delta W^* = \lambda_g \Delta \Pi + \Delta S(p(q)) + \tfrac{1}{2}[L_g + L_p][w(L_p) - w(L_g)]$$

$$+ \gamma_p^i L_p[w_p - w(L_p)] - \gamma_g^i L_g[w_g - w(L_g)]. \tag{6.10}$$

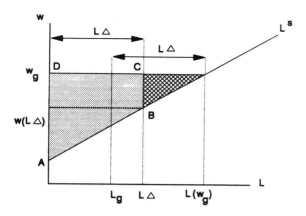

Figure 6.5
Rationing in reverse order of reservation wages

If labor hiring occurs only in the order of reservation wages, then this expression becomes:

$$\Delta W^* = \lambda_g \Delta \Pi + \Delta S(p(q)) + \tfrac{1}{2}[L_g + L_p][w(L_p) - w(L_g)] + L_p w_p - L_g w_g.$$
$$(6.10a)$$

Corresponding to (6.5b), if hiring is only in the reverse order of reservation wages, then

$$\Delta W^* = \lambda_g \Delta \Pi + \Delta S(p(q)) + \tfrac{1}{2}[L_g + L_p][w(L_p) - w(L_g)].$$
$$(6.10b)$$

Equations (6.10a) and (b) are completely analogous in contents and interpretation to the cases of output rationing described by equations (6.5a) and (b).

6.1.2   Indirect and Rent-Seeking Costs of Rationing

There can be other costs associated with rationing besides those measured by $S(p_g, q_g, R_g^o)$ and $M(w_g, L_g, R_g^i)$. For example, the enterprise may have to print and issue rationing coupons, and the consumers may have to queue or incur costs for alternative supplies. More specifically, electricity consumers in many countries have auxiliary power generators for the many times that their electricity is turned off.

As long as these other costs are borne by the enterprise, they are correctly captured in profits and therefore pose no new problems. Rationing costs borne by consumers and input suppliers, however, are often of a rent-seeking nature and may have to be considered separately. These costs will, in particular, be substantial for inputs such as labor. If the public enterprise hires labor at above-market wages but employs only a limited number of workers, then workers will be willing to incur costs to acquire these attractive jobs. For example, they may acquire additional credentials, spend time in employment queues, or bribe officials, all in an effort to become employed by the public enterprise. Once they are employed, their efforts are rewarded because they will then enjoy substantial rents. Similar behavior may be found among any other input suppliers when input markets are imperfectly competitive. We first elaborate on the nature of rent-seeking and then modify our equations accordingly.

Rents are gravy—that is, they are returns to actors in this activity that exceed those available to them elsewhere. It is, therefore, hardly novel to suggest that people seek rents. What the burgeoning literature on rent-seeking contributes is the insight that a lot of the gravy gets sopped up in the process.[13]

Are you willing to pay something for $100,000 in rent? Of course. How will you pay it? You will pay it in two fundamentally distinct forms. First, as a client (or potential client) you will make transfer payments to the producers and distributions of discretionary rents—patrons who protect a monopoly position or who control the allocation of tariff, tax, credit, licensing, or other benefits. Note that these payments need not—and often will not—go to the individuals themselves, but to political parties, charitable causes, or other "worthy endeavors" espoused by the patron. Second, you will incur real resource costs to identify these people, gain access to them, acquire their trust, or fend off competing bidders.

What are the relative magnitudes of the two components? Focusing on a single transaction, we may think that transfer payments are the dominant element. However, two other considerations greatly increase the role of real resource costs. First, the recipients of the transfer payments are also receiving rents as a result of their official position, and they are willing to pay a price for this. Governors, police officers, and other officials have been known to pay for so-called wet positions in some countries at some times, and politicians almost always pay for theirs. As the original transfer payment passes through successive hands, more and more is likely to leak into real resource costs. The second source of real resource expenditures is competitors for the $100,000. Many will seek rents, but few will find; yet all will expend resources in the process.

What might the resulting resource costs total? In the extreme, if markets for rents and patrons were both perfectly competitive, then competitive pressures would ensure that no one would receive more than their opportunity cost, and all potential rents would be eaten up in the quest. This is patently absurd, but extremes serve to make the point.

In sum, the fundamental contribution of this literature is that some—and theoretically all—potential rents are dissipated in the quest to obtain them.[14] Thus, for example, the traditional story that the evils of monopoly appear as a little triangle of welfare loss and a large rectangle of a transfer of surplus is wrong. In the extreme, both the triangle and rectangle are deadweight losses, substantially increasing our estimate of the evils of monopoly—and of any other rent-generating market imperfections.

Now, one may or may not agree that rent-seeking constitutes "one of the most stimulating fields of economic theory in recent years," but it is clearly a handy notion to have around.[15] There are two distinct sets of benefits. First, rent-seeking provides a properly pedantic euphemism that allows academics to talk about patronage, kickbacks, and other forms of corruption without sounding like journalists. Second, in forcing us to take a hard look at the distinction between "neutral" transfers and evil deadweight losses, it leads us to new calculations of the cost-benefit ratios of various public policies. Typically, this means that since the costs of discretionary market failures are understated, the returns to reform are likewise understated. Sadly, the reverse can be true in the case of divestiture.

The simplest, although perhaps unrealistic, assumption on an upper bound for real rent-seeking costs under rationing is that they equal the rents that are generated by the rationing. Under any nonprice rationing scheme for an output, the excluded customers would then get no consumer surplus at all. Such customers would be willing to pay up to the amount of surplus available to them if they could get the commodity at price p, whereas those happy customers that get the right to buy the commodity are willing to pay up to their surplus to defend this right. If consumers correctly weigh their chances of ultimately getting the commodity and if they are risk-neutral, then the total rent-seeking expenses will not exceed the additional consumer surplus at price p that is potentially generated by the nonprice rationing scheme. This is the lower shaded area in figure 6.1.

As a consequence, under the extreme case of "efficient" rent-seeking we can expect that the commodity will end up with those consumers that value the commodity most. Also, jobs in the enterprise will be given to those who are willing to sacrifice the most to get them. Assuming that rent-seeking costs are not just transfers but require real resources, we would then simply deduct rent-seeking costs borne by (potential)

consumers from the consumer surplus levels under rationing in the order of
willingness to pay or from the rent levels under queuing in order of
reservation wages. This means that under output rationing we will always
end up with an additional welfare loss that can be as large as the lower
shaded area in figure 6.1. The welfare change due to divestiture would then
be given by equation (6.5b) respectively (6.10b) rather than equation (6.5a)
respectively (6.10a).

However, normally we would expect rent-seeking costs to be only a
fraction κ of the distributable rent to be dissipated in rent-seeking cost.
This fraction will depend on how successful rent-seeking is perceived to be
and how strictly, for example, rationing rules are enforced. With two
simplifying assumptions we can include κ in our framework of rationing
without any major change of our formulas. First, we assume that rent-
seeking costs are proportional to the marginal rents. That means they are
proportional to the difference $p(q_g) - p_g$ in the case of output rationing
and to $w_g - w(L_g)$ in the case of job rationing. Second, we assume that
rent-seeking costs are borne by the (potential) consumers or (potential)
workers. Hence, the shadow price of funds spent on rent-seeking activities
is assumed to be equal to one. Under these two assumptions rent-seeking
costs simply enter formulas (6.3) and (6.8) in the following way:

$$S(p_g, q_g, R_g^o, \kappa^o) = S(p(q_g)) - [\mu^o - \kappa^o]q_g[p_g - p(q_g)] \tag{6.3a}$$

and

$$M(w_g, L_g, R_g^i, \kappa^i) = M(w(L_g) + [\gamma^i - \kappa^i]L_g[w_g - \gamma(L_g)]. \tag{6.8a}$$

This means that the rent-seeking cost parameters κ^o and κ^i for output
and input rationing simply enter as corrective factors of the rationing rule.

A third type of rationing important for divestiture is the rationing of
shares of the divested enterprise in the case of $Z < Z_p$. The rent-seeking
costs arising in this case are treated in chapter 10 as transaction costs.

6.2 Indirect Taxes

So far we have assumed away indirect taxes, which has led to two simplifications. First, the producer price was always equal to the consumer price.
This equality facilitated calculation of profits and consumer surpluses.
Second, we did not have to consider the tax consequences of price and
quantity changes. However, if $\lambda_g \neq \lambda_p$, these tax consequences matter.

Two simple types of indirect taxes allow us to make this case. We
denote indirect taxes by x^i. Ad valorem taxes at a rate x_v^i are relevant as

tariffs or general sales taxes. Specific unit taxes at a rate x_u^i are relevant for particular commodities such as gasoline or cigarettes. We assume that indirect taxes are not necessarily set optimally, so that there is no pre-specified relationship between the levels of individual taxes and λ_g.

First, assume the indirect tax rate is x_v^i on the value of output. If, therefore, the firm receives a price p, the consumers have to pay $p(1 + x_v^i)$. This means that the demand curve faced by the firm is proportionally lower by $1/(1 + x_v^i)$ than the demand curve of consumers. Accordingly, consumer surplus is still measured on the true demand curve of consumers, but firm profits are calculated using the shifted demand curve and the net prices received by the firm. For simplicity we omit time subscripts and assume that the same tax would be levied under both public and private operation. We also simplify notation by writing p_v for $p(1 + x_v^i)$. That is, p is the price at factor cost and p_v is the price at market cost. The three fundamental valuations of the firm are then

$$V_{sg} = \sum_{t=0}^{T} \rho^t \{S(p_{gv}) + \lambda_g \Pi_g(p_g) + \lambda_g x_v^i p_g q(p_{gv})\}, \tag{6.11}$$

$$V_{pp} = \sum_{t=0}^{T} \rho^t \{\Pi_p(p_p) - X_p^d\}, \tag{6.12}$$

and

$$V_{sp} = \sum_{t=0}^{T} \rho^t \{S(p_{pv}) + \lambda_p \Pi_p(p_p) + [\lambda_g - \lambda_p] X^d + \lambda_g x_v^i p_p q(p_{pv})\}. \tag{6.13}$$

When interpreting this and subsequent equations, bear in mind that in our notation we evaluate the output prices at factor cost rather than at market prices. Assuming that the public enterprise is sold at the private reservation price $Z = V_{pp}$, we can write

$$\Delta W^* = \sum_{t=0}^{T} \rho^t \{\Delta S(p_v) + \lambda_g \Delta \Pi(p) + \lambda_g x_v^i [p_p q(p_{pv}) - p_g q(p_{gv})]\}. \tag{6.14}$$

The first two terms in equation (6.14) correspond to similar terms in equation (5.10). They are adjusted by the effect of the taxes on output prices. The third term is simply the change in ad valorem tax evaluated at λ_g. Because tax is on revenues, the tax change is proportional to the change in firm revenues as a result of divestiture.

Second, let us consider the case of a specific unit tax x_u^i. In this case consumers pay $p + x_u^i$ if the firm receivers a price p. For the firm this means a parallel downward shift of the demand curve by x_u^i. Corresponding to equations (6.11) through (6.14), this shift leads to equations (6.11a) through (6.14a):

$$V_{sg} = \sum_{t=0}^{T} \rho^t \{S(p_{gu}) + \lambda_g \Pi_g(p_g) + \lambda_g x_u^i q(p_{gu})\}, \tag{6.11a}$$

$$V_{pp} = \sum_{t=0}^{T} \rho^t \{\Pi_p(p_p) - X_p^d\}, \tag{6.12a}$$

$$V_{sp} = \sum_{t=0}^{T} \rho^t \{S(p_{pu}) + \lambda_p \Pi_p(p_p) + [\lambda_g - \lambda_p] X_p^d + \lambda_g x_u^i q(p_{pu})\} + \lambda_g Z. \tag{6.13a}$$

Assuming again that the public enterprise is sold at the private reservation price $Z = V_{pp}$, we can write

$$\Delta W^* = \sum_{t=0}^{T} \rho^t \{\Delta S(p_u) + \lambda_g \Delta \Pi(p) + \lambda_g x_u^i [q(p_{pu}) - q(p_{gu})]\}$$

$$= \sum_{t=0}^{T} \rho^t \{\Delta S(p_u) + \lambda_g \Delta \Pi(p) + \lambda_g x_u^i [\Delta q(p_{pu})]\}. \tag{6.14a}$$

Again, the first two terms of (6.14a) correspond to (5.10). They are adjusted by the effect of the tax on output prices. The third term is simply the change in indirect tax evaluated at λ_g. Because the tax is on units of output, the tax change is proportional to the *output* change.

In the preceding formulas we have considered only taxes on outputs as final goods. Taxes and tariffs on inputs obviously carry just as much importance. They can be treated in a symmetrical fashion.

6.3 Shadow Prices Proper

Differences between private and social evaluation of inputs and outputs can be the result of constraints (policy or otherwise—e.g., monopoly power) or externalities or linkages. Typically the shadow prices corresponding to social evaluation are derived from a model outside our framework, but we can apply the results to our partial equilibrium setting.

Clearly, differences between the prices applied by the enterprises and the corresponding shadow prices affect welfare. How then do differences in social valuation affect our formulas? First, let us consider shadow pricing of outputs only, which applies mainly to cases such as externalities, linkages, or exports at distorted exchange rates. In exact terms, for the case where only the output price is different from its shadow value, we get

$$\Delta W^* = (\lambda_g - 1)\Delta\Pi_m + \Delta\Pi_s + \Delta S_s(p_s), \tag{6.15}$$

where the subscripts m and s indicate that the respective variables are calculated at market prices or shadow prices. The formula says that all changes have to be evaluated at shadow prices. Profits at market prices appear in this formula only because the government as shareholder or as seller of the public enterprise receives these profits in nominal terms and evaluates them with λ_g in the form of cash. λ_p does not appear because in the calculation of ΔW^*, the terms containing λ_p (that is, Z and Π_p) cancel out.

Now we may want to subdivide equation (6.15) into two changes. One is the change discussed in chapter 5, which is expressed only in market prices, ΔW_m. Here we have the familiar $\Delta W_m^* = \lambda_g \Delta\Pi_m + \Delta S_m(p_m)$. The other is the adjustment necessary for shadow pricing, ΔW_s. Thus $\Delta W^* = \Delta W_m^* + \Delta W_s$, and so

$$\Delta W_s^* = \Delta W^* - \Delta W_m^* = [\Delta\Pi_s - \Delta\Pi_m] + [\Delta S_s(p_s) - \Delta S_m(p_m)]. \tag{6.16}$$

Note that λ_g is irrelevant for the adjustment ΔW_s because no payments enter the calculation of ΔW_s.

Equation (6.15) says that one has to know the shadow demand and supply *schedules* in addition to mere shadow *prices* in order to derive the exact welfare effects—rather exacting requirements. However, as long as we are content with a good approximation, the introduction of shadow values requires only a very simple change to our previous results in chapter 5. This can be seen in figure 6.6, which portrays the case in which the public enterprise is capacity constrained while the private firm exercises market power. As usual, we assume constant average and marginal cost c_g and c_p for the public enterprise and the divested firm, respectively. Private and social prices are denoted by the first price subscript, whereas the second subscript refers to ownership. The market demand curve is D_p, and the shadow demand curve is D_s.

The change in welfare at market prices (ΔW_m) is given by the difference between the two lightly shaded areas. There is a welfare increase from divestiture due to the cost decrease from c_g to c_p, but there is a welfare decrease due to the reduction in quantity from q_g to q_p. By construction the net result is a slight welfare gain in nominal prices.

The change resulting from shadow evaluation is

$$\Delta W_s = (\Delta\Pi_s + \Delta S_s(p_s)) - (\Delta\Pi_m + \Delta S(p_m)) \tag{6.17}$$

and is given by the heavily cross-shaded area between the two demand curves, which shows a substantial welfare decrease. This just wipes out the

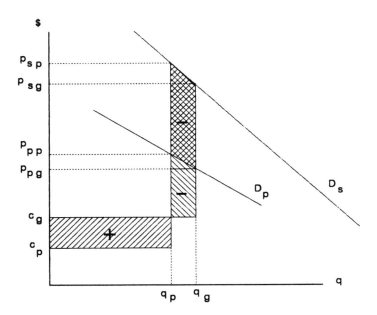

Figure 6.6
Welfare adjustment for shadow pricing

slight welfare increase ΔW_m in terms of market prices. In our illustration ΔW_s turns out to be approximately equal to the difference between the shadow price and the market price charged (paid) by the public enterprise times the quantity increase (decrease) effected by divestiture. Therefore,

$$\Delta W_s \simeq (q_p - q_g)(p_s - p_g). \tag{6.18}$$

Shadow pricing for inputs is also important. For example, firms often receive underpriced energy, or credit at rates that have little to do with the social cost of providing capital. The same can be true for imports for which a firm may collect quota rents on import licenses. It is good to know, then, that a symmetrical argument to the one for outputs holds for inputs. Again, we can get a similar approximation and, therefore, within some range of values, we have to know only the shadow prices of inputs, not the shadow demand schedules. Adding shadow prices for inputs to equation (6.18), we get[16]

$$\Delta W_s = (q_p - q_g)(p_s - p_g) - \Sigma(L_p - L_g)(w_s - w_g). \tag{6.19}$$

In this formula the summation sign indicates the variety of inputs that may be shadow priced.

The simplicity of (6.18) and (6.19) derives from the fact that we are looking at the effect only of a *change* in quantity on the difference in evaluations. The difference in slope between the private and public evaluation of surplus then becomes a second-order effect. This will be negligible as long as the quantity change due to divestiture is small and/or the slopes of the private and social demand (supply) curves are similar.[17] The simplest case of such a similar slope is a unit tax on inputs or outputs, in which case the slopes are in fact equal. There are definitely cases, however, where the slopes are not similar. For example, the pay schedule of a public enterprise may be independent of the scarcity of labor in the geographic or skill area in which it operates. If it hires more workers, the nominal wage will therefore not change. However, the shadow wage may rise if it is not a labor surplus economy. Still, the effect of this change is only second order as long as the change in employment is not enormous. Hence, it usually suffices to know only shadow prices, not shadow schedules.

If quantity changes are large, however, some information on shadow schedules may be required. Estimating such shadow schedules is likely to be difficult. The difficulty may be further increased by the fact that the relevant variable is the *difference* between the shadow schedule and the market schedule, both of which can be estimated only with a considerable margin of error. However, some shadow schedules are naturally proportional to the nominal schedules. This is true not only for ad valorem taxes but also for other items that depend on revenues rather than on quantities, such as scarce foreign exchange. If one is confident about proportionality, a Turvey-type approximation can be used.

Under our simplifying assumptions it is easy to construct a numerical example. To do so we take the flows from the monopoly case in chapter 5 particularly table 5.2, which provides us with the market price data and, therefore, with a discounted figure of

$$\Delta W_m^* = \frac{(1.3)(2,880) - 4,390}{1.1} = -588.$$

Now, this firm could be a public utility producing a nontradeable service with positive linkage effects, or it could be the domestic monopoly for a protected import-competing good. In either case the shadow value of its output is assumed to be above the sales price p. In particular, at q_g we assume $p_s = 1.25$, meaning that the shadow price is 25 percent above the price charged by the public enterprise. We know that after divestiture its output price has been increased, and output quantity has been reduced from 18,191 units to 12,458 units. Then equation (6.8) implies that

$$\Delta W_s = \frac{0.25(12{,}458 - 18{,}191)}{1.1} = -1{,}303.$$

Therefore, under shadow pricing of the output the welfare loss from divestiture is increased from 588 to 1,891 monetary units. Now assume that the opportunity cost of labor has been 25 percent below the wage paid by the public enterprise, and assume further that the savings in the wage bill by the divested firm occur only by laying off employees and workers, not by reducing wages. Then equation (6.9) gives us the total adjustment necessary for shadow pricing of the output and labor,

$$\Delta W_s = \frac{0.25(1{,}014 - 1{,}631)}{1.1} - 1{,}303 = -1{,}443.$$

Hence, in this case laying off workers further increases the welfare loss, because these workers lose their producer rents. Thus in terms of shadow prices the total welfare loss due to divestiture would be 2,301 monetary units, as compared with 588 units under market prices.

6.4   Conclusion

In this section we have extended our framework to include nonprice rationing, indirect taxes, and shadow pricing of outputs. Conceptually, these extensions are straightforward and highly compatible with our framework. However, approximations have to be used in order to deal with problems of complicated functional forms and of imprecise empirical measurement.

7   Synergies

7.1   Definitions

We have already noted that different private buyers will value the public enterprise differently. Aside from different preferences, risk attitudes, and states of information, such different private evaluations can derive from synergies that a private buyer hopes to realize by acquiring the public enterprise and merging with it. A celebrated example of this phenomenon in the United States was the sale of Conrail.

This cargo railroad company had quite a different value if it was sold to the general public as opposed to another railroad, in particular to Norfolk Southern. In the first case, Conrail was valued on a stand-alone basis, whereas in the second case its value depended on the substitutabilities and complementarities it would have had with the operations of Norfolk Southern. The combined Conrail/Norfolk Southern could have saved real resources by producing essentially the same transportation output as the sum of the two separate systems, at considerably lower cost. Parallel tracks could, for example, have been closed down; the turnover of railroad cars could have been increased; duplicate overhead costs for scheduling, systems expansion planning, and the like, could have been eliminated. At the same time, the combined system would probably have gained market power because the number of competing suppliers along parallel tracks would have been reduced by one. In many cases this could have led to monopoly supply. Also, the combined system could have saved on taxes by shifting old Conrail losses over to the profitable Norfolk Southern.

This combination of advantages increased the value of Conrail to a company such as Norfolk Southern, as compared with unaffiliated buyers. Such factors also affect social valuation. In general, real resource savings increase the social value of the combination, whereas increases in market power tend to have the opposite effect. Thus we can speak of *private* and *public synergies* in connection with divestiture.

We define an economic synergy of a merger (1) as positive if $V^{A+B} > V^A + V^B$ for two companies A and B that have merged into company A + B and (2) as negative if $V^{A+B} < V^A + V^B$.

Now we can apply the same subscripts to the various valuations defined in chapter 2. A positive private synergy is defined by $V_{pp}^{A+B} > V_{pp}^A + V_{pp}^B$ and a positive public synergy by $V_{sp}^{A+B} > V_{sp}^A + V_{sp}^B$. Note that in the case of the sale of a public enterprise, some positive synergies may be lost as a result of divestiture. This is particularly important for partial divestiture. In this case, *A* stands for the divested part and *B* for the part that remains in the public domain. We might call synergies that are lost through divestiture *ex-ante* synergies, as opposed to *ex-post* synergies, those that develop after divestiture. As an example, postal and telephone services are often organized jointly in a PTT (post, telegraph, and telephones entity). Divestiture here usually is considered only for the telephone services (and here often only for the part involving the sale and servicing of terminal equipment). The question then arises whether synergies between postal and telecommunication services influence the social evaluation of the enterprise division that is divested.

7.2   A Classification of Synergies

Given that synergies occur whenever the value of the combination of two companies is different from the sum of the values of the two companies as separate entities, the following questions arise: What are the sources of synergies? When do the private and social valuations of synergies coincide?

We propose a classification based on the private valuation of synergies and suggest that all private synergies may be classified into one of the following three categories:

1. Synergies that operate through costs of production,

2. Synergies that operate through changes in market power, or

3. Financial synergies that affect only the distribution of social surplus.

This classification is analytically convenient in that it categorizes different synergies according to their source in an economically meaningful way. In particular, we may think of the different components of a firm's profits in the following way:

$$\Pi = R - C - X.$$

That is, net profits are equal to total revenues minus costs minus taxes. Then, for instance, positive private synergies arise if

$$\Pi^{A+B} > \Pi^A + \Pi^B,$$

that is, if

$$R^{A+B} - C^{A+B} - X^{A+B} > (R^A + R^B) - (C^A + C^B) - (X^A + X^B).$$

A simple way to classify synergies would be to say positive synergies exist if, ceteris paribus,

$$C^{A+B} < C^A + C^B \quad \text{(cost synergies)},$$

$$R^{A+B} > R^A + R^B \quad \text{(revenue synergies)},$$

$$X^{A+B} < X^A + X^B \quad \text{(financial synergies).}[1]$$

Negative synergies would simply require reversal of each of the preceding inequalities. Of course, actual cases will not be so simple, because there may be simultaneous effects on all three components of revenue. The classification would be based on the primary or most important source of the synergy.

In addition to providing an economically intuitive set of categories, our classification also yields categories that differ according to whether the social value of such (positive) private synergies is positive, negative, or neutral, respectively. Our argument can be illustrated by use of the Conrail example, where all these types of synergies can be seen.

Under cost synergies, we would place a wide range of possible synergies, including economies of scale, economies of scope, benefits from horizontal or vertical integration, and so on. The key aspect of such synergies is that total costs of production are lower in the combined firm than in the separate firms. If Norfolk Southern had bought Conrail, for example, the cost of transport between, say, Florida and New England would have been lowered, because freight would have stayed on one railroad throughout the journey. This could be seen as a case of vertical integration, where the "upstream" firm provided transport from Florida to Washington, and the "downstream" firm transported the goods from Washington to New England. Other cases of cost synergies may well have arisen if the combined firm had benefited by scale economies or by economies of scope. Closing down parallel tracks is an example of enjoying scale economies. In general, cost reductions are, of course, socially desirable, so this category of private synergies would have the same sign in the social evaluation. That is, when synergies are due to cost reductions (or increases), then positive private synergies will result in positive social synergies, whereas negative private synergies will likewise be undesirable socially.

Revenue synergies depend upon rising profitability, because the combined firm has increased market power. The most obvious, simple example is that of a duopoly that becomes a monopoly through merger. In the Conrail example, if Conrail and Norfolk Southern were the only two railroads providing services in a particular sector, the combined firm would have been a monopoly and would likely have had profits in that sector higher than the sum of the two separate firms' profits. To the extent that this rise in profits stems from scale economies (such as the closing down of parallel tracks mentioned earlier), they are socially desirable at the same time that they are privately profitable. The more important source of synergy, however, is likely to be the greater ability of the combined firm to exploit its market power. This kind of positive private synergy has a decidedly negative impact socially, because of the increased deadweight losses that enhanced market power causes. The issue of market power was central in the discussion of the Conrail sale. In fact, it may safely be assumed that the main reason the U.S. government decided not to sell Conrail to Norfolk Southern was precisely the fear of the effects of reduced competition in the railroad industry.

The third category of synergies are purely financial. The most important examples are situations where the tax liabilities of the acquiring firm can be reduced considerably through merger. In the Conrail case, Norfolk Southern stood to gain tremendously by acquiring Conrail, because Conrail had large amounts of accumulated losses carried over allng with the possibility of sizable depreciation allowances. Norfolk Southern could in principle have offset its own profits against Conrail's losses and depreciation. Note that, in general, such synergies are not specific to a particular acquiring firm; rather, any profitable firm can take advantage of most of the available deductions.

In any case, from the social point of view, such synergies may be undesirable. To the extent that it will reduce its tax liability by buying the public enterprise, an acquiring firm will be willing to pay more for the enterprise. Thus government should, in principle, receive the "future tax payments" up front in the form of the sale price of the enterprise. If this happens, then there is no net effect from these synergies. This means that not only will government receive the full revenue it is due, but also the firm will not actually realize any ex-post benefit. Thus it is unlikely to happen. In other words, government will generally not receive the full willingness to pay of the buyer. Rather, the sale price may reflect only part of the financial synergy that the company will enjoy. In that case, as long as $\lambda_g > \lambda_p$, the realization of such synergies by the acquiring firm is socially undesirable, because it amounts to a transfer from the government to the private firm.[2]

7.3 The Measurement of Synergies

How can we incorporate synergies in our measurement system? Conceptually, this is quite straightforward: we simply have to add in the valuation of the other affected firms. The simplest case is one where there are no ex-ante synergies to worry about, but where the potential buyer has some synergies with the public enterprise. If we denote the public enterprise by A and the acquiring firm by B, then

$$V_{sg} = S_g + \lambda_g(R_g^A - C_g^A + X^B) + \lambda_p(R_p^B - C_p^B - X^B), \tag{7.1}$$

$$V_{sp} = S_p + \lambda_g X^{A+B} + \lambda_p(R_p^{A+B} - C_p^{A+B} - X^{A+B}), \tag{7.2}$$

$$V_{pp} = (R_p^{A+B} - C_p^{A+B} - X^{A+B}) - (R_p^B - C_p^B - X^B), \tag{7.3}$$

where, as before, S represents consumer surplus, R represents revenue, C is cost, and X refers to tax payments. Note that (7.3) can also be written in the form

$$V_{pp} = (R_p^{A+B} - R_p^B) - (C_p^{A+B} - C_p^B) - (X^{A+B} - X^B). \tag{7.4}$$

Equation (7.4) shows clearly the gain in private profits as the sum of three terms corresponding to the three potential sources of synergies.

Using equations (7.1), (7.2), and (7.4) we can write the change in welfare as a result of the divestiture. As before, this expression reduces to

$$\Delta W = \Delta S + \lambda_g \Delta \Pi + (\lambda_g - \lambda_p)(Z - Z_p).$$

Thus the presence of synergies makes no fundamental difference to the analysis and can be handled quite easily. The change in welfare can, as before, be represented as the sum of changes in consumer surplus, profit, and private rents, weighted as before. Differences may arise in the signs of the various terms, however.

There are two important cases when a divestiture that is privately profitable may not be socially desirable for reasons of synergies. First, if the synergies stem from the increased market power enjoyed by the buyer, then $\Delta \Pi$ may be positive at the expense of a negative ΔS. Clearly, ΔW

may then be negative. Second, we could well have a situation where V_{pp} is positive only because of the financial synergy $(X^{A+B} - X^B) < 0$. For example, the public enterprise may serve merely to reduce the buyer's tax liability. In this case, $\Delta W = 0$, so that the divestiture is not desirable if there are any transactions costs associated with it.

In considering more complicated cases, we may need to consider ex-ante synergies also. Thus, including synergies at the public enterprise stage, we would include those parts of the public (and private) sector that have particularly strong linkages with it. Similarly, for the acquirer we have to include its other operations in our valuation exercise. This means that generally we have to look at both the public enterprise and the acquirer in a multiplant or multiproduct setting.

Suppose the public enterprise being discussed has two parts, only one of which is being considered for divestiture. Suppose we indicate the potentially divested part by A, the rest of the enterprise by C, and the acquiring firm by B. For simplicity, we ignore tax and other financial considerations. Assuming that government receives the full willingness to pay Zp, the change in welfare resulting from the divestiture decision would then become

$$\Delta W^* = V_{sp}^{A+B} + V_{sg}^{C} - V_{sg}^{A+C} - V_{sp}^{B}$$

$$= \Delta S + \lambda_g \Delta \Pi$$

$$= S_p^{A+B} + S_g^{C} - S_p^{B} - S_g^{A+C}$$

$$+ \lambda_g (\Pi_p^{A+B} + \Pi_g^{C} - \Pi_p^{B} - \Pi_g^{A+C}). \tag{7.5}$$

This assumes that all private synergies are fully reflected in the bid price offered for it. Also the summation of consumer surpluses over potentially many products requires that demands for these products be independent of each other.[3]

While writing formulas to incorporate synergies is not too difficult, the quantity of information needed actually to calculate ΔW with synergies can easily be a multiple of the information needed for a calculation without synergies. In addition, the information on synergies is especially vague and hard to come by. However, it appears that by and large the synergies that are the most difficult to estimate are also likely to be the least important, whereas the largest synergies may be relatively easy to estimate.

Consider, for example, cost-reducing synergies. How can one know the extent to which cost savings will be realized from a private merger? The answer requires speculation on future events. There is considerable discussion of this issue in the U.S. antitrust literature on mergers. The empirical consensus is that such cost reductions are notoriously hard to predict and that predicted cost savings rarely occur.[4] That is, acquiring firms seldom actually enjoy the cost savings that they had expected; rather, the realized cost savings are mostly of second-order magnitude. If so, then we can ignore this category of synergy in most, if not all, cases.

Revenue synergies arise when the acquiring firm gains market power through the acquisition of the public enterprise. The simplest case is the one where the enterprise presently has only one competitor, and it is this competitor who is the potential buyer. Thus a monopoly would be created through the divestiture. A more complicated case would be sale of the enterprise to a firm that gains market power but does not become a monopoly. Analyzing such cases requires just a simple adaptation of our methodology. In chapter 5 we discussed the mechanics of evaluating monopoly behavior on the part of the divested enterprise. We also discussed the analysis of oligopoly situations. In the case where the acquiring firm would gain market power, we simply have to compare the option of divestiture to that firm against divestiture to some other firm or group that would be a competitor. Whereas selling to the potential monopolist will likely result in a higher price and hence loss of consumer surplus, it may also result in lower costs (say, because of the monopolist's superior knowledge of the industry), and it would pay more to the government in purchase price. This increase in purchase price is valuable if $\lambda_g > \lambda_p$. Thus we face the classic kinds of trade-offs discussed in chapter 5.

Finally, financial synergies can well be quite large and important in divestiture decisions. These are, however, quite easy to calculate. The loss carryover and depreciation situation of the public enterprise are available in the company's books, and tax benefits that might then accrue to any acquiring firm can easily be calculated and added in as an element of the buyer's willingness-to-pay.

7.4 Strategic Behavior

In discussing the maximum amount that any potential buyer would be willing to pay for a public enterprise, we have so far taken this to be the present value of any increase in after-tax profits that the firm would enjoy. In the case of an unaffiliated buyer, this is simply the present value of the after-tax profits of the divested enterprise. When synergies are introduced, that measure needs to be modified by any increase in after-tax profits of the parent organization.

The implicit assumption is that the alternative from the point of view of the buyer is that if he or she chooses not to buy the enterprise, things will go on as before. But this counterfactual is not realistic, because it ignores the announced intention of the government to divest the enterprise. The appropriate counterfactual therefore is the level of profits that the firm will enjoy if some *other* buyer buys the enterprise.

Let us illustrate this point with the specific example of Conrail. Suppose the potential bidders are Norfolk Southern and another railroad, say CSX.[5] Suppose Conrail, Norfolk Southern, and CSX all compete with one another in certain regions; they can therefore be considered competitors. Suppose Π_c, Π_n, and Π_x represent the levels of after-tax profits of the three companies prior to divestiture. Now consider the maximum amount that, say, Norfolk Southern, may be willing to pay for Conrail. If Π_{nn} represents the profits of the enlarged company that Norfolk Southern will make if it acquires Conrail, we have implicitly assumed so far that the willingness to pay for Conrail would be the present value of the difference $\Pi_{nn} - \Pi_n$. But this is not correct. If the alternative that Norfolk Southern faces is for CSX to buy Conrail, then Π_n is no longer relevant to the calculation. Rather, Norfolk Southern needs to estimate what its profits will be once CSX has acquired Conrail, say Π_{nx}. Its willingness to pay would then be the present value of the stream represented by $\Pi_{nn} - \Pi_{nx}$. In general, we may expect that $\Pi_{nx} < \Pi_n$ because the now-more-powerful CSX will be able to exercise its market power somewhat to the detriment of Norfolk Southern's interests. In that case, the maximum willingness to pay under strategic behavior will be greater than the nonstrategic case. At the same time it is possible that $\Pi_{nx} > \Pi_n$, say, because of the simple fact that there are now only two competitors in the market rather than three.[6] In this event, the maximum willingness to pay will be lower under strategic behavior.

In conclusion, we would argue that the analysis of synergies is easily accommodated within our methodological framework. As is inherent in the calculation of future values, we cannot be sure of the accuracy of our calculations. Knowledge of the particular case combined with the use of our framework is required.

8 Valuation Algorithm and Sensitivity Analysis

Thus far, our examples have been limited to a single company and to changing one or two variables at a time. While useful for expository purposes, this method has obvious practical limitations. In this section we therefore generalize the empirical portion of our approach by outlining a valuation algorithm (section 8.2). The procedures are computerized (as a Lotus 1-2-3 template) allowing application to various data sets under various sets of assumptions.[1] The various text examples are first replicated to show how the template works, and other features are illustrated with nontext examples. The algorithm is then used to conduct a sensitivity analysis to identify just which variables are critical in the valuation process (section 8.2).

8.1 Valuation Algorithm

8.1.1 Assumptions

The valuation algorithm is simply a cookbook summary of the text thus far, specifying the ingredients (data requirements) and the processing procedures (formulas) necessary to produce a particular set of outputs (the various values and prices of the enterprise).

For present purposes we need be concerned only with the front end of the template, as illustrated in table 8.1 (which mimics chapter 4's assumptions of competitive equilibrium except for a government revenue multiplier).[2] The company and run are identified first, followed by a statement of the principal assumptions. On the left are "dynamic assumptions" that cover efficiency and demand shifts persisting for more than one period. For example, an entry of

Table 8.1
Illustrative valuation run

1. BASIC INFORMATION

Company name: Corporation A	Run name: Perf Comp + LAMG > 1

2. BASIC ASSUMPTIONS

DYNAMIC

INDICATOR	YR MLT	TAU
Private Efficiency Multiplier	1.000	1
Government Efficiency Multiplier	1.000	1
Private Annual Demand Shift	1.000	1
Government Annual Demand Shift	1.000	1

MARKET STRUCTURE	VALUE
Private Price Formation	
Market = 0, Regulated = 1	0
If Mkt: Mnp = 1 > olgp > 0 = C	0.0
If Reg: give price	
If Reg: RatRl WP = 1 > > 0 = 1/WP	
Government Price Formation	
Market = 0, Regulated = 1	0
If Mkt: Mnp = 1 > olgp > 0 = C	0.0
If Reg: give price	
If Reg: RatRl WP = 1 > > 0 = 1/WP	
Base Price Formation	
Excess Capacity	0
Excess Demand	0
If XD: RatRl WP = 1 > > 0 = 1/WP	

STATIC

INDICATOR	VALUE
Gov Rev Mult	1.30
Pvt Rev Mult	1.00
D Elasticity	4E + 49
Life (max = 25)	1.00
G Corp Tax	0.33
P Corp Tax	0.33
G Indirect Tx	0.00
P Indirect Tx	0.00
G OpCst Wrk Cptl	0.10
P OpCst Wrk Cptl	0.10
G Discount Rate	0.10
P Discount Rate	0.10
G Loan Rate	0.10
P Loan Rate	0.10
NonOp Asset Adj Fct	1.00
Wrk Asset Adj Fct	1.00
Shd Mlt: Output	1.00
Shd Mlt: Intrmdt	1.00
Shd Mlt: Labor	1.00
Shd Mlt: Wrk Cpt	1.00
G Trnsct Costs	0.00
P Trnsct Costs	0.00

3. SUMMARY OF RESULTS

		TOTAL	TRNSCT	PRDCTN	FNCNL
VALUES					
TO PRIVATE OF PRIVATE	V_{pp}	101	0	3,439	-3,338
(TO SC OF PVT) - (TO SC OF GVT)	$V_{sp} - V_{sg}$	-30	0	-1,032	1,002
PRICES					
PRIVATE MAXIMUM (=OPTIMAL)	Z_p	101	0	3,439	-3,338
GOVERNMENT MINIMUM	Z_g	101	0	3,439	-3,338
CHANGE IN WELFARE					
MAXIMUM (at Z_p)	ΔW^*	0	0	0	0
MINIMUM (at Z_g)	ΔW^-	-0	0	-0	-0

	Year multiplier	τ
Private efficiency	1.10	3
Private demand shift	1.05	5

says that under private operation, efficiency will increase 10 percent annually for three years, whereas demand will expand five percent a year for five years. On the right side of the table, "static assumptions" give important parameters that are assumed not to change. At the lower left the critical elements of market structure are entered. The specifics of the cryptic notation are summarized in table 8.2 and will become clear as we move along. Note that any or all of the assumptions can be modified (at the top of the page) so as to explore the resulting values (at the bottom of the page) under a wide variety of circumstances.

8.1.2   Results Using Text Examples

First let us consider the interpretation of the results at the bottom of table 8.1. The first line (V_{pp}) says that with no transaction costs, the company will be valued by the private sector at 101^3 with a positive value on the production side (3,439) nearly offset by a negative value on the financial side ($-3,338$), where debts exceed assets other than fixed capital. The second line ($V_{sp} - V_{sg}$) says that society is worse off after divestiture, ignoring the sale price ($V_{sp} - V_{sg}$ is negative). Because of the government revenue multiplier, there is a gain in welfare from the financial transfer ($+1,002$), but this is more than offset on the production side ($-1,032$).

The prices for the firm then follow directly from the relationships spelled out in chapter 2. The private maximum willingness to pay (Z_p) is identical to V_{pp}, but the government's reservation price is ($V_{sp} - V_{sg})/(\lambda_g - 1)$, or, in this case, 101.

The last two lines show the maximum and minimum welfare changes. In this case both are zero because we have a zero-sum game, since flows will be identical under both public and private operation. The best the government can do is to capture the buyer's entire willingness to pay (Z_g), and this just compensates for the net loss in future revenues ($\Delta W^* = 0$). The last line (ΔW^-) will always be zero because that is the welfare change associated with Z_g by construction.

Now let us assume that the private sector is more efficient. We simply go to the assumption section and change the private efficiency multiplier to 1.1 to reflect an annual efficiency increment of ten percent for one

Table 8.2
Variables in valuation algorithm

1.	Private Efficiency Multiplier	Yearly multiplier (YR MULT) gives the factor by which efficiency improves annually for τ years. Tau is a maximum of five years; beyond that, fifth-year values are repeated. The efficiency multiplier is applied to all the following ratios: Capacity fixed capital; production/intermediates; production/wages; production/rentals production/output inventories; intermediate/input inventories; and (intermediates + production)/financial working capital.
2.	Government Efficiency Multiplier	
3.	Private Annual Demand Shift	Annual factor by which demand shifts out for τ years. Factor is applied to equilibrium quantity at previous year's prices and slope is assumed unchanged, creating different percentage quantity changes at all other prices. An exception is made for infinitely elastic demand (anything greater than 9^{50}), where the factor is applied to price at last year's quantity.
4.	Government Annual Demand Shift	
5.	Private Price Formation	a. The first variable tells whether price will be formed by the market (0) or by regulation (1).
6.	Government Price Formation	b. If price is set by the market, the second variable tells where it is formed on a continuum from monopoly (0) to perfect competition (1).
		c. If price is set by the regulator, the third variable gives the price.
		d. If price is set by the regulator, the fourth variable tells how rationing of excess demand is accomplished on a continuum from willingess to pay ($wp = 1$) to the inverse of willingness to pay ($wp = 0$).
7.	Base Price Formation	To identify supply and demand curves, it is necessary to know whether or not they both passed through the base year price and quantity. If not, then there is either excess capacity or excess demand, which is entered here. If the latter, then the rationing value must also be entered.
8.	Gov Rev Mult	Gives the factor that converts government and private income into the consumption numeraire. See chapter 3.
9.	Pvt Rev Mult	
10.	Elasticity	Absolute value of own-price elasticity of demand at the base price.
11.	Life	Remaining years of life of project for which cash flow is to be discounted. Maximum of 25.
12.	G Corp Tax	Rate at which corporate tax will be paid under future government and private operation. Tax base calculated as revenues at factor cost less intermediates, employment costs, rentals and depreciation. Deductibility of interest treated as subsidy to debt and so reduces financial costs (FNCNL in results section) rather than increasing production benefits (PRDCTN).
13.	P Corp Tax	
14.	G Indirect Tax	Rate at which indirect taxes will be levied under future government and private operation. If indirect subsidies, enter negative number.
15.	P Indirect Tax	

Table 8.2 (*continued*)

16. G Op Cost Wrk Cptl	Opportunity cost of holding working capital under public and
17. P Op Cost Wrk Cptl	private operation.
18. G Discount Rate	Rate at which future cash flows are discounted under public
19. P Discount Rate	and private operation.
20. G Loan Rate	Gross rate of interest paid for debt under public and private
21. P Loan Rate	operation.
21. Non Op Ast Adj Fct	Factor by which book value of nonoperating and variable operating (working) assets must be multiplied to reach fair
22. Net Ast Adj Fct	market value.
23. Shd Mlt: Output Shd Mlt: Intrmdt	Factor by which market price of Output, Intermediates, Labor, and Working Capital must be multiplied to reach true social
24. Shd Mlt: Labor	value.
25. Shd Mlt: Wrk Cpt	
26. G Trnsct Costs	Value of transaction costs incurred by government and private
27. P Trnsct Costs	buyer, expressed arbitrarily as share of base production at factor costs.

year. New results (production side only) are given in line 3 of table 8.3. Now we have a positive-sum game with a maximum welfare gain of 2,185. Because it is more efficient, the private buyer's willingness to pay has gone up (from 3,439 to 4,560). Society values the efficiency increment even more highly (because of taxes), and so V_{sp} rises even more than V_{pp}. With V_{sg} unchanged, $V_{sp} - V_{sg}$ rises to a positive value (to 817 from $-1,032$), meaning society will be better off as a result of the transfer of ownership. Accordingly, the government minimum sale price is *negative* 2,724. The negative sign tells us that social welfare will be improved even if the government pays the private sector to take over the company. Since society will be better off after divestiture, it should be willing to pay something to achieve that state. How much? With a government revenue multiplier of 1.3, every dollar paid to the private sector results in a social loss of \$0.30. If, therefore, the government pays $1,817/0.30 = 2,724$ to the private sector to take the company, then society's gains from the asset transfer ($+817$) will be precisely balanced by the loss from the sale subsidy ($0.30 \cdot 2,724$). This point (where society's gains just equal losses) is precisely the minimum price (Z_g^π). At any higher price, society is better off from the sale, and at any lower price, worse off. The maximum gain to society ($\Delta W^* = 2,185$) occurs if the private maximum price is extracted. In sum, the result here illustrates a positive-sum game in which the price can

Table 8.3
Summary of text examples (production only)

Assumptions changed (from previous run)	V_{pp}^{π}	$V_{sp}^{\pi} - V_{sg}^{\pi}$	Z_p^{π}	Z_g^{π}	ΔW^*	ΔW^-
1. Base (Competitive Equilibrium)	3,439	0	3,439	ERR	0	ERR
2. Government Revenue Multiplier = 1.3	3,439	−1,032	3,439	3,439	0	0
3. Private Efficiency Shift = 1.1	4,560	817	4,560	−2,724	2,185	0
4. Private Market Structure = Monopoly; Elasticity = 1.1	5,184	−2,143	5,184	7,144	−588	0
5. Regulated Price (PVT and GVT) at 1.0; Rationing by willingness to pay	4,189	206	4,189	−686	1,462	0
6. Base excess demand = 3,638	4,560	1,005	4,560	−3,350	2,373	0
7. Rationing by inverse of willingness to pay	4,560	2,133	4,560	−7,109	3,501	0
8. Private Competition (as in 3) Shadow Output Mult = 1.25 Shadow Wage Mult = 0.75	4,560	1,231	4,560	−4,102	2,598	0
9. Private Monopoly (as in 4)	5,184	−3,772	5,184	12,575	−2,217	0
10. Indirect Tax after privatization (otherwise, competition as in 3)	3,347	1,181	3,347	−3,937	2,185	0
11. Private Rev Mult = 1.3 (else 3)	4,560	2,185	4,560	ERR	2,185	ERR
12. Private Rev Mult = 1.6 (else 3)	4,560	3,553	4,560	11,843	2,185	0

Note: Runs correspond to text sections, as follows:

1. Chapter 4.1.1   5. Chapter 6.1   9. Chapter 6.3
2. Chapter 4.1.2   6. Chapter 6.1   10. Chapter 6.2
3. Chapter 5.2   7. Chapter 6.1   11. None
4. Chapter 5.3   8. Chapter 6.3   12. None

fall anywhere in the wide range from $-2,724$ to $4,560$ and still make divestiture socially desirable.

If, on the other hand, we maintain the efficiency differential but convert private market structure to monopoly (If Mkt Mnp $= 1$ with a demand elasticity of 1.1), then divestiture is no longer desirable (line 4 of table 8.3). This condition is reflected in a negative value for ΔW^* (-588), which says the enterprise *shouldn't* be sold (at any price a rational buyer would be willing to pay). Equivalently, it *can't* be sold, because the private maximum (5,184) exceeds the government's minimum (7,144).

The reasonable response to this situation is to exploit the private efficiency differential but control the monopoly exploitation through price regulation (at, say, the old level of 1). Assuming this can be accomplished without eroding the efficiency differential (a very strong assumption), results are given in line 5 of table 8.3. As expected, divestiture now has considerable potential ($\Delta W^* = 1,462$), and there is considerable range for negotiation ($Z_p = 3,439 > Z_g = -686$). Note, however, that the gains are less than in the competitive case (line 3) because the private sector's ability to produce more cannot be exploited, given the fixed price and noninfinite demand elasticity. This emphasizes the point that demand conditions do affect both the private sector's willingness to pay and the public sector's reservation price.

So far we have assumed that the base price and quantity are set by market forces, but that need not be the case. What if the base state is the result of price regulation at 1.0 and that there is underutilized capacity of, say, 20 percent? This is not unrealistic, because a fair number of public enterprises apply average cost pricing in a misguided attempt to cover fixed costs even in the presence of excess capacity. If so, then divestiture under the previous assumptions has an additional advantage of expanding production, making divestiture still more desirable, as shown in line 6.

Thus far we have assumed rationing via willingness to pay. In the extreme case of perfect inverse rationing, we get the results of line 7 of table 8.3. The private valuation is unchanged, because the private shareholder doesn't care about the source of his or her dollar. From the public enterprise perspective, however, divestiture is even more desirable than in the previous case because the incremental output is valued more highly.[4]

Rationing need be neither symmetric nor extreme. For example, what if a portion of public output is distributed to the politically favored, while the private sector sells largely to those with the highest willingness to pay? The impact can be determined by setting $\mu_g^o = 0.25$ and $\mu_p^o = 0.75$.

Note that all these nonprice-rationing examples are unrealistic in ignoring rent-seeking. How does the private sector accomplish rationing via willingness to pay? Presumably, rationing occurs by actually charging the market-clearing price and capturing the increment off the books. This raises V_{pp} and ΔW^* above the levels specified. On the other hand, the dead-weight loss associated with real resources expended in rent-seeking lowers V_{sp}, Z_g, and ΔW^*.

Now we consider the impact of shadow pricing, returning to the competitive environment of line 3 but with output undervalued by 25 percent and workers overpaid by 25 percent. As shown in line 8 of table 8.3, private willingness to pay is unaffected by shadow pricing, because only the market prices affect the private decision. The public numbers change considerably, however. Market price underestimates benefits and overestimates costs, so shadow pricing increases the gains from the output expansion effect while somewhat reducing the credit for cost reduction. On balance, $V_{sp} - V_{sg}$ rises from 817 to 1,231, making divestiture even more desirable than appears to be the case at market prices. If, on the other hand, the private sector behaves as a monopolist (line 4), then shadow pricing increases the loss due to reduced output, making divestiture even less desirable than at market prices (line 9).

Next we consider the impact of an indirect tax imposed in conjunction with divestiture. In the competitive case (which is supply constrained), V_{pp} falls without altering ΔW^* (line 10). The government has simply taken some of the gains as taxes, reducing Z_p by an equivalent amount.

Transaction costs also need to be considered. In private placements these have been reported to fall in the range of 10 percent to 20 percent of proceeds, with clear evidence of economies of scale.[5] Reports on the U.K. divestitures are in the 3 percent to 11 percent range, *excluding* costs borne by the company itself.[6] Accordingly, we assume illustratively that these amount to 10 percent and are evenly split between buyer and seller. Returning to case 3 (competition without shadow pricing), the effects are straightforward.[7] Value to the private sector falls (from 1,221 to 1,130), and value to the government falls even more (from 1,819 to 1,610) because the full transaction costs are a loss to society, and a portion of those are valued at the government revenue multiplier. Accordingly, the maximum welfare gain is reduced (from 2,185 to 1,945), and the bargaining range ($Z_p - Z_g$) narrows (from 7,083 and 6,495). In this particular case there remains plenty of scope for a mutually beneficial transaction to occur, but in close cases the transaction costs could make ΔW^* negative. This is more likely for smaller enterprises, insofar as there is a high fixed component in the transaction costs, making it a large percentage of smaller transactions.

Finally, we consider the impact (on case 3) of a change in the private revenue multiplier. Line 11 shows a rise in the private revenue multiplier to the level of the government multiplier (1.3). The private valuation is unchanged, but the government valuation rises (from 817 to 2,185) because of higher societal evaluation of the return to the private sector. As in case 1, Z_g and ΔW^- are undefined because with money in public hands equivalent to money in private hands, the magnitude of the sale transaction is irrelevant. Line 12 shows the effect of a further rise in λ_p, so that it exceeds λ_g. Again, this does not matter to the private buyer, but there is a further rise in the social valuation (from 2,185 to 3,553). The perverse effects of $\lambda_g < \lambda_p$ show up in Z_g and ΔW^*. As explained in section 2.8, Z_g now becomes the maximum the government is willing to accept, because the more the private sector pays, the worse off society is. At this price ($Z_g =$ 11,843), society is just neutral about the whole transaction ($\Delta W^- = 0$), but now it is higher prices that bring lower welfare, and lower ones that increase welfare. Accordingly, lowering the price to the private buyer's maximum willingness to pay now increases welfare (to $\Delta W = 2,185$). This is no longer the maximum ΔW, however, because still lower prices are still more beneficial.

In this section we have changed one variable at a time from the base state to show how the template works. In the following section we shift all variables at the same time to reflect a prototypical LDC context and then conduct a sensitivity analysis.

8.2   Sensitivity Analysis

8.2.1   Overview

What is the relative importance of the various variables involved in the divestiture calculation? This question is of obvious practical importance, because—given scarce analytical resources—we need to know just where to focus our efforts. It makes little sense to waste time perfecting our estimate of a variable that doesn't really make much difference to the bottomline. Accordingly, in this section we conduct a sensitivity analysis to get a feel for the relative impact of various variables on ΔW^*. Specifically, we calculate the percentage change in ΔW^* resulting from a 1 percent change in each variable and report the result as an arc elasticity.

Use of the phrase "get a feel for" is purposeful because there can be no general result independent of the specific context. Sensitivity of ΔW^* to a particular variable is calculated holding all other variables constant; if the other variables are different, then sensitivity will generally be different. This is of course a source of concern in any sensitivity analysis, but it is particularly important in the present context because of the critical role of discontinuous market structure variables. For example, in a competitive environment with excess demand, indirect taxes make little difference because quantity is not affected, and all that changes is that the government gets more in future taxes but less in present sale price.[8] In a noncompetitive market, on the other hand, quantity also changes, with a significant welfare impact. In the first case, sensitivity to indirect taxation is low, but this result cannot be extrapolated to a different market structure where it could be extremely high.

In sum, the detailed results of this subsection should not be taken as definitive but rather as indicative of general orders of magnitude and illustrative of an approach that can and should be used in any particular context.

8.2.2 Basic Assumptions

As the starting point for our sensitivity analysis we once again use corporation A but now with a life expectancy of twenty-five years. The assumption section of table 8.4 reflects the following—and not uncommon—view of the public/private environment in LDCs.

Reforms can improve efficiency in the public sector (gvrmnt. efficiency multi. = 1.025) but to a lesser extent than under private operation (private efficiency multi. = 1.05). Demand will expand with national income under both public and private operation (government and private annual demand. shifts = 1.01).

Because divestiture is not very controversial in a competitive setting, we use a noncompetitive environment (D elasticity = 1.1), with price formation via the market (market = 0). Private market power, however, is only partially exercised (if market = 0.3), either because there are several producers or because of fear of government regulation. Public market power is not exercised at all (price set at realized marginal cost). We also assume that in the original base state, output was supply constrained rather than demand constrained (base excess demand = 1,909).

Turning to the static indicators, we assume that the government revenue multiplier is somewhat larger than the corresponding private multiplier,

Table 8.4
LDC base run

1. BASIC INFORMATION

Company name: Corporation A   Run name: LDC base

2. BASIC ASSUMPTIONS

DYNAMIC

INDICATOR	YR MLT	TAU
Private Efficiency Multiplier	1.050	5
Government Efficiency Multiplier	1.020	5
Private Annual Demand Shift	1.010	5
Government Anual Demand Shift	1.010	5

MARKET STRUCTURE	VALUE
Private Price Formation	
Market = 0, Regulated = 1	0
If Mkt: Mnp = 1 > olgp > 0 = C	0.3
If Reg: give price	0.00
If Reg: RatRl WP = 1 > > 0	0.00
Government Price Formation	
Market = 0, Regulated = 1	0
If Mkt: Mnp = 1 > olgp > 0 = C	0.0
If Reg: give price	0.0
If Reg: RatRl WP = 1 > > 0	0.00
Base Price Formation	
Excess Capacity	0
Excess Demand	1,909
If XD: RatRl WP = 1 > > 0	0

STATIC

INDICATOR	VALUE
Gov Rev Mult	1.30
Pvt Rev Mult	1.10
D Elasticity	1.1
Life (max = 25)	25.00
G Corp Tax	0.33
P Corp Tax	0.25
G Indirect Tx	0.10
P Indirect Tx	0.10
G OpCst Wrk Cptl	0.10
P OpCst Wrk Cptl	0.20
G Discount Rate	0.10
P Discount Rate	0.20
G Loan Rate	0.10
P Loan Rate	0.05
NonOp Ast Adj Fct	2.00
Wrk Asset Adj Fct	0.50
Shd Mlt: Output	1.50
Shd Mlt: Intrmdt	1.25
Shd Mlt: Labor	0.75
Shd Mlt: Wrk Cpt	1.00
G Trnsct Costs	0.02
P Trnsct Costs	0.02

3. SUMMARY OF RESULTS

		TOTAL	TRNSCT	PRDCTN	FNCNL
VALUES					
TO PRIVATE OF PRIVATE	V_{pp}	30,624	-327	24,324	6,628
(TO SC OF PVT) - (TO SC OF GVT)	$V_{sp} - V_{sg}$	3,175	-786	4,754	-793
PRICES					
PRIVATE MAXIMUM (=OPTIMAL)	Z_p	30,624	-327	24,324	6,628
GOVERNMENT MINIMUM	Z_g	-15,875	3,929	-23,768	3,963
CHANGE IN WELFARE					
MAXIMUM (at Z_p)	ΔW^*	9,300	-851	9,618	533
MINIMUM (at Z_g)	ΔW^-	0	0	0	0

with both exceeding unity (gov. rev. mult. = 1.3 > pvt. rev. mult. = 1.1). The effective corporate tax rate is lower under private ownership (G corp. tax = 0.33; P corp. tax = 0.25), reflecting the view that private owners are somewhat more creative in utilizing accounting practices that avoid taxes. Indirect taxes, on the other hand, are the same in both environments (G indirect tax = P indirect tax = 0.1). The government discount rate (and opportunity cost of capital) is lower than in the private sector, reflecting both the Arrow and Lind normative view and the positive statement that private investors in LDCs expect to get their money back in three years, given uncertainty. A differential loan rate (G loan rate = 0.1; P loan rate = 0.05) is included to suggest that as part of the negotiating process, the government may offer to refinance the original loan at a lower subsidized rate. The book value of nonoperating assets is below its market rate (Nonop. ast. adj. fc = 2), reflecting inflation. However, the market value on working capital is lower (wrk. asst. adj. fc = 0.5) because of over-optimistic estimates of receivables. The real scarcity value of output is above its market value (shd. mlt.: output = 1.5), but this is partly offset by the enterprise receiving subsidized inputs, especially energy (shd. mlt.: intrmdt. = 1.25). Labor is overpaid (shd. mlt.: labor = 0.75) and we have no priors on working capital (shd. mlt.: wrk. cpt. = 1.00). Transaction costs are 4 percent of base sales equally shared between buyer and seller.

8.2.3   Basic Sensitivity Results

For the basic assumptions just described, sensitivity results are given in table 8.5. Interpretation is straightforward: a sensitivity (elasticity) of $+5.0$ says that a 1 percent rise in the variable increases ΔW^* by 5 percent, whereas a sensitivity of -0.50 says that a 1 percent rise in the variable reduces ΔW^* by 0.5 percent. Results are easily summarized in three groups. First, variables that matter quite a bit (absolute sensitivities greater than one) are efficiency, demand, market power, and working capital. Second, revenue multipliers, discount rates, demand elasticity, and shadow multipliers for output and inputs are moderately important (absolute sensitivities in the range from about 0.2 to unity). Results are much less sensitive to other variables (absolute sensitivities well below 0.2).

The critical importance of efficiency and demand shift parameters will come as no surprise to those familiar with the ex-post project evaluation literature. When the actual project outcome differs considerably from that projected, it is far more commonly due to errors in forecasting demand, costs, and gestation periods than to whether the shadow multiplier for un-

Table 8.5

SENSITIVITY RESULTS

	RUN 1	RUN 2	RUN 3	RUN 4	RUN 5
Private Efficiency Multiplier	5.77	2.14	-17.82	3.55	4.53
Government Efficiency Multiplier	-2.60	-0.66	7.14	-1.72	-1.95
Annual Demand Shift: PVT	1.40	0.39	-4.09	2.21	0.98
Annual Demand Shift: GVT	-1.36	-0.35	3.83	-2.21	-0.99
PVT: If Mkt: Mnp = 1 > olgp > 0 = Cmpt	-1.86	-0.50	10.14	0.00	-1.31
PVT: If Reg: give price	0.00	0.00	0.00	-26.17	0.00
PVT: If Reg: RatRl WP = 1 > > 0 = 1/WP	0.00	0.00	0.00	0.00	0.00
GVT: If Mkt: Mnp = 1 > olgp > 0 = Cmpt	0.00	0.00	0.00	0.00	0.00
GVT: If Reg: give price	0.00	0.00	0.00	18.49	0.00
GVT: If Reg: RatRl WP = 1 > > 0 = 1/WP	0.00	0.00	0.00	0.00	0.00
BASE: Excess Capacity	0.00	0.00	0.00	0.00	0.00
BASE: Excess Demand	0.19	0.13	-0.61	0.10	0.00
BASE: If XD: RatRl WP = 1 > > 0 = 1/WP	0.00	0.00	0.00	0.00	0.00
Government Revenue Multiplier	-0.35	-0.08	0.66	-0.49	0.11
Private Revenue Multiplier	0.20	0.05	-0.66	0.26	0.07
Demand Elasticity	0.82	0.33	-4.39	-0.12	0.21
Government Corporate Tax	0.00	0.00	0.00	0.00	0.00
Private Corporate Tax	0.12	0.03	-0.39	0.15	0.03
Government Indirect Tax	0.00	0.00	-0.01	0.01	0.00
Private Indirect Tax	-0.05	-0.00	0.68	0.16	-0.04
Gov Oppty Cost Working Capital	0.79	0.20	-2.32	0.87	0.75

Table 8.5 (*continued*)

SENSITIVITY RESULTS

	RUN 1	RUN 2	RUN 3	RUN 4	RUN 5
Pvt Oppty Cost Working Capital	−1.43	−0.34	4.10	−1.41	−1.27
Government Discount Rate	−0.97	−0.92	−0.43	−0.72	−1.08
Private Discount Rate	−0.47	−0.13	1.51	−0.59	−0.18
Government Loan Rate	−0.00	0.00	0.00	−0.00	−0.00
Private Loan Rate	0.03	0.01	−0.10	0.04	0.03
Nonoperating Asset Adj Factor	−0.00	0.00	0.00	−0.00	−0.00
Working Assets Adjment Factor	−0.00	0.00	0.00	−0.00	−0.00
Shadow Multiplier: Output(mc)	−0.01	0.23	2.59	−0.00	−0.24
Shadow Multiplier: Intermediates	0.31	0.08	−1.48	0.33	0.36
Shadow Multiplier: Labor	−0.05	−0.01	0.22	−0.05	−0.05
Shadow Multiplier: Working Cap	0.00	0.00	0.00	0.00	0.00
Government Transaction Costs	−0.05	−0.01	0.13	−0.05	−0.03
Private Transaction Costs	−0.05	−0.01	0.13	−0.05	−0.03
Memo: ΔW^*	9,300	36,067	−3,223	8,085	9,860

Notes: Elasticity of ΔW^* with respect to a 1 percent change in the indicated variables. Note that a 1 percent change is a good deal greater if the original variable is listed as a multiplier (1.10) rather than as an equivalent increment (0.10). To increase comparability, the 1 percent increase was therefore calculated on the basis of the value minus one for all multiplier-type variables.

Run 1: Base run.

Run 2: Private efficiency parameter rised from 1.05 to 1.075.

Run 3: Greater exercise of private market power, from 0.3 to 0.5.

Run 4: Regulated price at 1.0.

Run 5: Base state changed to a loss-making enterprise.

skilled labor was 0.3 rather than 0.7. The importance of the market power variables will likewise come as no surprise to readers of this volume.[9]

The importance of the opportunity cost of working capital, however, may at first glance be somewhat more surprising. At least three factors are at work. First, as with any other cost increase, a relatively small shift in a large number (total costs) has a relatively large impact on residual small numbers (such as profits). Second, under the current market structure, this matters a great deal, as it raises prices and reduces quantity (unlike, say, shadow multipliers, consumer surplus, or profit). Under other market structures (inelastic demand or price regulation), it is much less important. Third, each of the opportunity cost variables affects only one ownership form and operates in only one direction, with no offsets. For example, raising the shadow multiplier for intermediates has a higher effect on V_{sp} and V_{pp} as compared with raising only the cost of working capital, but this is in part offset by its simultaneously raising V_{sg}.

No great emphasis should be placed on the relative magnitudes of the public and private multipliers. These derive primarily from differences in the base assumptions. For example, the absolute value of the efficiency sensitivity is 5.77 for private versus only 2.60 for public largely because we assumed 5 percent annual private improvement versus 2 percent public; 1 percent of 5 percent is more than double 1 percent of 2 percent and hence has more than double the impact on ΔW^*. Public and private efficiency changes both matter a great deal.

Signs on the efficiency shift elasticities are readily interpreted: the more efficiency improves under private operation, the greater the potential gains from divestiture; but the more efficiency improves under public operation, the less the potential gains from divestiture. The same is true for the sign on the demand shift parameter. Under private management, greater demand means fuller utilization of the expanded capacity, increasing both V_{pp} and V_{sp} (without altering V_{sg}) and, therefore raising ΔW^*. However, under government operation, greater demand raises V_{sg} (without altering V_{pp} or V_{sp}), thus lowering ΔW^*. The one sign that appears counterintuitive is the negative sign on the shadow output multiplier. This can be more readily understood if we compare it with a case where the sign is positive. We therefore defer this discussion until the end of the next section.

8.2.4   Sensitivity of Sensitivity Results

As with any elasticity measurement, responsiveness varies substantially with the starting level of the responding variable. In the present case, this means that if we start with a ΔW^* that is extremely high, nothing much matters; conversely, with a small ΔW^*, everything matters. This is illustrated in column 2 of table 8.5, where the assumed annual private efficiency multiplier has been increased to 1.075, greatly increasing ΔW^* (from 9,300 to 36,067). As expected, the whole set of elasticities has been made smaller with the relative importance of most parameters largely left unchanged. Notable exceptions include the government discount rate (which is basically unchanged in absolute terms and thus several times as important in relative terms), base excess demand (which changed much less than the average), and the shadow output multiplier (which actually reversed its sign).

None of these relative changes are straightforward. Consider the government discount rate. This is negative in both runs, because net benefits are deferred (government operation is superior in the earlier years, until the cumulative impact of the efficiency differential dominates) and thus the higher the discount rate, the lower the net present benefits from divestiture. If the stream were a perpetuity, then the drop in ΔW^* would be inversely proportional to the rise in the discount rate in both runs. However, the present streams persist for only twenty-five years, the two streams have different crossover points (private begins to dominate public in year 4 in run 1, but in year 2 in run 2), and private willingness to pay (Z^*) increases dramatically, but undiscounted, from run 1 to run 2.

Nonetheless, the relatively stable elasticity of the government discount rate is more or less predictable, as opposed to the relative stability of the base excess demand multiplier, which is the accidental result of a number of offsetting changes. Note that in the current case, output is supply constrained under government output but demand constrained under public operation (because efficiency gains shift capacity beyond the demand constraint under private operation but not under public). Greater demand therefore increases price and quantity in all years under private operation but increases only price under government operation. As a result, V_{pp}, V_{sp}, and V_{sg} all increase but by different magnitudes, exaggerated by the different multipliers.

This result is distinct from the effect of changing the shadow output multiplier, which also shifts the real demand curve out in terms of measuring consumer surplus but not the effective demand curve, which determines price and quantity. As a result, V_{pp} is unchanged, and the rises in V_{sp} and V_{sg} are smaller than when the market demand curve shifts out. Whether V_{sp} or V_{sg} changes more in a given year depends on which one was larger in the first place. In run 1 public operation is superior to private operation in the first four years, making V_{sg} grow by more than V_{sg} during this period, which more than dominates the offsetting changes in later years, making the net effect negative (barely). In run 2 on the other hand, the reversal takes place after year 2, and the present value of the positive later-year impact dominates the negative effect of the earlier years. The result is the sign reversal described in the previous section.

If this seems complicated, that is only because it is. It can get worse as we alter other variables. In run 3 we assume a greater exercise of private market power (0.5 versus 0.3 in run 1). In run 4 we control market power with a regulated price (0.9) that is identical under public and private operation. Comparison of results shows additional diversity in the elasticity patterns. Some of these are obvious: for example, the importance of the regulated price and the rationing rule under regulation or, in run 3, the sign reversal on most elasticities as a result of the negative base value of ΔW^*.[10] Others are less obvious and require detailed investigation to understand what is really going on—for example, the relatively high sensitivity of ΔW^* to private indirect taxes and base excess demand in run 3 or the absence of sign reversal on the shadow output multiplier in run 3. Examples could be multiplied, but the basic lesson is clear: sensitivity is in large part a function of the starting point.

Thus far we have altered only environmental data, but we can also alter the company data. Run 5 retains the environmental assumptions of run 1 but converts corporation A from a profitable to a loss-making firm in the base year: sales are reduced considerably (from 18,191 to 13,000), with some of the drop absorbed by dropping taxes and dividends to zero and the balance passed through to retained earnings (which falls from -809 to $-2,937$). Column 5 of table 8.5 shows the resulting additional sensitivity variety. Note that this is a straightforward illustration of the point that it is possible to sell a losing enterprise. As shown in table 8.6, the private sector is willing to pay a substantial positive price ($Z_p = V_{pp} = 13,812$), more or less evenly divided between productive (7,444) and financial (6,628) assets. On the financial side the market value of the nonoperating assets and the working capital substantially outweigh the present value of the debt incurred. On the production side the exercise of market power and improved efficiency are sufficient to more than wipe out the losses in the base state. The transaction is also socially desirable ($\Delta W^* = 10,269$), and almost all this is on the production side. That is, society values the gain in efficiency (lower unit costs and increased capacity) more than the loss of consumer surplus due to exercise of market power.

Table 8.6
Selling a loss-making enterprise

1. BASIC INFORMATION

Company name: Corporation B   Run name: Losing company + LDC base

2. BASIC ASSUMPTIONS

DYNAMIC

INDICATOR	YR MLT	TAU	STATIC INDICATOR	VALUE
Private Efficiency Multiplier	1.050	5	Gov Rev Mult	1.30
Government Efficiency Multiplier	1.020	5	Pvt Rev Mult	1.10
Private Annual Demand Shift	1.010	5	D Elasticity	1.1
Government Annual Demand Shift	1.010	5	Life (max = 25)	25.00
			G Corp Tax	0.33
			P Corp Tax	0.25
			G Indirect Tx	0.10
			P Indirect Tx	0.10
			G OpCst Wrk Cptl	0.10
			P OpCst Wrk Cptl	0.20
			G Discount Rate	0.10
			P Discount Rate	0.20
			G Loan Rate	0.10
			P Loan Rate	0.05
			NonOp Ast Adj Fct	2.00
			Wrk Asset Adj Fct	0.50
			Shd Mlt: Output	1.50
			Shd Mlt: Intrmdt	1.25
			Shd Mlt: Labor	0.75
			Shd Mlt: Wrk Cpt	1.00
			G Trnsct Costs	0.02
			P Trnsct Costs	0.02

MARKET STRUCTURE

	VALUE
Private Price Formation	
Market = 0, Regulated = 1	0
If Mkt: Mnp = 1 > olgp > 0 = C	0.3
If Reg: give price	0.00
If Reg: RatRl WP = 1 > > 0 = 1/WP	0.00
Government Price Formation	
Market = 0, Regulated = 1	0
If Mkt: Mnp = 1 > olgp > 0 = C = 1/WP	0.0
If Reg: give price	0.00
If Reg: RatRl WP = 1 > > 0	0.00
Base Price Formation	
Excess Capacity	0
Excess Demand	1,909
If XD: RatRl WP = 1 > > 0 = 1/WP	1

3. SUMMARY OF RESULTS

		TOTAL	TRNSCT	PRDCTN	FNCNL
VALUES					
TO PRIVATE OF PRIVATE	V_{pp}	17,127	−252	10,751	6,628
(TO SC OF PVT) − (TO SC OF GVT)	$V_{sp} - V_{sg}$	6,434	−605	7,832	−793
PRICES					
PRIVATE MAXIMUM (=OPTIMAL)	Z_p	17,127	−252	10,751	6,628
GOVERNMENT MINIMUM	Z_g	−32,172	3,024	−39,159	3,963
CHANGE IN WELFARE					
MAXIMUM (at Z_p)	ΔW^*	9,860	−655	9,982	533
MINIMUM (at Z_g)	ΔW^-	−0	−0	0	0

8.3   Conclusion

In this chapter we presented a valuation algorithm and illustrated its utility in a variety of contexts. Two general conclusions emerged. First, the importance of the various assumptions varies considerably with the particular circumstances, meaning that a priori assumptions are dangerous in empirical work. Second, the least dangerous assumptions are that results will be relatively sensitive to efficiency multipliers, demand shift factors, market structure variables appropriate to the context, the opportunity cost of working capital, and the discount rates. A final use of the algorithm is to assess the impact of discretionary policy variables, a subject to which we will turn after looking at the political economy of divestiture.

9   Winners and Losers

Thus far we have taken a rather narrow view of divestiture from the perspective of a neutral technocrat carrying out antiseptic cost-benefit calculations. Fortunately, the real world is more interesting. Divestiture creates winners and losers: Some are witting, others unwitting; some are influential, others disenfranchised; some are affected in their pocketbooks, others in their political or ideological agendas; some are concentrated, others diffuse. The machinations of these groups to alter the outcome in their favor, at someone else's expense, we call politics. The intersection of the technocratic and political perspectives we call political economy, which is the subject of this chapter.

In one brief chapter we do not pretend to accomplish a comprehensive treatment of the political economy of divestiture; for that one may turn to the volumes edited by Vernon and by Suleiman and Waterbury.[1] Instead, we merely endeavor to link our technocratic framework to the broader structure of political economy. The first step is to expand our earlier work to incorporate distributional considerations. The most relevant use of the resulting framework is for ex-ante or ex-post analysis of actual cases, something we do not at present have to offer. Instead, we utilize the framework at a more aggregate level to examine the genesis of the current wave of divestiture and the differential responses between LDCs and MDCs.

9.1   Analytics: Distribution

9.1.1   Issues

Results in the earlier part of this book were derived using an implicit assumption of distributional neutrality in consumption. An incremental dollar of consumption was of equal worth regardless of who consumed it (so long as it was not a foreigner). Dollars were different in so far as they were used for different purposes (for example, investment versus consumption), and this led to efficiency multipliers. In this section we incorporate distributional considerations, leading to multipliers that reflect both equity and efficiency. As a starting point we use equation (5.21), since it incorporates the rents we view as central to the political economy story that we wish to tell.[2]

9.1.2   Income Distribution

The mechanics of introducing income distribution is a four-step process:

1. *Redefine the numeraire* to represent a dollar of consumption accruing to a particular group. Ideally, we like to use as numeraire an allocation that does not change the distribution of consumption. A simpler and more pragmatic possibility[3] is a dollar accruing to the "average"[4] consumer, as utilized in Squire and van der Tak.[5]

2. *Calculate the multipliers.* Discrete multipliers may be assigned to some groups (e.g., foreigners equal zero) or regions. For the rest, we need a continuous distribution as a function of consumption. This is commonly captured in a single parameter for the consumption elasticity (n) of the marginal social utility (δU) of consumption (C):[6]

$$\delta U_c = C^{-n}$$

If $n = 0$, then the marginal social value of consumption is independent of the level of consumption, we do not care about distribution, and the shadow multiplier for consumption (λ_s) equals unity. Greater levels of n yield exponentially greater levels of redistributional weight. For example, if the target group's consumption is half of the median, then their consumption is twice as valuable if $n = 1$ and four times as valuable if $n = 2$.

3. *Insert the consumption multiplier* thus calculated into the consumer surplus term in equation (5.21).

4. *Reinterpret the existing multipliers* in equation (5.21) to incorporate both the previous efficiency effect and the new distributional impact.[7]

There is a bit more to it than this, but the first two steps are a staple of the cost-benefit literature, and the last two are straightforward. Before we start to interpret our basic distributional equation, we need to identify the actors in our story.

9.1.3   Actors

We identify seven classes of actors. The first four share the costs and benefits of divestiture:

1. *Citizens* are the ultimate beneficiaries of funds accruing to the government, be it in the form of reduced taxes, greater consumption of public goods, or reduced inflation.

2. *Consumers* are affected insofar as divestiture alters the price/quantity/ quality bundle offered by the enterprise.

3. *Purchasers* of the enterprise benefit from the sale insofar as the actual sales price falls short of their maximum willingness to pay.

4. *Providers* of inputs lose insofar as divested cost-cutting efforts reduce rents previously accruing in such forms as excess wages, overbilling for intermediates or construction contracts, excess profits to intermediaries, kickbacks to providers of credit, and side payments to signers of various official pieces of paper. They may also gain, for example, if profit shares and incentive payments are offered to employees after sale.

The second set of actors is involved in the decision-making process:

5. *Patrons* are broad-minded political agents who make the ultimate decisions about public enterprises, taking into account both their ideological priors and explicit effects on the general interests of citizens and the narrower interests of various special-interest groups.

6. *Technocrats* are narrow-minded economic agents who attempt to influence patrons to act in the interest of citizens.

7. *Clients* are the special-interest groups of providers, consumers, and purchasers who attempt to influence patrons to act in their interest.

This morphology is imperfect in that the categories are neither mutually exclusive nor exhaustive. In part, this is trivial: for example, almost all[8] actors are citizens, but if a provider gets 1/100 of the benefits, we can safely ignore the fact that he or she also pays 1/10,000,000 of the costs. In part, it is by design: patrons can also be providers, and therein lies part of the story. In part, it is a simplification designed to draw attention to certain fundamentals: for example, providers are a rather heterogeneous group encompassing selected unionists, capitalists, and bureaucrats, among others. Depending on the political bargains struck to gain support for divestiture, some may actually gain while others lose. Their interests will, therefore, ultimately have to be separated, but as a starting point it is useful to call attention to their common interest in opposition to simple divestiture. The proof of the pudding, however, is in the eating, so let us see how this particular classification works as a starting point.

9.1.4 Distributional Equation

Given our choice of actors and the introduction of the new multipliers, a simple rearrangement of equation (5.21) yields our basic distributional equation (9.1) completely allocating the change in welfare resulting from divestiture:[9]

$$\Delta W = \underbrace{\underbrace{\underbrace{\Delta S}_{} + \underbrace{Z_p - Z}_{} + \underbrace{\Delta M}_{\text{Providers}}}_{\text{Purchasers}}}_{\text{Consumers}}$$

$$+ \underbrace{[\lambda_g(\Delta\Pi + Z - Z_p) + (\lambda_p - 1)(Z_p - Z) + (\lambda_m - 1)\Delta M + (\lambda_s - 1)\Delta S]}_{\text{Citizens}}.$$

$$(9.1)$$

In other words,

1. *Consumers* receive the change in consumer surplus. This is positive to the extent that greater efficiency or competition reduce prices, negative to the extent that prices rise due to exploitation of market power or abolition of price subsidies.

2. *Purchasers* benefit to the extent that their willingness to pay (Z_p, the present value of future profits) exceeds the price actually paid (Z). Since they are not coerced into buying, the expected value will be nonnegative.

3. *Providers* receive any change in rents accruing to suppliers of inputs. This will most commonly be negative but can be positive for particular subgroups in so far as facilitating side payments are agreed to in advance or their bargaining power is maintained and they receive a share of increased enterprise rent after divestiture (witness the increased returns to labor after divestiture raised profits at Jaguar).

4. *Citizens'* returns are, not inappropriately, somewhat more diffuse and harder to interpret. The first term says that in the unlikely event that bargaining extracts the purchaser's full willingness to pay ($Z = Z_p$), citizens receive the entire stream of enhanced profitability, evaluated at the shadow price of government funds. To the extent that the strike price falls short of

the buyer's willingness to pay, this benefit is reduced. The next three terms follow from the definition of the respective multipliers. Recall that a λ_p greater than one may mean that a dollar of investment is worth more than a dollar of private consumption because of capital market distortions. This excess accrues to citizens in the form of government revenue and/or greater investment, which creates more jobs and ultimately higher aggregate consumption levels. A similar argument holds for the efficiency component of λ_m. For λ_s (and the equity components of λ_p and λ_m) the interpretation is that whereas the individual consumer gets the extra surplus, society as a whole benefits from living in a more egalitarian society.[10]

This gives us a brief outline of the candidates for positions as winners and losers from divestiture. The next step is to study them further.

9.2   Distributional Realities

9.2.1   Issues

Where do the different actors fit into the income distribution of a country? Where do they fit into the power distribution? This section addresses these questions in turn. Particular attention is focused on the role of providers, a group that we view as central to the political economy of divestiture.

2.9.2   Divestiture and the Poor: LDCs

Where do the various actors appear in the income distribution? Mechanically, are λ_s and the distributional components of λ_p and λ_m likely to be greater or less than one? We begin with consideration of the LDCs.

Who consumes public enterprise products? With electricity, for example, some goes to consumers, who are disproportionately wealthy: the rich have air conditioners and stereos, the poor have one light bulb dangling on a wire or are not served at all. The rest of the output is sold to industry as an intermediate input and, depending on the degree of competition in their output markets, is shared between the owners (rich, obviously) and the consumers of energy-intensive projects (also relatively well-to-do). A similar analysis applies to the bulk of public enterprise products, which are capital and energy intensive. Even for foodstuffs, which do not fit this mold, relatively little goes to rural areas, where the bulk of poverty lies, and even within urban areas the well-to-do consume more than the poor.[11]

Exceptions may occur. Lifeline pricing in electricity may direct benefits to the poor. Profits from luxury housing may be used to cross-subsidize low income housing. The case is similar for first- and third-class rail or bus service. Even in these cases, it is by no means certain that the subsidized consumer is significantly below the median. While allowing for the possibility of such special cases, it seems that in general λ_s will be less than one in LDCs.

What of providers? Suppliers of inputs, contractors and approvers of credit, licenses, and other documents are obviously disproportionately at the top of the income distribution. Labor will at first glance seem to be less well off, but work in a variety of countries shows that even the lowest paid worker in a public enterprise is typically in the seventieth percentile of the income distribution and certainly in the top half. The distributional component of λ_m will generally be less than one.

What of purchasers? Sale to a single individual, family, or closely held corporation obviously affects only the very top of the income distribution. The sale of shares on the stock market moves down the distribution somewhat but still affects primarily the top decile. Even sale to employees still involves only the top three deciles. The distributional components of λ_p will certainly be considerably less than one.

What of citizens? Here, of course, the poor are represented. If, at the margin, additional government funds are used for purposes that benefit the lower half of the income distribution and if divestiture is implemented in such a way that the government captures a share of the benefits, then the poor can gain. However, this is not very likely. As we argue shortly, an environment facilitating extensive divestiture is likely to be characterized by fiscal stringency and/or ideological predilection for less government, not more. Under such conditions, then, additional government revenues are more likely to reduce taxes than to increase services to the poor. If so, the segment of citizens benefiting at the margin from additional government revenues is likely to be taxpayers, whose mean position on the distributional scale is well above the median. In sum, the distributional component of λ_g can in principle be greater than one but in the environment of extensive divestiture is likely to be somewhat lower.

The bottom line is that in LDCs divestiture is a game played primarily between the rich and the upper middle class. This is not to say that income distribution cannot be improved in the process. Transferring resources from the top 1 percent to the seventieth percentile may be worthwhile. However, if the bottom half of the population is to be directly benefited, then one must look to the benefits to citizens and not those accruing to consumers, purchasers, or providers. For divestiture to help the poor, the primary route is indirect: matters must be arranged so that the government gets a substantial share that is then used for services to the poor.

9.2.3 Divestiture and the Poor: MDCs

How do things differ in MDCs? Qualitatively, the same situation holds, but quantitatively, costs and benefits are dispersed far more widely. In MDCs the relevant actors are spread across the income distribution; hence the distributional impact of divestiture is much less concentrated than in LDCs.

Because public utilities form a major group of public enterprises in such countries, practically every household is a customer of the public sector. Businesses are also customers, but they in turn sell throughout the income distribution. Further, because of the more competitive nature of business in such countries, the owners of industry receive less of the surplus generated by public enterprises than in LDCs. The same sorts of arguments also apply to other types of public enterprises. For example, the big manufacturing or mining enterprises, such as steel mills, shipyards, aerospace companies, and coal mines, sell their outputs to a broad spectrum of firms, which then sell to most income classes. Consequently, λ_s can be greater or less than one in MDCs, depending on the income elasticity of demand for public enterprise products and the skewness of the income distribution. It will, however, be far closer to one than in the LDCs.

Providers are major beneficiaries of public enterprises in MDCs, particularly the work force. In some cases (coal mining in Britain and Germany) the work force may be the primary beneficiary. Compared with the private sector, wages and salaries in the public enterprise sector are more compressed, so that both the upper and lower tails of the distribution are missing. Consequently, any rents received by public enterprise employees exclude the lowest two or three deciles of the wealth distribution in MDCs. Divestiture will partially reduce these rents through layoffs, lower pay for some employees, and an increase in work effort. There may also be scope for larger rents to go to managers in so far as ownership is divorced from control, and/or output markets are regulated in a cost-plus fashion. On balance, therefore, there may be some worsening of the income distribution from divestiture as far as providers go, leading to a distributional parameter of slightly greater than one.

Selling public enterprises in MDCs has been an opportunity for governments to increase the appeal of the stock market to the "general" public. In countries such as Great Britain and Germany, general has meant about 10 to 20 percent of all households who purchased the shares. In some cases public enterprises are sold to other corporations. In any case, with the exception of one Canadian divestiture, where the enterprise was handed over to the taxpayers,[12] the purchasers are clearly concentrated in the upper half of the wealth distribution. Thus the distributional component of λ_p will be lower than one.

If the financial benefits from divestiture are used by governments mostly to reduce taxes, then it is worth noting that the tax systems in MDCs are regressive. However, the very poor tend to receive net transfers. It is unlikely that citizens' benefits from divestiture will lead to an increase in these net transfers in the political context of divestiture. We would therefore argue that, once again, the very bottom of the wealth distribution is not going to benefit from divestiture, whereas the rest of the distribution will be largely unaffected. The net result will be a distributional impact of something less than one.

Basically, in MDCs the benefits of divestiture will be spread over the majority of citizens, with some concentration at the top (depending on the method/price of sale) and the very bottom left largely unaffected.

9.2.4   Inefficiency and Rent-Seeking

In chapter 6 we summarized the theory of rent-seeking, noting that, in forcing us to take a hard look at the distinction between "neutral" transfers and eveil deadweight losses, it led us to new calculations of the cost-benefit ratios of various public policies. Typically, this means that because the costs of discretionary market failures are understated, the returns to reform are likewise understated. Sadly, the reverse can be true in the case of divestiture.

Briefly, the argument is this. If seekers of rents find them in public enterprises, then they are entered on the books as a cost. A major perceived benefit of divestiture is improved efficiency, but a portion of that is rent reduction, and a portion of that is transfers. Some—we argue a considerable portion—of the ostensible benefits from divestiture are therefore not deadweight gains but transfers. This result has two central implications for our analysis. First, technocrats must not neglect to deduct ΔM in calculating ΔW. Second, since there is no danger that clients will ignore ΔM and neglect to convey this awareness to patrons, any divestiture strategy must include explicit attention to dealing with the interests of clients. In the balance of this subsection we therefore examine in more detail the relationship between rents and inefficiency.

Public enterprise inefficiencies can be thought of as reflecting potential rents and quasi-rents that do not accrue to capital. An analysis of sources of inefficiency is then a description of the existing distribution of those rents. Improvement of efficiency means returning those rents to the owners of capital. As usual in a rent-seeking context, we must be careful to distinguish two sorts of inefficiency: first, those whose removal involves merely a transfer of existing rents; and second, those whose removal creates rents via real resource savings. On the output side the difference is manifest in the traditional distinction between little triangles of deadweight loss and big rectangles of transfers when analyzing market distortions. The same distribution must be made on the input side, where costs can be reduced either by reducing input prices or by reducing quantities. As a first approximation, endogenous input price changes can be thought of as transfers, and quantity changes as real resource savings.[13] The price category includes the following, among other things:

1. Wages/benefits/perks above opportunity cost.[14]

2. Markups on contracts and intermediates.

3. Sales at below-market price to privileged intermediaries who resell at market.

4. Contributions to political parties and designated charities.

If cost reductions are achieved by reducing or eliminating such distortions, then rents are not created but merely transferred from one recipient to another. On the other hand, if costs are reduced by decreasing the quantities consumed (pure technical efficiency improvement), then it would seem that rents are created.

In the strictly neoclassical view, no such pure rent-creation can occur. The argument is that costs can be reduced only by the actions of individuals —especially managers—who work harder or smarter. The cost reduction is thus accompanied by a reduction in the welfare of the persons putting out more effort, in the form of sacrifice of alternative output, leisure, or psychic utility. If, in the extreme, all cost reductions are interpreted this way, then the net output (or welfare) of society is unchanged but is redistributed from employees to the enterprise. Either employees were previously earning a rent, which is now being taken away, or some market imperfection makes labor immobile, allowing the divested firm to reduce employees' welfare below their opportunity cost and thus charge a negative rent. This may be called the neoclassical theory of the exploitation of the masses. If X or cost inefficiency does not exist, then no real cost savings are possible from reducing slack.[15]

Note the symmetry with the rent-seeking extreme: in the perfect neoclassical world all rents disappear in the cost of seeking, but cost-saving efficiency changes become rent redistribution. As already noted, we do not espouse either extreme view as a reflection of the world of imperfect markets but merely note that some ostensible quantity savings may have (nonmonetary) resource-cost offsets.

Where does this leave us as regards inefficiency and divestiture? On the one hand, some apparent efficiency improvements (ostensibly cost savings) turn out, on closer examination, to be rent transfers. On the other hand, there are some apparent rent transfers (which therefore do not appear to be efficiency improvements) that in fact are reduced costs of rent-seeking. The relative size of the two components is presumably a case-by-case empirical issue. Here we note only that, in an imperfect world, some of what appear to be cost savings from the point of view of the enterprise are really rent transfers, and the resulting negative ΔM creates opponents to divestiture.

9.3   Why Divestiture Now?

9.3.1   Issues

There is a marked discontinuity in postwar world economic history: in the last decade the public enterprise sector has *contracted*, or remained the same in almost all countries; prior to that, it *expanded*, or remained the same in almost all countries in almost all subperiods. Such a strong statement obviously must admit important exceptions (for example, the United Kingdom's divestiture of British Steel in 1953 and the divestiture of Korea Airlines in 1968) and allow qualifications (for example, restricting the assertion to policy-generated change, recognizing that the sector can shrink absolutely as a result of recession and shrink relatively if large public-dominated sectors—read oil—are hit disproportionately). Nonetheless, the generalization holds surprisingly well across the world's 200-odd countries, be they socialist, LDC, or MDC.[16] The question is, Why the discontinuity?

One class of answers focuses on the role of ideological change and/or "great men or women."

Most analysts trace its beginnings to proposals stumbled onto and subsequently pushed with great zeal by the Thatcher government after 1979. In just a very few years, similar types of experiments could be found in dozens of countries and on every continent.[17]

A different class of answer is stressed by Vernon and his colleagues:

Thus, in interpreting the significance of the surge of divestiture programs all over the world, my colleagues and I have been strongly inclined to discount the possibility that the movement represents a basic ideological shift among the countries concerned. Instead, we see the programs as the result of a learning process stretching over two or three decades, a process that has given the governments involved a keener appreciation of the costs and benefits associated with their ownership and management of various enterprises.[18]

We see merit in both sets of explanations. In terms of our framework, there are three stylized classes of change that precipitate divestiture:

1. *Technocrats'* views may change because ΔW has changed as a result of real exogenous shifts in the costs and benefits.

2. *Clients'* effective views may change, either because their own net benefit position may have changed or because their political power has changed.

3. *Patrons'* positions may change, either because the previous two viewpoints have changed or because they themselves have changed their weightings.

We treat these possibilities in turn.

9.3.2 Change in Technocrats' Position

Overview
We have argued that there are two broad sets of factors that determine the welfare impact of divestiture: behavioral and fiscal. Both have changed in ways that might increase returns to divestiture. As regards behavior, a secular trend of increasingly competitive markets is the dominant factor, potentially increasing the various Δ's in ΔW. As for fiscal impact, increased fiscal stringency potentially increases λ_g and the efficiency component of the other λ's. These and other contributing factors are discussed below.

Increasing Effective Market Size
The potential number of firms in a market depends on the size of that market relative to the minimum efficient scale. There are two distinct sources of increasing market size and, therefore, increasing potential competition.

1. *Economic growth:* Over the last three decades, the world economy—and therefore the average economy—has roughly tripled in size.[19] An economy that was large enough to support only three cement plants in the late 1950s may be able to support nine today.

2. *Increased openness:* The fact that there are only one or two domestic producers of a commodity is not terribly significant if the bulk of produc-

tion is freely imported.[20] Increasing openness therefore increases competitive pressures. Our prior assumptions were that both technological change (decreasing transport and information costs) and policy change would have contributed to increased openness over the long term at the global level. Inconveniently, we cannot readily put together the data to test this. Nonetheless, it remains true that for many individual economies, especially in the last fifteen years, increased openness has increased competitive pressures.[21]

As a special case of the foregoing, the creation of a single market in Europe is important enough to warrant separate attention. After 1992, an inefficient European producer of tradables will die or require huge subsidies; inefficient producers of nontradables may survive but make it difficult for domestic producers of tradables to compete. For both sets of reasons, anticipation of 1992 should have produced major technocratic pressures for public enterprise reform.

Decreasing Minimum Efficient Scale
Whereas effective market size has clearly grown, economies of scale seem to have grown at a lesser pace or even declined. This growth pattern has, of course, been highly variable across industries but seems to have been particularly pronounced in the public utility sphere, where public enterprises are concentrated. One reason for this difference is the trade-off between the two-thirds rule and the strain on materials as machines or containers become larger and larger.[22] This trade-off has been used to explain the failure to build reliable thermal electricity generating units above 600-MW capacity. In telecommunications the natural monopoly argument has lost much of its validity largely due to technological advances such as microwave transmission, cellular radio, and satellite technologies (although fiber optics may re-create part of the natural monopoly). Another important development has been the use of computers as inputs in production processes. The ubiquity of personal computers and off-the-shelf hardware has reduced returns to scale across a large range of products requiring information, coordination, and control.

   In sum it seems safe to conclude that in the majority of countries for the majority of public enterprise products, the rate of growth of market size has substantially exceeded that of minimum efficient scale and that competition has accordingly increased dramatically. How does this factor affect the technocratic divestiture decision?

Competition and ΔW

Because competition is the economist's grail, it comes as something of a shock to inspect equation (9.1) and find that competition is a mixed blessing in terms of ΔW.[23] The positive side is obvious: the more competition in the output market, the less likely that the divested firm will exercise market power and create a negative ΔS. The neutral side is that the more competitive the output market, the less likely that any cost savings from divestiture will be passed on to consumers. The negative side is that under competition there is less likely to be any cost savings to pass on: $(\Delta M + \Delta \Pi)$ approaches zero. Why is this?

The answer can be seen in the following standard public enterprise issue: given that monopolies are inefficient and public enterprises are often monopolies, is the observed inefficiency of monopolistic public enterprises due to imperfect control from the market or to imperfect control from the government?[24] A substantial volume of empirical work tends to support a dominant role for the market, failing to find evidence of efficiency differentials between public and private firms after adjusting for the degree of competition in the market.[25] The literature is far from unanimous on this point, however, and it is not our intention to resolve the issue here. We note only that, to the extent that some of the observed public enterprise inefficiency is due to absence of market pressures, increasing competition alone will improve performance, and the efficiency returns to divestiture will be smaller than otherwise.

In sum the effect of competition is to reduce the range of ΔW: the downside potential is reduced, but so is the upside. Let us consider an extreme case in which the fundamental trade-off is the only issue (meaning, among other things, that fiscal effects can be ignored). Then competition means that one cannot lose from divestiture (ΔS will be nonnegative), yet the potential gain from efficiency improvements will be small, to the extent that competitive pressures have already affected or will in the future affect public enterprise behavior.

Improving Organizational Technology

In addition to technical change, organizational change also needs to be considered. Two forms can be distinguished: *internal*, affecting the ability of large organizations to control themselves, and *external*, affecting the ability of governments to control enterprises (regulation for private enterprises and oversight methods for public enterprises).

It can be argued that internal organizational change (such as the M-form structure emphasized by Chandler and the use of computers) has reduced

the managerial diseconomies of scale associated with very large organizations.[26] On the other hand, it can be argued that changes in communica-
tions, information management, marketing, and globalization combine to
make markets more dynamic and thus penalize the slower decision-making
that characterizes large mechanistic organizational structures. How these
two forces offset each other we leave to others to determine, because it
does not seem to be critical in the current context. Unlike technical change,
these organizational changes do not seem to be great enough to significantly alter the number of potential producers unless the number is already
large (that is, a change from ten to eleven participants is a reasonable
expectation, but from one to two is not). If so, then the innovation will not
alter market structure but only cost efficiency. The issue then becomes
the relative speed with which organizational innovations are accepted by
private as opposed to public firms. To the extent that public enterprises
tend to be slower in adopting such innovations, divestiture may be a way
to speed up their diffusion; correspondingly, ΔW will increase.

With regard to external organization, changes can be identified that
increase W under both private and public operation, making the ΔW
from divestiture unpredictable. On the private side, reforms of regulatory
mechanisms make possible increased W under private regulated monopoly.
Considerable advances have been made in regulatory theory in recent
years.[27] Of those that have been implemented, one of the better known
examples is the RPI-X formula used to control prices in the divested British
Telecom.[28] Although this scheme falls considerably short of the theoretical
ideal, it has major advantages over traditional cost-plus-fair-return regulation: the long period before regulatory review provides increased incentives for cost cutting, and the preset rate puts some limits on exercise of
market power.

Public enterprise control mechanisms have similarly been improved.
Broadly speaking, the reforms involve a philosophy of management by
objectives in which managers are granted increased autonomy over methods
in return for greater accountability (via incentives) for results. Examples
include the Program Contract system popular in Francophone countries,[29]
the recent Memoranda of Understanding (MOUs) in India,[30] and the
highly regarded Korean reform.[31]

In summary, the trend in external control mechanisms is that two imperfect mechanisms for dealing with imperfect situations are being modified
imperfectly albeit for the better. To the extent that the rate of imperfection
reduction under regulation exceeds that under public ownership, ΔW is
enhanced. While the difference may be significant in some countries, we

doubt that it has much explanatory power at the global level: the sign may well be wrong, and the magnitude of the difference is probably small.[32] We now turn to a more robust candidate for a causal factor.

Increasing Fiscal Stringency and λ_g

In many, if not most, countries, divestiture programs correlate with periods of fiscal stringency. Considerations of theory and fact lead many observers to attribute causality:

> The fact that so many countries showed signs of ... (divestiture) ... in the early 1980s, we believe, was a reflection largely of the drying up of cash in that period, a reaffirmation of the soundness of Samuel Johnson's observation that the prospect of being hanged in a fortnight wonderfully concentrates the mind. The pronounced slowdown in the growth of the world economy at that time, when coupled with the drying up of the international credit markets, provided the functional equivalent of a sentence of hanging.[33]

We do not question the conclusion that fiscal stringency played a major role but rather ask whether this was due to economic or political factors, or both. That is, to what extent do tough fiscal times increase technocrats' ΔW and to what extent merely patrons' perceptions?

At first glance the technocratic answer might seem clear. Let us consider an exogenous fiscal shock such as a fall in oil prices for an oil exporter. A rational government in equilibrium will respond either by cutting out lower-valued public expenditures or by raising money at greater cost. In either case the value of government funds (λ_g) rises at the margin and, as shown by equation (5.21), other things equal, so does ΔW.[34] That is, when times are tough, at the margin you spend only on more highly valued items and obtain funds at higher cost. Under such conditions the technocratic valuation of ΔW will rise simply because the marginal value of funds is higher for a poorer government.

In disequilibrium, of course, anything is possible. The government may respond to fiscal duress by spending more on tear gas and riot police to keep the masses quiet. If the technocrat evaluates this as a lower-yielding activity, then λ_g will fall. If you think this is a trivial example of declining λ_g in tough times under conservative leadership, consider how the Reagan administration adjusted at the margin.

Diminishing Returns to Government and λ_g

Diminishing returns is about as robust a law as economists have. It can be applied to the well-documented expansion of government worldwide from the 1950s through the 1970s. Other things being equal, expanding expenditures means undertaking progressively lower yielding projects, whereas expanding revenues means utilizing increasingly high cost alternatives. To the extent that this process continues into disequilibrium, marginal benefits from government expenditure are below the marginal costs of financing it.

Under these circumstances how will a technocrat value λ_g? At the low value implied by looking at expenditure? Or at the high value implied by looking at revenue? The answer depends on whether he or she believes the government will use an extra dollar (obtained from the divestiture) to cut high-value taxes or expand low-value expenditures. What government will do is probably a function of the nature of the government in power. It would not be unreasonable to expect a conservative government to reduce taxes and a liberal government to increase services. If so, then in a disequilibrium context of excess government, a change of regime from liberal to conservative will raise λ_g and increase the returns to divestiture. Thus a trend toward conservative governments might explain why divestiture actually becomes more rational from the economic (or technocratic) point of view. We therefore shift toward consideration of political issues.

Change in Technocratic Influence
The foregoing factors alter the judgments of technocrats. Two factors that might change the degree of influence they might have on patrons come to mind. First, in the LDC context a typical pattern has postindependence leaders focusing on problems of nation-building over economics, leading to economic decline and a second generation of leaders focusing on growth. Sukarno and Rhee Sung Man ignored technocrats; Suharto and Park Chung Hee did not. The second factor follows from our discussion of fiscal stringency: during difficult times, patrons are more likely to listen to technocrats. It is a common observation that in oil-rich countries a decline in oil prices may be a long-run boon because it facilitates needed reforms.

Technocratic Change: Summary
We have identified a number of factors that over time have on balance altered the cost-benefit calculation in favor of divestiture. Two stand out. First, as a long-term trend, increasing competition reduces the possibility of exploitation of market power by the divested firm, thus increasing returns to divestiture. Second, fiscal stringency can both enhance the returns to divestiture and increase the probability that it will be carried out.

9.3.3 Change in Clients' Position

Overview
Over time, clients' effective position on divestiture may change for two distinct sets of reasons. First, their own net benefit position may change. Second, their power to force patrons to consider their views may change. Both sets of reasons are considered in turn for the three classes of clients: providers, purchasers, and consumers.

Providers: Employees
We have already stressed that providers are major potential losers from divestiture and that what they stand to lose is not their total compensation but only its rent component. If rents decline over time in the public sector, then providers have less to lose, and their opposition may be expected to decline. We therefore first look for changes in the rent component of employees' wages. The following hypotheses seem relevant:

1. *Secular decline in rent component*: If we are correct that unskilled public enterprise workers in LDCs receive a far larger rent component than their counterparts in MDCs, and if cross-section data can be used to infer intertemporal change, then the rent component may decline over time.

2. *Unemployment*: The greatest rents accrue to those whose alternative is unemployment. If the probability of unemployment declines over time with economic development, then the rent component declines.

3. *Social insurance*: Similarly, the spread of unemployment insurance or other forms of welfare payments decreases rents to public enterprise employment.

4. *Changing skill mix*: It can be argued that rents are highest at the bottom end of the public enterprise pay scale and lowest (if not zero or negative) at the top. If so, then changes in technology that shift the mean employee toward the top will lower the mean rent. An example is the replacement of telephone operators by computer operators.

5. *Deteriorating enterprise financial position*: Rents must be paid from somewhere, either from a favorable enterprise market position or a sympathetic government. As markets become more competitive and as particular companies enter their geriatric phase and become less competitive, the capacity of enterprises to yield to union demands declines. Increasing fiscal stringency yields the same result.

In sum, we have a testable hypothesis: over time the share of rents in total employee compensation declines. If so, then the intensity of labor opposition to divestiture also declines.

For a given level of intensity of preference, how has employees' ability to influence patrons changed? One factor may be the declining share of unions in total employment, thus reducing the need for patrons to pay attention to the demands of particular unions.

Providers: Other
Rent extraction is facilitated by imperfect markets. Thus suppliers of inputs to public enterprises will likely enjoy fewer rents as they face more and more competition. A single bidder on a government supply contract is much more likely to extract rent and keep a large share than when there are multiple bidders. Subsidized interest rates by definition give someone a rent, but this condition is much less likely under what passes for market clearing rates. Increasing competition therefore reduces net rents over time.

Development of journalism also plays a major role. It is one thing to find rents; it is quite another to have the discovery announced on a public news program. Development of pluralistic political institutions plays a similar role. The existence of multiple competing centers of political power makes it more likely that rent-finding will be publicized and, in any case, causes the proceeds to spread more widely.

In sum, development of political, economic, and journalistic competition reduces the magnitude of rents and also spreads their benefits more widely, in both cases reducing the intensity of providers' resistance to divestiture. This is by no means to say that rents disappear with development. Readers of the *New York Times* are daily treated to announcements of rent-finding in the U.S. government, and this situation is even more pronounced in many U.S. state and local governments. The argument is only that rent-seeking is reduced in the process.

Purchasers
Purchasers present a puzzle. Barring bad judgment on their part, they can only win from divestiture. One therefore expects them not only to be pro divestiture but to be in the vanguard of the movement. Surprisingly, both the literature and oral traditional are silent on their role.[35] One exception occurs when previous owners of nationalized firms clamor for reprivatization. Otherwise, divestiture leaders tend to be politicians, technocrats, and academic scribblers, with busninesspersons playing at most a supporting

role. Accordingly, what needs to be understood first is not any trend in their interest/influence but their level.

One possibility is that the interest is there and we and others have missed it. If so, we would like to be informed. If not, then academic hindsight can be brought to bear using hypotheses such as the following:

1. *Dispersed benefits in MDCs*: Insofar as sale is through public share offerings to a dispersed public or as sale is to a publicly held company with similarly dispersed ownership, then we have the familiar free-rider obstacles to coalition-building. Purchasers, then, are much like the other set of potential winners, the citizens.[36]

2. *High opportunity cost in LDCs*: In LDCs it is more likely that sale will be to individuals or narrowly held family groups. In a number of countries, however, divestiture advocates have been disappointed at the distinct paucity of enthusiasm among potential buyers. Unsystematic interviewing among this clientele in various countries has yielded a composite response as follows: "When making an investment I except to get my money back in three years, but there's no way I can do this by buying a public enterprise; the opposition is already accusing the government of 'selling the national patrimony,' so the deal will be scrutinized very carefully; besides, the last thing I need is the hassle of dealing with such a work force." In short, there are plenty of ways for well-connected entrepreneurs to make money, and at first blush, taking over a public enterprise is not high on the list.

In any event, we detect little evidence that increasing returns to, or increasing influence of, purchasers has much to do with the divestiture wave.

Consumers

As a first approximation, whether consumers are likely to win or lose from divestiture is likely to have little impact on patrons' decisions because of the dispersed benefit problem. The most elaborate application of this line of thinking is due to Olson, who emphasizes the difficulty interest groups have in overcoming their internal free-rider problem: any political gain achieved by the group is a public good from which all people with similar interests can benefit without necessarily having to pay their dues.[37] One corollary is that small groups form more readily than large groups both because the costs of organizing and policing the free-rider problem are lower and because the per-member benefits are greater. This leads to the result that inefficient policies whose costs exceed the benefits may nevertheless be adopted when the costs are dispersed over a large group while the benefits are concentrated on a small group. Public enterprise consumers are generally a large group relative to providers, and therefore their interests are liable to be subordinated.

One major exception occurs if the product has been heavily subsidized and an increase to something approaching market prices accompanies divestiture. Riots in the streets are a common result of such price increases in LDCs even without divestiture, and such occurrences certainly gain patrons' attention. A further corollary of Olson's work comes into play: "On balance, special-interest organizations and collusions reduce efficiency and aggregate income in the societies in which they operate and make political life more divisive."[38] Riots over price rationalization would seem to qualify. Further, one wonders how many purchasers would buy under such conditions. Accordingly, we would expect enterprises whose prices are hugely out of line not to be candidates for divestiture.

A second exception occurs when output is subsidized only to a moderate degree, but the bulk of output is sold to a small number of downstream users, who in turn sell in imperfectly competitive markets. Now the benefits of the subsidies are concentrated in a few hands, and opposition to divestiture is likely to be communicated to patrons.

A third possible exception occurs if, as Olson also argues, more and larger interest groups can be organized in stable societies through innovation and reduced organizational costs.[39] Is it possible that some of the observed increase in divestiture in MDCs represents the rise in the power of consumer groups relative to providers?

9.3.4   Change in Patrons' Position

The Fundamental Problem
In the previous two subsections we identified a number of reasons why the returns to divestiture may have increased over time and why the coalitions opposing divestiture may have become weaker. There is, however, a fundamental flaw in attributing causality to these factors because we would be using a set of largely continuous phenomena to explain a discontinuous event. That is, most of the factors were rooted in an evolutionary process of growth and development, which would have predicted a smooth process of divestiture rather than the 1980s jump. We might therefore conclude that the causal factor is the one important discontinuous event in our list—fiscal stringency. This explanation is also less than perfectly satisfying, because in previous decades most countries went through tough times without divesting,[40] and in the 1980s, countries such as South Korea

divested even though they were by no means suffering from fiscal stringency. This would seem to leave a change in patrons—the Reagan-Thatcher bandwagon—as the dominant explanatory variable.[41] This theory, too, has its problems, however.

Ideology and Divestiture

A number of authors have stressed the striking lack of correlation between ideology and divestiture/nationalization. Bermeo is worth quoting at length:

... periods of expansion and contraction of public enterprise are not related in any simple way to whether the ruling party is socialist or non-socialist. Spain's public enterprise sector was initiated by a right-wing authoritarian regime, expanded by a democratically elected center-right government and then successfully challenged, for the first time in history, by a democratically elected Socialist party. In Greece, New Democracy, a democratically elected center-right party, expanded the much smaller public sector during the mid 1970's and the Socialist PASOK expanded it further in the 1980's. In Portugal, the Socialist Party supported the nationalization of banking and industry and then maintained tacit support of a massive state enterprise sector, for at least twelve years. For these cases, at least, a ruling party's position on the ideological spectrum tells us little about national policy toward public enterprise.[42]

The only thing wrong with this statement is the modesty in confining the conclusion to those cases. Boneo documents a similar phenomenon for Argentina, noting that the share of public enterprise in the economy does not fluctuate with (dramatic) political change but steadily increases. His explanation is that liberal regimes add enterprises, whereas conservatives add value—added via pricing and management reforms—but neither divests.[43] Turning from time series to cross section, Jones and Mason begin by documenting the remarkable similarity in the size, structure, and growth of public enterprise in the ideologically diverse pairings of India and South Korea.[44] They go on to identify similar patterns across a broad spectrum of LDCs and attribute this to common responses to common problems of market and organizational failure.

A Synthesis

The question then becomes, If ideology was impotent elsewhere at other times, what made Reagan, Thatcher, and others different? Our answer is, timing.

Our case hinges on the dialectics of diminishing returns to government. As described earlier, expansion of government involves increasing costs and decreasing benefits. This process continues well past equilibrium and into disequilibrium because of inertia, discontinuous political change, the time necessary for a problem to build to such a magnitude that it passes the threshold of citizens' consciousness, and the fact that any change involves substantial economic, political, and psychological costs. The process of diminising returns to government thus creates the internal contradictions for its own destruction, spawning Thatcher and Reagan, who then appear not as exogenous causal forces but as endogenous trigger mechanisms.

9.4   LDCs versus MDCs

9.4.1   Rhetoric versus Reality

Turning to LDCs, we find a striking gap between rhetoric and reality. On the rhetoric side, many—and perhaps most—LDCs have announced ambitious divestiture programs. A comprehensive World Bank listing identifies more than seventy LDCs with divestiture platforms.[45] On the reality side, developments have been somewhat less impressive. First, some of the most important LDCs with the largest public enterprise sectors have not even indulged in the rhetoric of divestiture to any major extent—India, Indonesia, and Egypt come to mind. Even more importantly, among those who have announced programs there has been considerably more talk than action.

The experience of the World Bank is instructive, because it is one of the alleged transmission mechanisms for the Reagan-Thatcher bandwagon effect. Nellis has examined 101 different structural-sectoral adjustment loans with public enterprise components signed by the bank from 1978 to 1988.[46] On the rhetoric side, divestiture is the most common single element of conditionality, appearing in 40 percent of the cases. On the reality side, details are provided for nine countries selected for intensive study. Among these, four are identified as relatively successful: Jamaica sold a $0.5 billion worth of enterprises; Togo leased four enterprises, shut down five, and has twenty on the block; Niger divested three companies fully and eight partially; and Panama sold five. Even the successes represent only a small fraction of the total number of public enterprises in the respective countries and a far smaller fraction of total sector sales or value added. Further, in many cases the sales were accompanied by side conditions that considerably reduced any positive welfare effect: for example in Guinea, five of fourteen divested firms maintained monopoly positions, and a fifth was granted the right to import oil duty free for fifteen years.[47] Much less happened in the other five countries.

Turkey is perhaps prototypical and certainly well documented.[48] Divestiture was a major component of Turkey's liberalization program as early as 1980. By 1986 a $2 million master plan had been developed with World Bank assistance. As of 1988 all that had been accomplished was sale of the first tranche of a portion of the government's minority share holding in Teletas, the telecommunications company. If this is slow going, then how can it be explained? It has been suggested that the rhetoric-reality gap can be explained by the fact that the divestiture announcements do not reflect the true beliefs of the nation's leaders but are merely intended to placate and gain funding from alleged transmission mechanisms of the Reagan-Thatcher bandwagon, such as USAID and the World Bank. While this may indeed have been a factor elsewhere, it was not so in Turkey, where it had the full support of Turgut Ozal, first as senior civilian in the military government and later as elected prime minister. Further, many other elements of the liberalization program were implemented, and Turkey has generally been considered a success story of economic rationalization. Why not in the field of divestiture?

Turkey is not alone. We ask the question, In which LDC's has divestiture been significant to reduce the size of the public enterprise sector by, say, 10 percent of its GDP share? It is a measure of our ignorance that the literature is largely silent on this sort of question. We are told how many firms are involved and occasionally how much their sales are but are seldom given a sense of the basic empirical magnitude. Just how much of the sector are we talking about here, anyway? We believe that as of 1990 the number of LDCs passing the 10 percent test are few and probably consist only of Chile and Mexico.

Regardless of the accuracy of this last guess, the basic question remains, Why in the LDCs has there been far more smoke than fire? Asking this question should not obscure the fact that previous decades did not even witness much smoke. That programs were widely announced, that some divestitures actually occurred, and that others are likely to follow in the future still represents a clear break between the 1980s and previous decades. What needs to be explained is why the process progressed so little or at least so slowly in the LDCs as opposed to the MDCs.

9.4.2   Time-Series Arguments

Our basic answer is simple. In the previous section we argued that as economies grow, markets become more competitive. This competition increases the technocrats' estimate of ΔW, but it reduces rents and spreads them more widely, thus reducing clients' opposition and their ability to impose that opposition on patrons. This class of arguments applies with still greater force to the LDC/MDC comparison. If per capita GDP is a proxy for market forces, then we are talking about perhaps a threefold differential over three decades, whereas we are talking about perhaps a fortyfold differential across countries.[49] If there is any explanatory power in the time-series argument, then there is a lot in the cross-section variant.

In sum the essential argument of this section can be obtained by rereading the market development arguments of the previous section and multiplying by (or even compounding by a factor of) ten. A few areas merit additional emphasis, however.

9.4.3   Fiscal Stringency in LDCs

The fiscal stringency argument would seem to cut the other way in LDCs. If you think Thatcher faced fiscal problems, imagine being a Latin American finance minister in the 1980s. Accordingly, one would predict more, not less, action in LDCs.

The fact that the reverse has occurred suggests at least two possibilities. The first is that the fiscal effect is dominated, at least in LDCs, by the behavioral effect. This is consistent with Leeds's report that sixteen senior government officials ranked revenue generation dead last of fourteen possible divestiture objectives in Turkey.[50] A second possibility is that the fiscal impact primarily benefits citizens and that citizens' interests are poorly represented in LDCs as opposed to MDCs.

9.4.4   Capital Markets

Observers of LDC divestiture are virtually unanimous in identifying capital market imperfections as a major obstacle.[51] Equity markets are thin, characterized by few participants, low volume, and impacted information. Debt markets are fragmented, with many submarkets clearing by executive decision rather than price. The magnitude of these imperfections is sometimes hard for Westerners to appreciate. One manifestation is the Saõ Paulo exchange (Brazil's largest), where price tripled in six months and then plunged 61 percent in a week, allegedly because of the manipulations of one individual, whose transactions accounted for half of the market during the run-up (and involved a major play on Val do Rio Doce, a public enterprise).[52] Are there any LDC markets without similar episodes in their history? The point is not that this case is any different from the early history of Western exchanges or that things won't improve over time.

Rather, the point is that only rather special individuals will willingly participate in such a market, the information imposed by share prices is limited, and the discipline imposed by being responsible to a market is suspect. Among the specific implications for divestiture are the following:

1. It is hard to sell the largest enterprises: if British Telecom had to be split into two tranches to avoid disrupting the capital market, imagine the problem in LDCs, where the 1988 trade volume in twenty-seven LDCs as a group was only one-tenth that of London's.[53]

2. If you do sell parts of the largest enterprises you are not going to get people's capitalism. Several writers see major political/social/economic externalities of divestiture from broadening stock market participation.[54] In the United Kingdom divestiture led to significant expansion of share ownership among workers and the middle class. In the LDC context, you are going to be selling to a minority at the top. If you try to sell to workers, they might prefer to buy food; if you induce them to buy by offering a premium, they are likely to resell quickly, because at their income levels the demand for savings for old age is modest. If you force them to keep the shares (commonly, through sales to a workers' pension plan), you may well have accomplished something, but still only among the top third of the distribution.

3. If you do manage to sell parts of any enterprise to a dispersed public, you may not get much change in behavior. In an MDC selling some shares on the market is thought to provide an element of market discipline to offset bureaucratic indiscipline: managers will be more attentive to the movement of share prices and the elected representatives of the shareholders and less attentive to that of the minister. In many LDCs, the thought that a manager appointed by the government—who remains the dominant shareholder—will respond to minority shareholders rather than the minister who appoints him is humorous.

4. If you do manage to sell parts to a dispersed public, it is likely to be accomplished by underpricing the sale, thus reducing the return to divestiture (assuming $\lambda_g > \lambda_p$).

5. If you do sell to an individual or corporation, it will likely be to a distinct minority: foreigners, an ethnic minority, or the top 20/30/40/50 families. This argument may be objected to on noneconomic grounds: in Indonesia, a standard explanation for the lack of enthusiasm for divestiture is that the only buyers are Chinese. It also may be objected to on Jeffersonian grounds—that is, by concern for the effect of concentrations of wealth on a free society. It may also be objected to on economic

grounds: concentrations of wealth lead to privileged access to credit, protection, licenses, and other scarce commodities, which distorts behavior
across many markets (more on this in the next subsection).

6. If you prohibit any one group from getting a controlling interest, they
may well get it anyway. In South Korea the government prohibited any
group from amassing more than a small percentage of the shares in any
divested bank. However, the use of friends, dummies, and relatives has
reputedly allowed each of the biggest business groups to obtain a controlling interest in a different bank.

7. If you want to sell to smaller buyers, they may not have the capital and
may be unable to raise it on the stock market, so government or other
banks may have to loan it to them. If these lenders are unaccustomed to
making careful creditworthiness evaluations, the result may be a bankruptcy. The first wave of Chilean divestitures were heavily debt financed,
and subsequent widespread failures led to renationalization of the banks
and with them most of the companies.[55] In Bangladesh oral tradition has it
that divested firms were typically purchased with 10 percent or even less
in effective equity, giving substantial motivation to mine the firm of its
assets and declare bankruptcy for a tidy profit.

8. If you do sell to an individual and he or she does not go bankrupt but
turns a tidy profit, then you are going to be accused of corruption and
giving away the national patrimony. Absent a stock market to set the price
and a fully functioning press to disclose any side deals, questions about
favoritism and/or collusive bidding are going to arise, whether or not they
are true.

We do not contend that these bold assertions hold across all countries
and all times. Markets in NICs and Latin American countries with per
capita GDPs in the thousands of dollars are far different from those in
countries with GDPs in the hundreds. Public enterprises have been divested,
and more will be as clever people create clever ways of overcoming the
sorts of problems enumerated here. Our only purpose has been to suggest
that capital market problems exist, that they are rather more severe in
LDCs as opposed to MDCs, and that therefore somewhat slower progress
is to be expected.

9.4.5   The Private "Alternative"

It is not just capital markets that are imperfect in LDCs. This is made
clear in the divestiture context in an article by Manual Tanoira, formerly

undersecretary for divestiture to Argentina's Raul Alfonsin. He begins by quoting a colleague of a colleague as saying: "First, we've got to privatize the private sector."

He elaborates on this theme at length. The following quote conveys the essence of the argument:

Privatization might mean no more than an expansion of not-so-private enterprise, or an expansion of government by another name. This is the best reason I can offer for the perpetuation of unprofitable state-owned enterprises (SOE's) in Argentina. To the people, privatization is less likely to be seen as a means for *eliminating* the enormous subsidies received by SOE's than as a means for *transferring* the protection of the state to private (in other words, not-so-private) firms.[56]

In terms of our framework we take this statement to emphasize the importance of focusing on ΔW: welfare under public operation is suboptimal, but so also is welfare under private operation. In particular, both public and private enterprises operate in a highly imperfect environment in LDCs, reducing the technocratic return to divestiture. Transfer of rents from citizens to patrons is by no means confined to the public sector.

9.4.6   Competitive Enterprises

If the foregoing arguments help explain the slow pace of divestiture of enterprises that are large relative to product and factor markets, they do not explain the reluctance to divest small-scale competitive establishments. It is difficult to construct a technocratic argument for a negative ΔW for Venezuela's love motel, Peru's pornographic movie house, or any of the other small-scale establishments that litter the public enterprise rolls in many LDCs. Getting rid of these establishments would not only have a positive welfare effect but would free bureaucratic and technocratic resources to concentrate on the 20 percent of the companies that generate 80 percent of the value added and involve real trade-offs.

9.5   Conclusion

In this chapter we developed a distributional version of our cost-benefit framework and used it to help explain broad trends in divestiture over time and across countries. A quite different application of this framework is to aid the technocrat who is interested not simply in understanding outcomes but in altering them. We therefore turn next to the policy implications of our analysis.

10 Divestiture Policy in a Cost-Benefit Framework

10.1 Dimensions of Divestiture Policy

It follows from our political economy analysis that it may not be politically feasible to divest a public enterprise even if net benefits from divestiture are positive; on the other hand, a divestiture decision may go through with negative net benefits. Just looking at the aggregate net benefits therefore is definitely too narrow. Political feasibility requires considering the effect of divestiture on group benefits as well.

At the same time, the status quo and simply selling the public enterprise are not the only relevant alternatives. The politician may have to consider government policy measures besides the divestiture decision itself for three reasons. First, public enterprise policies less drastic than divestiture, such as reorganization, worker layoffs or wage reductions, that hitherto were prevented by political constraints suddenly may become feasible once divestiture is considered as an option. Second, there may be politically motivated constraints, for instance, in the form of a minimum selling price Z. That is, even with a positive net benefit of divestiture, the resulting Z may be too low; then the government will have to find ways to increase Z without making ΔW nonpositive. Third, there may exist policies to improve the net social benefit of divestiture for a given V_{sg}. This would be in line with our normative stipulation (in equation (2.2)) that the government's goal for divestiture is

$$\max \Delta W = V_{sp} - V_{sg} + (\lambda_g - \lambda_p)Z. \tag{10.1}$$

Thus far we have assumed that the government takes the right-hand-side variables of equation (10.1) as exogenous. We now endogenize them and ask how V_{sp}, V_{sg}, and Z can be altered by governmental policy decisions.

V_{sg} is influenced by the counterfactual policies taken *instead of* divestiture. V_{sp} is influenced by the policies affecting the period *after* divestiture, whereas Z is influenced by both of these plus by sale-related policies for the time *before* divestiture.

As noted in chapter 2, V_{sg} differs from V_{sp} for two quite distinct sets of reasons: (1) for a given economic environment, private behavior will differ from public behavior; and (2) as part of the terms and conditions of sale, the economic environment will change.

The objective of the private negotiator trying to buy the public enterprise will be to maximize $V_{pp} - Z$. Once V_{sg} is fixed, analysis focuses on raising V_{sp} as a way to increase social welfare and on increasing Z as a way of making the transaction politically acceptable.

We have to interpret Z as the net sale price of the public enterprise, that is, net of transaction costs. Optimizing the divestiture decision with respect to Z then involves two different factors. First, it is desirable to increase V_{pp} in order to increase the private willingness to pay. Second, the government may need to expend resources in the selling process in order to reduce the difference between Z and V_{pp}. For example, lining up more potential buyers increases the expected sale price, but at the same time the search for additional buyers increases the transaction cost of the sale.

Regarding the value after divestiture there are then five broad classes of policies to be considered:

1. Policies that raise both V_{sp} and V_{pp}.
2. Policies that raise V_{sp} but lower V_{pp}.
3. Policies that lower V_{sp} but raise V_{pp}.
4. Policies that lower both V_{sp} and V_{pp}.
5. Policies that raise Z for given V_{pp}.

The fourth category is, of course, of interest only in identifying policies that should always be avoided.

Government policy instruments for the situation after divestiture can be categorized into one of the first three classes. For example, there are policies that unambiguously increase efficiency, thereby raising both V_{sp} and V_{pp}. Under certain market conditions, reductions in regulation may be of this kind, especially because rent-seeking activity may be reduced. Devices that shift risk to the government may frequently be of this nature also, as is discussed in greater detail shortly. A third, somewhat more subtle, example is the creation of favorable expectations. If government can assure the potential buyers of stability in future policy, particularly regarding the possibility of renationalization, estimates of V_{pp} and, implicitly, V_{sp} will be higher.

For the second class of policies, there exist many situations where government intervention in markets is desirable from the social point of view. Regulation may be desirable if the divested enterprise will be a monopoly, such as British Telecom. In this kind of situation, regulation is likely to raise V_{sp} at the cost of lowering V_{pp}. Policies that increase the net inflow into (or reduce the outflow from) the treasury without creating too much distortion also fall in this category.

A wide range of policies fall in class three (that is, lower V_{sp} but increase V_{pp}). For example, the provision of import protection (either tariffs or quotas), exclusive licensing arrangements, or established price floors all tend to raise V_{pp} at the expense of V_{sp}. Of course, this may be true only in the short run. In the long run such policies may be justified if they increase the dynamic capability of the economy. In fact, that is one of the reasons why we expect λ_p to be greater than one.

Because policies in class five contain two elusive elements, benefits in terms of a higher sale price and transactions costs, they are hard to exemplify. Two interesting features emerge immediately from our framework, though.

First, to the extent that transaction costs require real resources on the part of the government, they receive a weight of λ_g, whereas the increase in the sale price receives a weight of only $\lambda_g - \lambda_p$. For the private negotiator, transactions costs weigh the same as reductions in Z. Also, the government values private transactions costs with λ_p. Thus we should expect the private purchaser to negotiate harder than the government, according to our framework.[1]

Second, bargaining often results in some focal point formula, such as fifty-fifty splitting of the difference between Z_g and Z_p. In this case any policies that increase either of these two variables will lead to an increase in Z that is only 50 percent of the increase of the variable (as long as $V_{pp} > Z_g$).

The effects of all the policies described can, in principle, be simulated by extending the model of chapter 8. Each policy set, however, consists of a myriad of options, which can be combined in innumerable ways and which, therefore, ultimately have to be considered on a case-by-case basis. These options will depend on variables such as market structure, size of firm, type of product (for instance, tradable versus nontradable), or the firm's financial situation. In this section we therefore raise only the major issues for each of the policy steps and show the applicability of our framework via example.[2]

We categorize these issues by the three sets of policies mentioned at the beginning of this chapter. The first set consists of policies as alternatives to divestiture. The second set consists of policies that improve the net benefits of divestiture. And the third set consists of policies to overcome political constraints to divestiture. In the first two sets our emphasis is on the efficiency issue, whereas in the third set we focus on the interaction between efficiency and group benefits. Of course, the last two sets of policies may overlap because improvements in net benefits may increase feasibility of divestiture.

10.2 Lifting Constraints on Public Enterprise Behavior

In this section we assume that some of the political constraints on public enterprise behavior have been lifted. It is then useful to distinguish between two alternative values under continued public operation:

V_{sga}: Value under continued operation "as is."

V_{sgr}: Value following restructuring under conditions paralleling those of divestiture.

Such restructuring should be undertaken instead of divestiture if $V_{sgr} > V_{sga}$ and if, as a result, $Z_{gr} > Z$, where $Z_{gr} > Z_p > Z_{ga}$ is the minimum acceptable sale price after restructuring and Z_{ga} is the minimum acceptable sale price before restructuring. This restructuring can be internal or external to the firm. First, let us consider an example of internal restructuring.

10.2.1 Effect of a Change in Hiring Policy on V_{sg}

There exist good theoretical reasons and some empirical evidence that cost inefficiency is the major problem of public enterprises.[3] Constraints on input prices and input quantities, in particular for labor, may well be responsible for this cost inefficiency. Without the threat of divestiture, these constraints are politically well established. Public enterprise employees in many countries cannot be fired, and their pay (especially in lower ranks) is above that in comparable private industry jobs. Under the threat of divestiture employees may then accede to some reduction in pay and in job security. How does this affect V_{sg}? Assuming that workers in the reference situation (denoted by the superscript 0) were paid above their social opportunity wage, we have $w_s < w_g^0$. In the counterfactual scenario their wage is reduced. In this new situation (denoted by the superscript 1) $w_g^1 < w_g^0$. At the same time the work force is reduced. We now make the following assumptions: (1) The alternative wage for laid-off workers is $\underline{w} \leqslant w_g^1$; (2) the private buyer pays $Z = V_{pp}$; and (3) output price and quantity do not change.

Then the resulting change in ΔW^* can be expressed as

$$\Delta W^{*1} - \Delta W^{*0} = -\Delta V_{sg} = (1 - \lambda_g)(w_g^0 L_g^0 - w_g^1 L_g^1) + \underline{w}(L_g^0 - L_g^1)$$

$$= \lambda_g \Delta \Pi + \Delta M. \tag{10.2}$$

Equation (10.2) says the following: The change in the public enterprise wage bill is a saving to the treasury weighted by λ_g and a loss to the workers weighted by one.[4] The loss to workers, however, is reduced because those laid off receive the alternative wage $\underline{w}$.

How does this counterfactual policy compare with the divestiture option? Clearly, if divestiture will result only in the same layoff as is now being considered by the public enterprise, and if there are no behavioral changes, then $Z_{gr} = Z_p$. Therefore, if the cost saving achieved through the layoff is not fully reflected in Z, then $\Delta W^{*1} < \Delta W^{*0}$ as a result of the layoff policy. More generally, if the public enterprise can successfully mimic the behavior of the firm after divestiture, then divestiture does not pay in terms of net benefits.

Next, we consider two examples of external policy changes. The first one concerns a change in the regulated price of the output, and the second one consists of a reduction in tariff protection for the public enterprise.

10.2.2   Effect of a Change in p on V_{sg}

In chapter 5 we assumed that, after divestiture, the monopoly firm would raise the price for the output. What if the firm under continued government operation were allowed to do the same? Assume the simple one-period case without discounting and without adjustment for shadow prices. In this case the effect of a price change for the public enterprise output can be expressed as the derivative

$$\frac{\partial V_{sg}}{\partial p} = \frac{-\partial \Delta W^*}{\partial p_g} = \frac{\partial \lambda_g \Pi_g}{\partial p} + \frac{\partial S}{\partial p}$$

$$= (\lambda_g - 1)q + \lambda_g \left(\frac{\partial q}{\partial p}\right)\left(p - \frac{\partial C}{\partial q}\right). \tag{10.3}$$

Equation (10.3) is quite familiar from the literature on optimal public enterprise pricing. In the case when $\lambda_g = 1$ it simply says that the effect of a price change on V_{sg} is proportional to the difference between price and marginal cost. Marginal cost pricing is then implied as the optimal government policy, whereas $\lambda_g > 1$ leads to an optimal price above marginal cost.

This result can be seen by looking at case 4 in table 8.2. Here the public enterprise charges a price of $p_g = 1.00$, whereas marginal cost is $MC = 0.73$. In this case the welfare change through divestiture is $\Delta W^* = -588$. Had the government enterprise charged a marginal cost price of $p_g = 0.73$ and had there been no binding capacity constraint, then divestiture would have resulted in a positive net benefit, $\Delta W^* = 1,507$. Thus charging a price of $p_g = 1.00$ turns out to be better than divestiture (without price regulation). In fact, the optimal price for the public enterprise to charge is $p_g^* = 0.93$. In this case divestiture would reduce welfare by $\Delta W^* = -613$.

Another way of describing the effect of alternative pricing policies by the public enterprise is in terms of Z_g. Under $p_g = MC = 0.73$ we get $Z_g = -3,176$. That is, government would be willing to pay to divest the enterprise. Under $p_g = 1.00$, Z_g is increased to $Z_g = +3,805$, while $Z_g = +3,889$ at the optimal $p_g = 0.93$. Obviously, the type of output pricing policy makes quite a difference here.

10.2.3   Effect of Reduced Tariff Protection on V_{sg}

In a developing country one of the most powerful policy tools applied by governments is tariff protection. A public enterprise that is, for instance, the only domestic producer of a tradable homogeneous commodity, may frequently enjoy some tariff protection. Let us assume that this is currently enough to keep imports out, and let us assume that domestic price equals the world market price plus the tariff and that the shadow price of foreign currency is the exchange rate. The domestic price is above marginal cost. The country is small in the world market, and local average production costs of the public enterprise are above the world market price. Now let us consider a reduction in the tariff. What will be the likely effects?

First, the price of the commodity will go down, and the total quantity consumed will go up. This will increase consumer surplus.

Second, at the old cost level, the profit of the public enterprise is likely to go down. This will hold whether imports actually occur or not. If no imports occur, it will hold, because otherwise the old price would have been above the profit-maximizing level. This is entirely possible but unlikely because it would not make sense for either the firm or the government to charge such a high price. If imports occur, the public enterprise will lose output, and thus profit is likely to be reduced further. However, the resulting tariff revenues may actually lead to a net financial gain for government.

Third, a reduction in tariff protection may actually affect the public enterprise's cost level. Empirical comparisons of public versus private enterprise cost levels indicate that the amount of competition in a market may have more influence on productive efficiency than ownership per se.[5] Reduced tariff protection increases competition and puts pressure on the public enterprise management to increase X-efficiency. It can therefore lead to a more diligent resource use by the public enterprise. Such a cost reduction will be smaller than the tariff reduction but can still be substantial. There may also be an increase in effective capacity of the public enterprise.

10.3   Improving the Net Benefit of Divestiture

10.3.1   The Effects of Price Regulation after Divestiture

The monopoly case is the obvious one, where the government would not want the firm after divestiture to choose the unconstrained profit-maximizing price. The question then arises, What is the effect on the divestiture decision of regulating price after divestiture where regulation is fully anticipated by all parties concerned? For the moment, let us assume that price regulation has no effect on the X-efficiency of the firm. Although the U.S. literature on rate-of-return regulation suggests that price regulation increases costs relative to unregulated firms, there may also be the opposite effect due to additional pressure on the firm to survive.[6] Also, there may exist less distorting forms of price regulation than those experienced in the United States. One such type may prove to be price capping, as introduced in Great Britain along with the divestiture of British Telecom. While there have been several attempts at evaluating this particular experience, the results are naturally inconclusive.[7] The main reason is that one cannot separate the effect of divestiture from the effect of the regulatory scheme on prices and productivity.[8] There is reason for optimism insofar as administrative costs of the scheme have been minuscule, productivity has increased by more than expected, and prices have stayed below the caps.

For the one-period case with a proportional corporate income tax, we find that a marginal change in p results in

$$\frac{\partial V_{sp}}{\partial p} = \frac{\lambda_p \partial \Pi_p}{\partial p} + (\lambda_g - \lambda_p)\frac{\partial X^d}{\partial p} + \frac{\partial S}{\partial p}$$

$$= \left[q + \left(\frac{\partial q}{\partial p}\right)\left(p - \frac{\partial C}{\partial q}\right)\right][\lambda_p + (\lambda_g - \lambda_p)x^d] - q \qquad (10.4)$$

and

$$\frac{\partial V_{pp}}{\partial p} = \frac{\partial \Pi_p}{dp} - \frac{\partial X^d}{\partial p} = \left[q + \left(\frac{\partial q}{\partial p}\right)\left(p - \frac{\partial C}{\partial q}\right)\right][1 - x^d]. \qquad (10.5)$$

We know that $\partial \Delta W/\partial p = \partial W/\partial p = \partial V_{sp}/\partial p + (\lambda_g - \lambda_p)\partial Z/\partial p$. Assuming that $Z = V_{pp}$, we then get

$$\frac{\partial W^*}{\partial p} = (\lambda_g - 1)q + \lambda_g\left(\frac{\partial q}{\partial p}\right)\left(p - \frac{\partial C}{\partial q}\right). \qquad (10.6)$$

Thus, under otherwise similar conditions, a price change after divestiture has the opposite effect of a price change under continued public operation (equation (10.3)). A welfare-enhancing price change under continued public operation makes divestiture less attractive, whereas the same type of price change for the divested firm would make divestiture more attractive. Aside from the sign, the difference between equations (10.3) and (10.6) is only that the effects may have to be evaluated at different levels for the price and cost variables.

A simulation of price regulation after divestiture is provided by case 5 of table 8.2 and was discussed in chapter 8.

10.3.2   The Effects of a Foreign Buyer for the Public Enterprise

Should the public enterprise be sold to a foreign buyer or not? If the public enterprise is acquired by a foreign buyer, then profits no longer accrue to the domestic economy. This situation can change our calculations. It is therefore important to know the effects of buyer nationality in order to assess whether the government should establish a policy of favoring domestic acquirers.

The main effects of foreignness are that the social value of the firm after divestiture no longer includes profits going to the foreign owner and that funds coming from foreign countries are valued at $\lambda_f = 0$.[9] Therefore, the formula for private valuation will stay as in equation (4.2) in the one-period framework (without discounting), $V_{pp} = \Pi_p - X^d$, whereas the social value after divestiture becomes

$$V_{sp} = S_p + M_p + \lambda_g X^d.$$

Thus under foreign ownership, denoted by the subscript f,

$$\Delta W_f = V_{sp} - V_{sg} + \lambda_g Z. \tag{10.7}$$

This differs from our previous formula, because the sale price Z is not paid by domestic agents; thus Z gets the full weight λ_g rather than $(\lambda_g - \lambda_p)$. Similarly, for the case of $Z = V_{pp}$ we get a different formula. However, in this case the net result stays unchanged:

$$\Delta W_f^* = V_{sp} - V_{sg} + \lambda_g V_{pp} = \lambda_g \Delta \Pi + \Delta S + \Delta M. \tag{10.8}$$

As noted in earlier sections, ΔW^* is independent of the size of λ_p. A difference through foreign ownership ($\lambda_p = \lambda_f = 0$) arises only if government cannot capture all the rents of the purchaser in the sales price. Thus if government can capture only a fraction θ, $0 \leq \theta \leq 1$, of the firm's rent, V_{pp}, in the purchasing price, then

$$\Delta W_f = \Delta S + \Delta M + \lambda_g (1 - x^d)(\theta \Pi_p - \Pi_g) + \lambda_g x^d \Delta \Pi. \tag{10.9}$$

In comparison, the welfare change from selling to a domestic buyer will be

$$\Delta W = \Delta S + \Delta M + [1 - x^d][(\theta \Pi_p - \Pi_g)\lambda_g + \lambda_p(1 - \theta)\Pi_p] + \lambda_g x^d \Delta \Pi$$

$$= \Delta W_f + \lambda_p(1 - x^d)(1 - \theta)\Pi_p. \tag{10.10}$$

In the absence of special efficiency gains coming from the foreign buyer and with the shadow price of foreign currency being the exchange rate, the government will do worse by selling to a foreigner as long as the sale price Z is the same and $\lambda_p > \lambda_f = 0$. The difference in net benefit from selling to a foreigner is directly proportional to the selling price for the firm. The conclusion thus is not, "do not sell to foreign buyers," but rather, "bargain more aggressively with a foreign buyer than with a domestic buyer."

10.4 Coping with Political Constraints on Divestiture

10.4.1 Coping with Public Enterprise Employees

Employees are the interest group most heavily affected by divestiture, and they may have wide-ranging interest. Therefore, policies inducing employees to cooperate are of ultimate importance to the political success or (even) feasibility of divestiture. Certainly, determined opposition from the employees can make divestiture difficult if not impossible.

The general discussion in chapter 9 of environmental changes affecting costs and benefits of divestiture leads us to expect the following distributional changes from a divestiture that is accompanied by liberalization of the market: First, production costs are expected to go down because (1) increased competitive pressure will reduce prices paid for inputs other than labor and (2) there will be some layoffs of employees due to increased opportunities and competitive pressure for the remaining employees. Under the threat of competition for the enterprise's services there is unlikely to be any major increase in the price level of the firm's products. Furthermore, there is likely to be a strong realignment in the firm's price structure, with stronger price differentiation than before and an abolition of cross subsidization. This has, for example, been the experience under British Telecom's divestiture. Last, if the divestiture involves placing any shares on the stock market, the sale price of the firm's shares will be somewhat below the subsequent stock market value because of the government's fear of unsold shares.[10]

To the extent that the various groups foresee this scenario, the potential private shareholders are likely to be a clear group of winners. In fact, once the governmental decision in favor of divestiture has been made, they are likely to be the only ones with a free choice. Citizens are also likely winners. As groups the largest losers will be privileged employees and the privileged consumers—that is, those groups receiving rents before divestiture.

What can the government do to alleviate these rent losses or to compensate the losers? Are there ways to force the winners to pay? The specific method obviously depends upon who exactly are the winners and losers from the divestiture.

Suppose the winners are the private shareholders and the citizens, whereas the major losing group is the employees. In this case one simple possibility is to reduce the gains of the potential private shareholders by handing out employee shares at a discount or giving them cash distributions from the proceeds of selling shares to others. The advantage of the first of these possibilities is that it makes employees oppose subsequent renationalization. Both methods will at the same time reduce the gains of citizens. However, in some sense this method is purely redistributive; it does not alter the fundamental postdivestiture equilibrium (although it may lower ΔW because citizens receive the special weight λ_g or increase ΔW if $\lambda_p > \lambda_g$).[11]

Another potential source of funds to finance employee layoffs is the holding back of liberalization in the firm's markets. By restricting entry competition after divestiture, the government could reduce pressures on the divested firm to reduce cost. The advantage of this apporach is its political feasibility in that potential entrants are not a powerful group initially. The disadvantage is that entry restrictions reduce the net gain of divestiture. To this extent this approach is less desirable than the earlier proposal to sell or give shares to employees. The relevant comparison here is between the cost to consumers and potential entrants of entry restrictions versus the cost of government funds.

10.4.2   Coping with Different Consumer Groups

Consumer fears about the effects of divestiture can largely be eliminated by price regulation after divestiture. If this turns out to be U.S. style rate-of-return regulation, then the price level will be cost based, whereas the price structure will be politically determined, as before. Regulation itself can have a cost-increasing effect. As mentioned previously, British divestiture has been accompanied by another type of price regulation. Experience with the specific new approach, which gives the firm leverage over its price structure, has been that changes in the price structure are likely to provoke political opposition at the time when they are made.[12] Reductions in the amount of cross-subsidization may therefore have to be limited as long as regulatory oversight over prices continues. Because we would expect the net welfare costs of cross-subsidization to be quite substantial, it is worth thinking of ways to compensate the beneficiaries of cross-subsidization.[13] One way to do this is via nonlinear tariffs that contain a refund component. Technically, this can be done by offering the beneficiaries of cross-subsidization an increasing block tariff with an extremely low price for the first units of services consumed and a higher price for the block of marginal services consumed.

10.4.3   Coping with Citizens

The Effects of a Change in Firm Debt on Z
Why is it that a major issue in divestiture negotiations is whether or not the government should take over the debt of the enterprise? In principle, this should make no difference, because the sale price of the enterprise should adjust to reflect the debt situation. Further, the public and private valuations of this adjustment would be similar, if not identical. There are,

however, a host of subtle points that do not permit this simple principle to work in practice.

First, as we mentioned earlier, there is frequently a tendency to focus on book value as the appropriate price; if the price is fixed in this way a priori, there will naturally be a reluctance on the part of the government to assume any debt. In such cases it is necessary to get away from this rigid notion of price.

Second, there may be political advantages to the assumption of debt. Having assumed the debt, government can raise the apparent sale price of the enterprise, thereby making the sale more acceptable politically. For example, when Great Britian divested the National Freight Company, the government assumed a £47 million pension fund liability (by actually pumping this amount of money into the pension fund). The company was then sold for £51 million. It is doubtful if it would have been politically feasible to simply sell the company for £4 million.

Third, one may argue that there may be some pure gain to government when it assumes the debt of a company. Government can borrow more cheaply than private firms can. More significantly, an improvement of the company's balance sheet in this way will lower the future cost of borrowing, at little or no cost to the government, because the cost of assuming the debt will be reflected in the sale price. Thus the assumption of debt can be seen as a device for shifting risk from the company to the government—a desirable policy that can raise both the social and private payoffs. There are several problems with this argument, though. First, if government is really so good at borrowing money, then it should profitably become a lender to all private firms.[14] Second, if the government pays off the debt of the enterprise, it must receive compensation in the form of a higher sale price. If the sale price doesn't rise by the full amount of the debt paid off, it is not an adequate compensation. If it does rise by the full amount, then the enterprise cannot enjoy any benefits of the debt payoff that it couldn't have otherwise. Specifically, if the buyer finances the purchase of the enterprise by issuing debt, then one form of debt is simply replaced by another. If the purchase is financed by equity, then the buyer could have paid off the debt anyway. In short, the company may not end up with an optimal debt/equity ratio. Third, if the government only guarantees the debt or replaces the debt with obligations to itself, there are likely to be adverse incentive effects on the firm. For example, the threat of bankruptcy becomes simply the threat of renationalization. Clearly, these are issues worth pursuing. However, solving them requires a model of financial markets that is outside our framework.

To illustrate some of the previous discussion, we simulated the effects of two policies to cope with the political constraint that Z be positive. One is a change in output price p after divestiture. The other is a change in the enterprises's debt-equity ratio before divestiture. The main assumptions for our simulations of these two policy options are those of the base case of chapter 8 with two qualifications: First, the public enterprise is assumed to charge the marginal cost price $p = 0.73$, and this has to be maintained after divestiture. There is no effective capacity constraint. Second, costs are decreased by 10 percent through divestiture. In the absence of any other policy adjustment, divestiture will then result in a net benefit of $\Delta W^* = 1961$. However, the maximum willingness to pay by the buyer will be $Z_p = V_{pp} = -1,884$. Thus divestiture may be difficult in such a case.

As a first policy option we allow the firm a price increase after divestiture to $p_p = 1.1$, which will lead to a private willingness to pay of $Z_p = V_{pp} = 1,424$. However, at the same time the net benefit of divestiture is reduced by 199 to $\Delta W^* = 1,762$. As an alternative, consider that the government increases the equity and reduces the debt of the firm by 4,311. Our simulation shows that this will lead to the same private willingness to pay of $Z_p = V_{pp} = 1,424$. However, this will leave the net benefit of $\Delta W^* = 1,961$ unchanged. The reason is clear: the increase in equity does not cost the government anything because it is fully reflected in an increase of the sale price Z.

The Effects of Trade Protection on V_{sp} and V_{pp}

As mentioned before, another way of bringing up Z to politically feasible levels may be through the grant of some additional tariff protection to the divested firm. Such trade protection can have various effects, not all of which we are able to trace here. For simplicity we make the following assumptions: The public enterprise is divested as a monopoly producer. The country is small in the world market. Before divestiture there is a unit tariff x_u^t. Thus the domestic monopoly firm faces a kinked demand curve with a horizontal section at $p = p_w + x_u^t$. We assume that before and after divestiture the firm produces in this horizontal range of its demand curve. Profit maximization after divestiture demands that either the firm chooses an output such that $p_w + x_u^t = MC$ or there will be no imports. For simplicity we assume that the firm has limited capacity, so that there will always be some imports. Average and marginal cost up to the capacity limit are constant, $AC = MC = c$. The effect of a tariff increase will be an increase in the firm's profit, a decrease in consumer surplus, and an uncertain change in government tariff revenues. For simplicity, we look at the one-period case.

Under our assumptions

$$V_{pp} = (p_w + x_u^t)\underline{q} - c\underline{q}, \tag{10.11}$$

where $\underline{q}$ is the capacity limit for output.

For small changes in x_u^t we get

$$\frac{\partial V_{pp}}{\partial x_u^t} = \underline{q}. \tag{10.12}$$

Equation (10.12) says that an increase in the tariff rate by one unit leads to an increase in profit of the firm by $\underline{q}$ units. This is due to our assumption that firm output is unaffected by the tariff. In terms of social valuation

$$V_{sp} = \lambda_p \Pi_p + S_p + \lambda_g x_u^t [q_D - \underline{q}], \tag{10.13}$$

where $q_D = q(p_w + x_u^t)$ is the total quantity traded in the domestic market (as a function of the domestic price). For small changes in x_u^t, this leads to

$$\frac{\partial V_{sp}}{\partial x_u^t} = \lambda_p \underline{q} - q_D + \lambda_g [q_D - \underline{q}] + \frac{\lambda_g x_u^t \partial q_D}{\partial x_u^t}$$

$$= [\lambda_g - 1][q_D - \underline{q}] + [\lambda_p - 1]\underline{q} + \frac{\lambda_g x_u^t \partial q_D}{\partial x_u^t} \tag{10.14}$$

The first part of equation (10.14) gives the government revenue increase on the imported quantity. This is borne by consumers, hence the weight $\lambda_g - 1$. The second part of (10.14) gives the net profit increase of the firm (which burdens consumers), and the third part gives the revenue reduction due the reduction in imports. The net effect can go in either direction.

We now come to the effect of a small change in x_u^t on the divestiture decision. For simplicity, we look only at the case where $Z = V_{pp}$. Then

$$\frac{\partial \Delta W^*}{\partial x_u^t} = \frac{\partial V_{sp}}{\partial x_u^t} + (\lambda_g - \lambda_p) \frac{\partial V_{pp}}{\partial x_u^t}$$

$$= (\lambda_g - 1)q_D + \frac{\lambda_g x_u^t \partial q_D}{\partial z_u^t}. \tag{10.15}$$

Thus the effect of a tariff increase on the divestiture decision may well be positive. Obviously, this will not hold if the tariff has been optimally set in the first place. Also note that it will generally not be optimal to increase the tariff up to a level where it no longer constrains the price setting by the domestic firm.

10.5   The Use of Our Framework as an Act of Economic Policy

A maintained hypothesis in the literature on the political economy of public enterprises and government regulation is that the influence of interest groups on policy decisions depends on the costs of organizing and informing group members and nonmembers. For example, the three theories by Peltzman, Borcherding, and Olson have in common the feature that they emphasize the redistributional influence of interest groups and that the losing groups, although almost always the majority, are powerless either because of their ignorance about the underlying economic relationships or because of the high transaction cost of organizing to influence political decisions.[15] To the extent that our framework influences information costs of users, it can be applied as a policy tool in itself.

Public choice theorists maintain that the normative approach of welfare economics to public policy issues is not likely to be relevant in a democracy because the economist's welfare function is derived exogenously, that is, outside the democratic process.[16] This view would validate the decision of a politician who discards economic advice because it does not conform to the evaluation of the polity as expressed in elections or in referenda. On the other hand one of the main ingredients of democratic processes is the openness of society and the concomitant uncovering of hidden information. Our method does precisely that. It allows decision-makers to bring together the relevant information in such a way that the decision to divest (or not) becomes more transparent. Parties negatively affected by the revelation of such information may oppose the use of our methodology but we cannot see how an oppression of the method would be more democratic than its use.[17] In fact we suspect that a policy decision based on our welfare-oriented analysis will be viewed as more legitimate than one that is based purely on speculation or on political power.

We define the objective of an interest group to be legitimate to the extent that an outside group will be willing to give up at least a small amount of its own welfare to help the first group. Redistribution in favor of disadvantaged groups is viewed as legitimate. Rents received under the status quo are legitimate to the extent that they have been accepted in the past or are the implicit price for some favor that the group is doing to the rest of society.[18] The creation of new rents is rarely regarded as legitimate. Under divestiture the suspicion usually arises that such new rents will be created for the new private shareholders. Here our framework comes in. It allows the government to derive a minimum sale price (Z_g) and the maximal willingness to pay of private buyers (Z_p) for the public enterprise. In countries with thin financial markets, such derived figures may be extremely important for providing a legitimate basis for the actual price Z at which a public enterprise will be sold.

11   Summary and Extensions

11.1   Chapter-by-Chapter Summary

11.1.1 An Economic Approach to Divestiture

Divestiture is the transfer of enterprises from government to private ownership. Although many countries have announced extensive divestiture policies, a much smaller number have, to date, implemented them successfully in the sense of significantly reducing the size of their public enterprise sectors. Further, the bulk of significant divestitures has taken place in MDCs, with Chile and Mexico being the notable LDC exceptions. This book attempts to both understand and reduce this gap between rhetoric and reality. The goal is to begin to do for the divestiture decision what the project evaluation literature has done for the investment decision: that is, introduce a systematic element of analytically based empiricism to an otherwise subjective process. The approach is that of applied theory, meaning that the lessons of theory are taken as far as they are likely to be usable in empirical fieldwork and no further.

The focus is on the determinants of the various values of the firm. Private exchange of assets occurs only when the buyer values them more highly than the seller, thus creating a positive-sum game. The strike price (or sale price) allocates the proceeds of the game within limits set by the minimum supply price and maximum demand price. Private/private exchange is thus rooted in two values and three prices.

Two additional elements must be added in public divestitures. First, the private sector may value the firm more highly because it plans to exploit monopoly power. The public seller may care about this, meaning that it must take into account a third value of the firm, namely, the value to society after divestiture. Second, the government must consider not only the impact of the transfer of physical assets but the reverse transfer of funds. If sale is financed by reducing private investment elsewhere, but the proceeds are used to reduce taxes, is society better off, worse off, or unchanged? Answers to this crucial question are summarized in the private funds multiplier and the government revenue multiplier. Public/private exchange is thus rooted in three values, three prices, and two inescapable parameters:

V_{sg}: social value under continued government operation,
V_{sp}: social value under private operation,
V_{pp}: private value under private operation,
Z_g: the minimum price acceptable to the government,
Z_p: the maximum price acceptable to the private buyer,
Z: the actual price at which the sale is executed.
λ_g: shadow multiplier on government revenue,
λ_p: shadow multiplier on private funds.

11.1.2   Basic Concepts

The government should sell a public enterprise if society will be better off as a result, taking into account both the physical exchange ($V_{sp} - V_{sg}$) and the financial exchange ($[\lambda_g - \lambda_p]Z$), or if [1]

$$(V_{sp} - V_{sg}) + (\lambda_g - \lambda_p)Z > 0. \qquad (2.2)$$

Rearranging yields the minimum government supply price:

$$Z_g = \frac{V_{sg} - V_{sp}}{\lambda_g - \lambda_p}. \qquad (2.6)$$

Note that whenever social welfare is higher under private operation than under public operation ($V_{sg} < V_{sp}$), and $\lambda_g > \lambda_p$, this price will necessarily be negative, meaning that the government should be *willing* to pay the private sector to take over the enterprise.

However, Z_g is not the price at which sale *should* occur, because (assuming $\lambda_g > \lambda_p$) maximum public benefit from sale occurs when

$$Z = Z_p = V_{pp}, \qquad (2.9)$$

making the maximum welfare increment (ΔW^*):

$$\Delta W^* = V_{sp} - V_{sg} + (\lambda_g - \lambda_p)V_{pp}. \qquad (2.10)$$

Ranking bidders according to this formula provides a starting point for selecting the "best" bid, but actual sale will occur in the range set by Z_p and Z_g, depending on relative bargaining strengths.

These basic concepts thus help answer the fundamental divestiture questions of whether to sell, to whom to sell, and at what price to sell. We can answer these questions if we agree on two parameters (λ_g and λ_p) and can estimate one value (V_{pp}) and one difference in values ($V_{sp} - V_{sg}$). Note that nowhere do we need to know either V_{sp} or V_{sg}, but only their difference. This is of enormous practical significance, because while the individual values are unknowable, analytic tools are available that allow reasonable approximations of the difference. The balance of the book specifies the determinants of the relevant values in increasingly complex environments.

11.1.3   Weights for Different Components of Welfare

Although the use of shadow multipliers for commodities is widely accepted, their application to such aggregate economic abstractions as investment and government revenue is far less familiar outside the project evaluation and taxation literatures. Since our analysis relies heavily on such multipliers, we explore the essential features of this literature.

The theory and measurement of λ_g, the shadow value of government revenue with respect to the consumption numeraire, builds upon the framework of applied welfare economics. For a fully optimizing government, the marginal social costs of all the different fund-raising activities have to equal the marginal social benefits of all the different expenditures. Because the raising of government revenues imposes excess burdens, $\lambda_g > 1$ for a fully optimizing government. If governments cannot fully optimize, then λ_g becomes a weighted average of the marginal social costs of fund-raising activities and the marginal social benefits of expenditures. We argue that in this case also, λ_g is likely on theoretical grounds to exceed a value of one; this in fact agrees with measurement results for λ_g found in the literature.

We then briefly consider the composition of λ_p, the shadow value of private funds, which in turn is largely a function of the shadow multiplier for investment (λ_i). We therefore proceed to consider both the theory and measurement of λ_i. Finally, we provide order of magnitude estimates of our critical parameter: $\lambda_g - \lambda_p$. The results are rather inconclusive because the values of λ_g and λ_p are likely to be quite close to one another. In particular, which of the two values is larger is actually an empirical question that must be settled for specific countries by careful analysis. However, as derived in chapter 2, $\lambda_p > \lambda_g$ would imply that the government should typically be willing to pay arbitrarily large sums to the private sector to take over the enterprise it is considering for divestiture. The fact that we do not observe such situations in reality suggests that it would be reasonable to take as our base case the one where $\lambda_g > \lambda_p$.

11.1.4 Competitive Equilibrium

The focus of this section is empirical, showing how to translate profit and loss statements and balance sheets into economic accounts and then into the various values of the firm. Computations are done for a hypothetical (or synthetic) public enterprise in the simplest possible case of competitive equilibrium (all prices are right, public behavior is the same as private behavior, etc.). Under these conditions, no sale will occur because the government's minimum selling price equals the private maximum price and therefore any transaction costs would create a negative-sum game.

11.1.5 The Fundamental Trade-off

A positive-sum game is created once private behavior differs from public behavior. Typically, it is expected that divestiture would increase efficiency, but it is feared that it might also lead to exploitation of consumers. Thus a trade-off is created. In this chapter, the theoretical results of chapters 2 and 3, and the empirical methodology of chapter 4, are extended to deal with this fundamental trade-off.

It is shown that the change in welfare depends upon the change in consumer surplus, the change in pretax profits, and the difference between the buyer's willingness to pay and what he actually pays, as follows;

$$\Delta W = \sum_{t=0}^{\infty} \rho^t \{\Delta S(t) + \lambda_g \Delta \Pi(t)\} - (\lambda_g - \lambda_p)(Z_p - Z), \tag{5.9}$$

where t indicates the time period, ρ is the discount factor, $\Delta S(t)$ is the change in consumer suprlus, and $\Delta \Pi(t)$ is the change in pretax profits. Note that the first term is negative when market power is exercised, the second term is positive when efficiency is increased, and the last term drops out when the strike price is the maximum willingness to pay.

The bulk of this chapter extends and quantifies the basic result of equation (5.9) under different market structures. In competitive output markets there is no market power, hence no trade-off, and divestiture is unambiguously good if efficiency improvements occur. In monopolistic markets, the trade-offs are fundamental and the results vary with empirical magnitudes. Oligopolistic and monopsonistic markets, intermediate goods, and quality changes are also treated.

11.1.6   Shadow Pricing

Public and private valuations can also differ if different prices are assigned
to inputs and/or outputs; that is, if the government uses shadow prices.
In public enterprise markets the common—not to say ubiquitous—
endogenous distortion is price regulation accompanied by nonprice rationing. Accordingly, we show how to estimate the various magnitudes
as a function of the nonprice-rationing schemes used before and after
divestiture.

Rent-seeking behavior is a critical component of divestiture since much
of the excess costs of public enterprises are not true resource cost but rents
accruing to overpaid workers, subsidized consumers, providers of various
inputs, or signers of various pieces of paper. To the extent that resources
are expended in pursuit of these rents, true resource savings result from
increased profitability after divestiture. To the extent that rents remain
after deducting the costs of rent-seeking, part of the apparent gains are
only redistributive transfers. We incorporate such considerations into our
analysis of rationing and shadow pricing. We also treat indirect taxes in the
public enterprise market and incorporate exogenous shadow prices made
necessary by distortions in other markets.

11.1.7   Synergies

Private valuation will vary to the extent that different buyers have ongoing
operations that are affected by the acquired enterprise: production costs
may be reduced through realization of economies of scope or scale; market
power may be increased by the merger; or the acquiring firm may be able
to utilize accrued tax liabilities. The stand-alone value of the firm must then
be adjusted to reflect the value of such synergies to the larger corporate
group, a process akin to shadow pricing on the public side.

11.1.8   Valuation Algorithm and Sensitivity Analysis

For expository clarity, earlier sections deal with only one or two complications at a time and give numerical examples for only a single company. In
this chapter we therefore generalize the empirical portion of our approach
in the form of a valuation algorithm embodied in a Lotus 1-2-3 template.
The interested reader may wish to turn back to Table 8.1 to inspect the
front end of this system, which gives the variables and assumptions that
the user may adjust, as well as summarizing results. The algorithm is used

to conduct a sensitivity analysis and to illustrate the impact of various combinations of assumptions, thus providing a policy-relevant tool for decision-makers.

11.1.9   Winners and Losers

Divestiture creates winning and losing groups. The machinations of these groups to alter the outcome in their favor we call politics. This chapter is about the intersection of political and technocratic aspects, which we call political economy. To this end we incorporate distributional considerations in our framework. The most relevant use of the resulting formula is for ex-ante or ex-post analysis of actual cases, something we do not at present have to offer. Instead we utilize the framework at a more aggregate level to examine the genesis of the current wave of divestiture and the differential responses of LDCs and MDCs.

11.1.10   Policy Implications

Technocrats are not simply interested in understanding outcomes, but in altering them. We therefore turn to selected policy implications of our analysis. Determinants of the various values of the firm are of course subject to government action, and an active divestiture policy means manipulating V_{sp}, V_{sg}, and Z to maximize the benefits of divestiture: V_{sg} is influenced by the counterfactual policies taken *instead of* divestiture (e.g., increasing autonomy or financial restructuring); V_{sp} is influenced by the policies affecting the period *after* divestiture (e.g., tariff protection or price regulation); and Z is influenced by both of the above plus sale-related policies for the time *before* divestiture (e.g., assuming part of corporate debt or pension funding). These and other policy options are explored using our cost-benefit analysis framework and valuation algorithm.

11.2   Extensions: Ex-post Evaluation

11.2.1   Overview

In this section we shift from the prescriptive task of suggesting *what should be done* in future divestitures to the descriptive task of ascertaining *what actually happened* in past divestitures: that is, *from ex-ante valuation to ex-post evaluation*. While this book has focused exclusively on the former task, the cost-benefit methodology is equally well suited to the latter.

11.2.2   Ex-post Evaluation: Goals

At present, divestiture can be supported or opposed only on the basis of ideology, theory, or politics, because there is only the most limited empirical support for either position. Serious and balanced studies of what actually happened in the wake of divestiture are not known to us. Instead, what we find is little more than elaboration on one side or the other of the following anecdotes.

Visit a country and be taken to see a "success story" of divestiture, where profits have risen dramatically thanks to both lower costs (attributed to more efficient use of all inputs) and higher sales (attributed to improved product quality and marketing). Then visit the opposition and be informed that of course sales rose, because as a side condition of sale, a high tariff was imposed on competing imports; and of course costs fell, because the sale contract included the government's taking over some debt and re-financing the balance at a lower rate.

Alternatively, visit a country where profitability has deteriorated in the wake of divestiture. Proponents attribute this to mismanagement of the economy by the government, making it impossible for even the most efficient businessperson to turn a profit. Opponents charge that the enterprises were sold at 10¢ on the dollar and that 9¢ of that was funded by a government-subsidized loan. As a result, purchasers were speculators who could turn a tidy profit by simply selling off easily liquidated assets at their market price (e.g., head-office real estate in the capital) and not worrying about the operations of the firm.

Certainly, such stories are true in some cases, and perhaps every divestiture involves many of the very different phenomena represented in such stories. The question is, How much? More precisely, for any given divestiture, one would like to know the answers to the following questions:

1.   What is the bottom line? Was the nation better off or worse off following the divestiture, and by how much?

2. How were the benefits and costs of divestiture distributed? Who was better off, who worse off, and by how much?

3. What variables actually changed: prices or quantities? exports or import substitution? lower inputs or higher output? explicit or implicit subsidies or real changes in efficiency? lower inventories or improved tax-avoidance accounting? greater adaptability to a changing environment or a more efficient response to the existing environment?

4. To what extent were the foregoing changes attributable to
  a. Divestiture itself, through improved management and motivation by the private sector;
  b. Discretionary changes in the economic environment (prices, financing, etc.) that accompanied divestiture but that could in principle have been accomplished under public operation;
  c. Exogenous changes in the economic environment that occurred independently of divestiture; and
  d. The cross-product interaction of the foregoing independent effects?

5. How do actual results compare with those envisioned at the time of the original divestiture decision? To what extent are any divergences explained by unexpected events and to what extent by failures in the bargaining process?

6. Given the actual distribution of benefits, could or should the actual sale price have been set higher or lower?

7. What do the achievements under private ownership tell us about priorities for reforming management practices in remaining public enterprises and about the potential gains from such changes?

Ex-post divestiture evaluation attempts to provide answers to such questions. The goal is to improve future divestitures by understanding historical divestitures.

11.1.3   Ex-post Evaluation: Methodology

The analytics of ex-post evaluation are a mirror image of those of ex-ante valuation: annual flows are compounded forward in the one case but discounted backward in the other. The relevant single-period flows themselves, however, are identical in the two cases.

The only thing distinguishing the two approaches is empirical detail. Ex-ange we necessarily rely heavily on assumption, whereas ex-post we rely more heavily on facts. Given the room for error in our ex-ante assumptions, it makes no sense to fine-tune them through great detail. This is equally true of divestiture valuation and project evaluation. Ex-ante we therefore assume a single set of shadow multipliers that do not change over time and one price index (or a very limited number of price indices) that do not vary over commodities. Ex-post this is ridiculous, since relative prices vary dramatically over commodities, and economic distortions vary substantially over time. To incorporate these differences, ex-post evaluation requires much finer detail in commodity categories, dynamic rather than static shadow prices, and much greater attention to empirical methodology (e.g., Divisia versus Laspeyres indexing procedures). These problems parallel those dealt with in ex-post performance evaluation, and the interested reader can find guidance there.[2]

The distinctions between the two approaches therefore involve mechanics rather than fundamental principles. Important though such issues may be, they are better treated by example in the context of an actual study. Such studies in four countries are currently taking shape in a project sponsored by the World Bank. It is hoped that they will result in follow-up volumes.

11.3   Conclusion

In sum, much remains to be done. Nevertheless, we hope we have achieved our initial goal of adding a pinch of analytically based empiricism to what has to date been primarily an ideological or political decision. Some public enterprises should be shut down, some divested, some revitalized, and some left as they are. Our goal has been not to act as advocates for any one view but rather to provide tools that inform the discussion.

Notes

Chapter 1

1. Or state-owned enterprise (SOE), or state-owned business (SOB), or government enterprise, or parastatal.

2. That is, ownership or internal managerial control of the enterprise is in government hands.

3. That is, output is sold in a market.

4. Diversiture of public enterprises is naturally termed "privatization" in many countries. However, in recent years the latter term has been expanded to include everything from mixed public/private hybrids (for example, management contracts or leasing) to anything that makes public entities behave more like private entities (for example, incentive systems), to anything that makes private enterprises behave in practice more like they are supposed to behave in theory (for example, liberalization). In its extreme forms, therefore, privatization has come to mean anything that is more privatelike or (since "private" in this literature is synonymous with "good") any positive economic reforms. To avoid being tainted with such ideological baggage, we eschew use of privatization in this volume and stick with divestiture of public enterprises, or divestiture, for short.

5. Reducing the sector by more than, say, 10 percent in terms of value-added or assets (but not in terms of number of enterprises).

6. The bibliography is a subset of a data base that runs to 970 items.

7. Raymond Vernon, ed., *The Promise of Privatization: A Challenge for American Foreign Policy* (New York: Council on Foreign Relations, 1988). Ezra Suleiman and John Waterbury, ed., *The Political Economy of Public Sector Reform and Privatization* (Princeton: unpublished manuscript, May 1989).

8. Dieter Bös, "Welfare Effects of Privatizing Public Enterprises," in *Welfare and Efficiency in Public Economies*, ed. D. Bös, M. Rose, and C. Seidel (Berlin: Springer-Verlag, 1988), pp. 339–362; Dieter Bös, "Privatization of Public Firms: A Government–Trade Union–Private Shareholder Cooperative Game," in *Public*

Finance and the Performance of Enterprises, ed. M. Neumann (Detroit: Wayne State University Press, 1988); Carl Shapiro and Robert D. Willig, "Economic Rationales for the Scope of Privatization," in Suleiman and Waterbury, *The Political Economy of Public Sector Reform and Privatization*.

9. John Vickers and George Yarrow, *Privatization: An Economic Analysis* (Cambridge, MA: MIT Press, 1988).

10. Divergence in valuation also arises from differences in expectations: the optimistic buyer might think he can make 15 percent, and the pessimistic buyer, 5 percent, when both can really only manage 10 percent.

11. The first two being the value to the buyer and the value to the government if it continued to operate the enterprise.

12. After work was well along on this volume, we did discover that elements of the analysis are contained in five paragraphs (pp. 152—154) in Simon Domberger and John Pigott, "Privatization Policies and Public Enterprise: A Survey," *The Economic Record* (June 1986): 145—162. For a different approach, focusing on the degree of privatization rather than the value of the firm, see Bös, "Welfare Effects of Privatizing Public Enterprises."

13. T. M. Ohashi and T. P. Roth, *Privatization: Theory and Practice* (Vancouver: Fraser Institute, 1980).

14. For elaboration on the implications of capital markets in an LDC context, see chapter 9, section 5.

15. Use of "often" does not signify simple academic wishy-washiness. There are certainly cases where the pure market mechanism might work. For example, in a newly industrialized country (NIC) such as Brazil, Mexico, or Korea, the government might first sell only a small fraction of the shares on the open market and later release more at the price thus determined. Even here, the initial offer price still needs to be set, and there remains the open question of whether or not this gradual process will really alter management conduct.

Chapter 2

1. The fundamental thrust of cost-benefit analysis is precisely the point that social valuation may differ from private valuation, necessitating the use of "shadow" or "accounting" prices. There is a huge literature on this subject. The basic references are Partha Dasgupta, Amartya Sen, and Stephen Marglin, *Guidelines For Project Evaluation* (New York: United Nations Industrial Development Organization, 1972); Ian Little and James Mirrlees, *Project Appraisal and Planning For Developing Countries* (London: Heinemann, 1974); and Lyn Squire and Herman van der Tak, *Economic Analysis of Project* (Baltimore: Johns Hopkins University Press, 1975).

2. See chapter 3 for further discussion on the choice of numeraire.

3. A complete description of the welfare effect of the transaction requires inclusion of the transaction cost of executing the sale. We treat this as a second-order effect and for the sake of simplicity, defer its introduction until later.

4. If not, see (2.7).

5. Note that this statement is not the same as saying "if the private operation is more efficient than public operation." The difference arises because of the presence of λ_g in the expressions for V_{sp} and V_{sg}. It is possible, for example, that there is an efficiency improvement from divestiture, yet V_{sg} is still greater than V_{sp}.

6. Algebraically, this follows from the fact that when dividing or multiplying both sides of an inequality by a negative number, the inequality sign is reversed.

7. Or, given a number of identical bidders, choose the one with the highest bid.

Chapter 3

1. Most microeconomics texts contain a detailed discussion of this concept and its pitfalls. See, for example, D. Hueth, R. Just, and A. Schmitz, *Applied Welfare Economics and Public Policy* (Englewood Cliffs, NJ: Prentice-Hall, 1982).

2. The optimal tax would then be the one for which, at the margin, $dW = 0$, where dW refers to the infinitesimal version of ΔW.

3. Dasgupta, Sen, and Marglin, Guidelines for Project Evaluation.

4. Squire and van der Tak, *Economic Analysis of Projects*.

5. See, for example, Anthony B. Atkinson and Joseph E. Stiglitz, *Lectures on Public Economics* (New York: McGraw-Hill, 1980).

6. This argument provides the justification for the usual practice of ignoring the differences between the different activities of the government. See, for example, Squire and van der Tak, *Economic Analysis of Projects*, p. 68.

7. Edgar Browning, "The marginal Cost of Public Funds," *Journal of Political Economy* 84 (April 1976): 283–298.

8. Harvey Rosen, "The Measurement of Excess Burden with Explicit Utility Functions," *Journal of Political Economy* 86 (April 1978): s121–s135.

9. Edgar Browning, "On the Marginal Welfare Cost of Taxation," *American Economic Review* 77 (March 1987): 11–23.

10. Charles Stuart, "Welfare Costs per Dollar of Additional Tax Revenue in the U.S.," *American Economic Review* 74 (June 1984): 352–362.

11. Charles Ballard, J. Shoven, and J. Whalley, "General Equilibrium Computations of the Marginal Welfare Costs of Taxes in the the United States," *American Economic Review* 75 (March 1985): 128–138.

12. The last number comes from an estimate based on a value of the parameter elasticities outside the range presented in table 3.1, specifically for a saving elasticity of 0.8 and a labor supply elasticity of 0.3.

13. See Ingemar Hansson and Charles Stuart, "Tax Revenue and the Marginal Cost of Public Funds in Sweden," mimeo, University of California at Santa Barbara, January 1983; and Harry Campbell," Deadweight Loss and Commodity Taxation in Canada," *Canadian Journal of Economics* (August 1975): 441–446.

14. They do, of course, have a downstream cost when payment of interest, debt, loan amortization, or capital repatriation costs domestic resources. This, however, is reflected in an appropriate share of V_{sg} being valued at $\lambda_f = 0$.

15. Further approximations would recognize that the foreign investment multiplier might differ from the domestic one (because of different values of r) and any possible distortions in the foreign exchange market.

16. In the U.N. system, gross *domestic* product is that produced within a country, whereas gross *national* product is that produced by factors owned by a country, wherever located.

17. For pedagogical reasons, we begin with a two-period model, deferring the extension to multiple periods to the following section.

18. Other reasons for a divergence could include transaction costs, risk, price regulation, and exercise of market power in the banking industry.

19. All three comprehensive systems (Squire and van der Tak; Little and Mirrlees; and Dasgupta, Sen, and Margin) use the same concept, though this is often obscured by differential emphasis, numeraire, notation, and exposition. For a comprehensive comparison, see A. Ray, *Cost-Benefit Analysis: Issues and Methodologies* (Baltimore: Johns Hopkins University Press, 1984), pp. 76–101.

20. However, neither of the authors notes that his methods are modifications of the standard literature or even recognizes the existence of that literature. Students of the sociology of economics may understand this omission if it is pointed out that Squire and van der Tak is often referred to as "the World Bank manual," Dasgupta, Sen, and Marglin as "the UNIDO manual," and Little and Mirrlees as "the OECD manual."

21. D. F. Bradford, "Constraints on Government Investment Opportunities and the Choice of Discount Rate," *American Economic Review* (December 1975): 887–889.

22. Robert J. Lind, "A Primer on the Major Issues Relating to the Discount Rate for Evaluating National Energy Options," in Robert J. Lind, ed., *Discounting for Time and Risk in Energy Policy* (Washington, DC: Resources for the Future, 1982).

23. The expression that, when multiplied by a single payment of an N-period annuity, gives the present value of the annuity discounted at the rate i.

24. And under the nonstringent conditions that $0 < t < 1, s < 1.00$, and $0 < \lambda_g$.

25. J. E. Stiglitz, "The Corporation Tax," *Journal of Public Economics* 5 (1976): 303–311.

26. J. E. Stiglitz, "The Rate of Discount for Benefit-Cost Analysis and the Theory of the Second Best," in Lind, ed., *Discounting for Time and Risk in Energy Policy*, pp. 151–204.

27. C. Bell and S. Devarajan, "Shadow Prices for Project Evaluation under alternative Macroeconomic Specifications," *Quarterly Journal of Economics* 98 (August 1983): 457–477.

Chapter 4

1. We use $\Pi - X^d$ rather than $\Pi(1 - x^d)$ because the applicable corporate tax rate x^d is not charged on quasi-rents but on Π less interest, depreciation, and other accounting charges. Also note that Π is defined as a quasi-rent (see section 4.3.4).

2. For simplicity, we exclude in this chapter any measure of consumer welfare, since this is unaffected by divestiture when behavior is unchanged.

3. Except for indirect taxes and subsidies, which generally do not appear on the profit and loss statement and must be obtained exogeneously if production at market cost is needed.

4. "The factors acquired for production which have not yet reached the point of the business process where they may be appropriately treated as 'cost of sales' or 'expenses' are called 'assets' and are presented as such in the balance sheet. It should not be overlooked, however, that those 'assets' are in fact 'revenue charges in suspense' awaiting some future matching with revenue as costs or expenses." William A. Patton and Aranias C. Littleton, *An Introduction to Corporate Accounting Standard* (Chicago: American Accounting Association, 1967). Cited in Stephen H. Penman, "What Asset Values?—An Extension of a Familiar Debate," *The Accounting Review* (April 1970): 333–346. For an excellent review of the literature in this field see T. A. Lee, *Income and Value Measurement: Theory and Practice* (Baltimore: Baltimore University Press, 1975).

5. In practice, things get a little more complicated because transfers from one account to another (e.g., from construction in progress to active), disposals (e.g., sales of capital goods and the associated depreciation stock adjustment), and adjustments to previous periods need to be taken into account. However, the basic principle remains applicable.

6. Within the rather broad limits set by generally accepted accounting standards.

7. By assumption, capital goods and intangibles have no liquidition value in this case; deferred accounts have no liquidation value by definition.

8. These obligations would normally be due early in 1987 and thus subject to a lower discount rate. We ignore this for computational simplicity (see table 4.1, assumption 4.A).

9. We assume these were declared prior to sale and thus are the property of the previous owners. Also, the earlier footnote on timing applies here as well.

10. Where capital gains equal the net benefits, reduced by dividends and by the original purchase price (which is just V_{ppc}).

11. Figures, direct from table 4.5, except as noted.

12. Net taxes are only 751, but the tax effect of the interest deduction $(1,029 \times 0.3333 = 343)$ is treated as reducing the cost of debt. The total tax on operations $(751 + 343 = 1,094)$ is entered here, with the 343 netted out of the cost of debt capital in step 4.

13. From table 4.5: $4,063 + 2,417$.

14. $(10,286 \times 1.1)/1.1$ less 343 from note 12. For non-interest-bearing, $2,817/1.1$.

15. Recall from table 4.1 that we arbitrarily set $\lambda_g = 1.3$ and $\lambda_p = 1.0$.

16. For example, if public and private discount rates differ (a price distortion), then there can be a motive for sale in the absence of behavioral change.

Chapter 5

1. An alternative formulation of the trade-off is due to Bös, who assumes (among other things) no government (so λ_g is irrelevant) and perfect capital markets (so $Z = Z_p$). Private shareholders vote to maximize profits, whereas public shareholders vote to maximize welfare. The optimal balance between allocative and cost efficiency is then obtained by divesting an optimal number of shares. See Dieter Bös, "A Theory of the Privatization of Public Enterprises," *Journal of Economics* (Suppl. 5, 1986): 17–40.

2. If r is the discount rate and is constant over time, then $\rho = 1/(1 + r)$.

3. Synergies are discussed in chapter 7.

4. More precisely, this is Z_p^π (willingness to pay for operating assets) to which we add Z_p^f (willingness to pay for financial assets) and from which we deduct transaction costs to reach Z_p, as explained in section 4.4.5. In this and the next two chapters we are concerned only with operating assets, so we drop the superscript.

5. It may be useful to give some background for this concept. Suppose the price of a good rises from p_0 to p_1. How much worse off are consumers as a result of this price change? We might attempt to answer this question by asking, How much would they have been willing to pay in order to prevent the price change from taking place? This amount is called the *equivalent variation* of the price change and is regarded as a reasonable measure of the welfare change experienced by consumers. Under certain conditions it can be shown that this dollar amount can be measured as the area under the demand curve for the good between the two price levels, which is known as the change in consumer surplus. Most microeconomics

text books contain a detailed discussion of this concept and its pitfalls. See, for example, Hueth, Just, and Schmitz, *Applied Welfare Economics*.

6. This assumption is, of course, not necessary, and we do not make it in the following example.

7. Previously, we used 11,011 of inputs to produce 18,191 of output—that is, 0.6053 per unit. Because there is a 10 percent increase in output per intermediate input, the per-unit requirement becomes $0.6053/1.1 = 0.5503$.

8. Previously we needed $1,631/18,191 = 0.0897$ labor per unit output. Again, divide by 1.1 to get the new per-unit requirement.

9. $(24/18,191)/1.1$.

10. Working capital includes input and output inventories, cash, demand deposits, and accounts receivable. We assume that input inventories are proportional to the level of intermediate input use, output inventories are proportional to the level of output, and financial working capital is proportional to the intermediate inputs and output. Allowing for the reduced use of inputs per unit output yields the figure of 0.0309 for the working capital requirement.

11. As before, obtained by applying the tax rate on quasi-rents minus economic depreciation.

12. The case where the enterprise has monopoly power in the output market and monopsony power in the input market is considerably more complicated. In this case the marginal cost curve of the enterprise will almost certainly be upward-sloping, which makes estimation of the new output and input quantities considerably more problematic. If the enterprise has monopoly power in the output market and no monopsony power but simply sets input price too high, then the approximation (4.26) may be used without difficulty.

13. Note that in the ensuing analysis, the consumer surplus measures S_g, S_p, and ΔS are defined over the output of *all* firms, that is, including the enterprise and the other firms in the industry.

14. See L. P. Jones and I. Vogelsang, *The Effects of Markets on Public Enterprise Conduct; and Vice Versa* (Ljubljana: ICPE Monograph Series, no. 7, 1983).

15. We follow here the development in Pankaj Tandon, "A Note on the Optimal Pricing of Publicly Produced Intermediate Inputs," *Atlantic Economic Journal* 17 (September 1989). Another source is Hueth, Just, and Schmitz, *Applied Welfare Economics*, chapter 9 and appendix D.

16. However, the analysis does not carry through if the downstream industry has *monopsony* power with respect to the upstream industry.

17. It is analogous to the problem of including new products in the calculation of price indexes or of allowing for quality improvements in such price index calculations.

18. For example, in what is rapidly becoming the standard text in industrial organization, Jean Tirole writes that there is "too much emphasis on the positive side. A more careful welfare analysis ... would be desirable." See Jean Tirole, *The Theory of Industrial Organization* (Cambridge, MA: MIT Press, 1989), p. 115.

19. See Kelvin Lancaster, "A New Approach to Consumer Theory," *Journal of Political Economy* 74 (April 1966): 132–157.

Chapter 6

1. The only exceptions are λ_g and λ_p, the shadow multipliers of public and private funds, which we introduced in chapter 2.

2. They may also use price rationing, with the proceeds going as rent to the hiring agent.

3. Cases of nonprice output rationing by private enterprises are not so exceptional, though. They include most service industries, where waiting is frequently involved, such as restaurants, movie houses, or airlines, and some manufactured products with order backlogs.

4. In the case of a convex demand curve, total consumer surplus would actually fall in response to rationing by reverse-order willingness to pay, compared to price rationing of the same quantity.

5. The leisure time lost in queuing offsets gains in consumer surplus. This loss is treated below as the cost of rent-seeking.

6. R. Turvey, "How to Judge When Price Changes Will Improve Resource Allocation," *Economic Journal* 84 (1974): 825–832.

7. Another approximation to the surplus change suggested in Finsinger and Vogelsang (F-V) is to use the Slutsky compensation $\Delta S = \Delta p * q_0$, where q_0 is the quantity demanded at the original price p_0. This approximation usually underestimates surplus increases and overestimates surplus decreases. See J. Finsinger and I. Vogelsang, "Alternative Institutional Frameworks for Price Incentive Mechanisms," *Kyklos* 34 (1981): 388–404.

8. The corresponding result for the F-V approximation is

$$\Delta W^* = \lambda_g \Delta \Pi + [p(q_p) - p][q_p - q_g].$$

This differs from equation (6.5.b) by the area of triangle CGD in figure 6.3. Note that the F-V formula is different if the private firm contracts output instead of expanding it.

9. The corresponding formula under the F-V approximation is

$$\Delta W^* = \lambda_g \Delta \Pi - q_g [p(q_p) - p(q_g)].$$

10. Note that we do not have to know λ_p in this case, because we are going to derive only ΔW^*.

11. The corresponding numbers for the F-V approximation are

$$\Delta W^* = \frac{2{,}404 + (1.0767 - 1)(20{,}010 - 18{,}191)}{1.1}$$

$$= \frac{(2{,}404 + 140)}{1.1} = 2{,}313.$$

Under this approximation the annual improvement due to the reduction in rationing is estimated to be 140 monetary units.

12. Similarly, the result for the F-V approximation is

$$\Delta W^* = 2{,}404 + \frac{\dfrac{18{,}191(20{,}010 - 18{,}191)}{24{,}012}}{1.1} = \frac{2{,}404 + 1{,}378}{1.1}$$

$$= 3{,}782.$$

13. An early statement is found in G. Tullock, "The Welfare Costs of Tariffs, Monopolies, and Theft," *Western Economic Journal* 5 (1968): 224–232. The notion received widespread professional attention only after the work of A. Krueger, "The Political Economy of the Rent-Seeking Society," *American Economic Review* 64 (1974): 291–303. Downstream results may be found in J. Buchanan, R. Tollison, and G. Tullock, *Toward a Theory of the Rent-Seeking Society* (College Station, TX: Texas A & M University Press, 1980).

14. Actually, one could imagine situations (overoptimistic rent-seekers) where the real resource costs are *more* than the potential rents.

15. Tullock, "Rent-Seeking," in *The New Palgrave: A Dictionary of Economics*, Vol. 4, ed. J. Eatwell, M. Milgate, and P. Newman (London: Macmillan, 1987), p. 149.

16. In a sense the different shadow prices act like different weights given to consumer surplus and wages.

17. There also exists a subtle issue of rationing under shadow pricing. Assume that the shadow value of an output is above the market price; then some consumers, whose social evaluation is above the market price, will be excluded. It is not clear that this rationing occurs according to social willingness to pay.

Chapter 7

1. Tax effects are not the only kind of financial synergy. There may be other purely financial synergies. For example, the debt rating of a company may change after it buys a public enterprise, thereby influencing the cost of borrowing. The debt rating may improve if it is felt the company now has greater assets; it may deteriorate if the company has borrowed heavily to finance the acquisition. In either event, we feel such effects are likely to be small.

2. A further problem will occur if the presence of such redistributive synergies results in rent-seeking behavior that dissipates some of the private benefits. Such rent-seeking will be a net loss socially.

3. If cross effects exist, calculating consumer surplus is more difficult. Nevertheless, the fundamental framework remains unchanged.

4. See Dennis Mueller, *The Determinants and Effects of Mergers: An International Comparison* (Cambridge: Oelgeschlager, 1980).

5. Note that, in fact, CSX announced early its intention not to bid for Conrail. The discussion here is for the express purpose of illustrating the idea of strategic bidding, not to represent any aspect of the actual bidding for Conrail.

6. This would be the prediction of some simple oligopoly models such as the Cournot model.

Chapter 8

1. The template is primarily intended to illustrate fundamental issues and should be extended to deal with real cases. For example, the template accepts only a single output and only a single efficiency shift parameter, whereas field work requires dealing with multiple products and differential efficiency shifts by year and by input.

2. The first step in using the template is to enter base state data for production and distribution flows and wealth statement. These are in a format identical to tables 4.4 and 4.5 and are not replicated here.

3. The section 8.3 result was reported as 100 (rounded from 100.42), whereas the 101 result here is rounded from 100.58. The difference is due in part to rounding and in part to the fact that our template does not deal very well with infinite elasticities, so we have to settle for 9^{52} as the highest approximation.

4. Note that the reverse is also possible. In the present instance marginal output under willingness to pay is to the right of marginal output under the inverse. That is, in terms of figure 6.2, D is to the right of G. If the quantity were much smaller (as shown in figure 6.2), extra output would be valued more highly under willingness to pay rationing.

5. Jay W. Ritter, "The Costs of Going Public," *Journal of Financial Economics* 19 (1987): 269–281.

6. Vickers and Yarrow, *Privatization: An Economic Analysis*, p. 181.

7. Transaction costs are treated as falling on the total value (financial plus operational less transaction costs) and so are not reported in figure 7.3, which covers only production value.

8. There will be some effect if discount rates differ, because the two transactors differ in their relative valuation of money now and money later. If the private

discount rate is higher, as we would expect it to be, then imposing an indirect tax on future output reduces current return to the government but increases future returns.

9. The elasticity of welfare with respect to government market power is zero here, but only because the base assumption is zero, and 1 percent of zero is still zero.

10. For example, if private efficiency is greater, and ΔW^* improves, the elasticity becomes negative, not positive, if the starting and ending points are both negative.

Chapter 9

1. Vernon, *The Promise of Privatization*, and Suleiman and Waterbury, *The Political Economy of Public Sector Reform and Privatization*.

2. $\Delta W = \Delta S + \lambda_g \Delta \Pi + \lambda_m \Delta M + (\lambda_g - \lambda_p)(Z_p - Z)$, where we have dispensed with the discount factor and therefore intend all the Δ's to indicate present discounted values.

3. Another possibility is to define a "base" consumer group whose welfare is just equal to $1 of government revenue, as advocated in the extended UNIDO method: *Guide to Practical Project Appraisal: Social Benefit Cost Analysis in Developing Countries* (New York: United Nations, 1978), chapter 5. This has the advantage of making λ_g equal unity. So long as everything else is redefined accordingly, this makes no difference, but we prefer the reminder effect of keeping an explicit λ_g greater than one.

4. Specifically, one in the fiftieth percentile of the income distribution—that is, the median consumer.

5. Squire and van der Tak, *Economic Analysis of Projects*, chapter 10.

6. For example, in Squire and van der Tak.

7. Note that the combination is not multiplicative but additive. That is, if the efficiency multiplier on profits is 1.5, and the distributional multiplier is 0.2, the net multiplier is not 0.3 but 0.7. That is, the consumption component is worth only 0.2, but the external effects on investment, taxes, and the like, is worth 0.5, for a total of 0.7.

8. Foreigners are excepted.

9. This simply means replacing ΔS in equation (5.21) with $\lambda_s \Delta S$. Note that in equation (9.1) this has been disaggregated and appears as ΔS on the left plus $(\lambda_s - 1)\Delta S$ on the right. Similar decompositions have been applied to other terms.

10. Alternatively, the multiplier can be left with the ΔS term, implying that the consumers themselves get the extra benefits.

11. For documentation and elaboration on this and other assertions in this subsection, see Leroy Jones, "Public Enterprise for Whom? Perverse Distributional

Consequences of Public Operational Decisions," *Economic Development and Cultural Change* (January 1985): 333—347.

12. This was the case of The British Columbia Resources Investment Corporation. For an account of this rather unusual divestiture, see Ohashi and Roth, *Privatization: Theory and Practice.*

13. It is an approximation for at least two reasons: first, because of the cross-product term, and second, because of the neoclassical possibility that any ostensible cost reduction includes rent transfer, as explained below.

14. We admit the theoretical possibility that efficiency wage arguments can justify above-market wages, but we judge its explanatory power in the market for sweepers in Bolivia to be of footnote proportions.

15. The only savings that remain are reductions in allocative efficiency. For the classic neoclassical exposition, see George Stigler, "The Xistence of X-Efficiency," *American Economic Review* (March 1976): 213—216.

16. For documentation through about 1980, see R. P. Short, "The Role of Public Enterprises: An International Statistical Comparison," in *Public Enterprises in Mixed Economies: Some Macroeconomic Aspects,* ed. Robert H. Floyd, Clive S. Gray, and R. P. Short (Washington, DC: IMF, 1984), pp. 110—194.

17. Speaking of the larger privatization trend and not merely its divestiture component. John Ikenberry, "The International Spread of Privatization Policies: Inducements, Learning and 'Policy Bandwagoning,'" in Suleiman and Waterbury, *The Political Economy of Public Sector Reform and Privatization,* chapter 3, p. 1.

18. Vernon, "Introduction," in *The Promise of Privatization,* pp. 18—19.

19. International Monetary Fund, *International Financial Statistics Yearbook: 1986* (Washington, DC: IMF, 1986). From 1959 through 1985 (their approximation to) "world" GDP grew at an average annual rate of 3.87 percent for a growth multiple of 2.68 over twenty-six years. Adding four years and cutting the growth rate a bit to reflect the assumption that the missing countries grew more slowly yields a rough tripling over thirty years.

20. Because monopoly profits are then limited to the transportation margin.

21. For the well-documented case of increasing competitiveness in the United States, see William Shepherd, "Increased Competition: Causes and Effects" (Louvain, Belgium, paper presented at the 9th EARIE Conference, September, 1982).

22. The two-thirds rule says that the surface area of containers grows at roughly two-thirds the rate of growth of their volume. Therefore, the cost of building containers such as boilers grows less than proportionally to their capacity.

23. Recall that we are here referring to the degree of competition that characterizes the market prior to divestiture. If divestiture itself is accompanied by policies that increase competition, this is a clear plus.

24. For elaboration, see Jones and Vogelsang, *The Effects of Markets on Public Enterprise Conduct; and Vice Versa.*

25. For example, see D. Caves et al., "Economic Performance of U.S. And Canadian Railroads: The Significance of Ownership and the Regulatory Environment," in *Managing Public Enterprises*, ed. W. T. Stanbury and Fred Thompson (New York: Praeger, 1982), pp. 123–151. For a survey see T. Borcherding, W. Pommerehne, and F. Schneider, "Comparing the Efficiency of Private and Public Production: The Evidence from Five Countries," *Journal of Economics*, Suppl. 2 (1982): 127–156. For theoretical arguments see L. DeAlessi, "On the Nature and Consequences of Private and Public Enterprises," *Minnesota Law Review* 67 (1982): 191–209. T. E. Borcherding, "Toward a Positive Theory of Public Sector Supply Arrangements," in *Public Enterprises in Canada*, ed. R. Prichard (Toronto: Butterworth, 1983), pp. 99–184. Vickers and Yarrow, *Privatization: An Economic Analysis.*

For empirical evidence see A. E. Boardman and A. R. Vining, "Ownership and Performance in Competitive Environments: A Comparison of the Performance of Private, Mixed, and State-Owned Enterprises," in *Journal of Law and Economics* 32 (April 1989): 1–36. R. Millward and D. M. Parker, "Public and Private Enterprise: Comparative Behavior and Relative Efficiency," in R. Millward et al., *Public Sector Economics* (Longman, 1983).

26. Alfred Chandler, *The Visible Hand: The Managerial Revolution in American Business* (Cambridge, MA: Harvard University Press, 1977).

27. For an excellent survey in the context of divestiture, see Vickers and Yarrow, *Privatization: An Economic Analysis*, especially chapter 4, "Theories of Regulation."

28. Price increases are limited to the rate of inflation in some consumer price index less a specified expected rate of productivity improvement, X percent.

29. John Nellis, "Contract Plans and Public Enterprise Performance," *World Bank Discussion Paper* No. 48, 1989.

30. Prajapati Trivedi, "Theory and Practice of the French System of Contracts for Improving Public Enterprise Performance: Some Lessons for LDCs," *Public Enterprise*, Vol. 8, No. 1 (1988): 28–40.

31. Y. C. Park, "Reform of Public Enterprise Sector in Korea," (Washington, DC: World Bank, Public Sector Management Division, August 1985).

32. Recall that we are talking about the rate of change here, not the level.

33. Vernon, *The Promise of Privatization*, p. 19.

34. Because λ_g appears twice in equation (5.21), once with a positive sign and once with a negative sign, it might appear that the impact on ΔW could go either way. However, the second term merely reduces the gains to government to the extent that they are passed to the purchaser via the process of bargaining over the price. Except in the unlikely event that the government actually accepts less than its minimum reservation price, the net impact of the two terms on ΔW will be

positive. The impact of the second term is further reduced by the fact that what matters is $(\lambda_g - \lambda_p)$, and as λ_g rises, so usually does λ_p.

35. A partial exception is due to Bermeo, who compares privatization episodes in Greece, Portugal, and Spain and emphasizes the much greater influence on policy of the Spanish business community. Nancy Bermeo, "The Politics of Public Enterprise in Portugal, Spain, and Greece," in Suleiman and Waterbury, *The Political Economy of Public Sector Reform and Privatization*, pp. 14–18.

36. After divestiture, however, purchasers may become an important interest group blocking renationalization. The critical factor would be the price at which shares would be redeemed. Opposition could be expected if increased prospects for renationalization resulted in lower market prices, or if the government considered redemption at a nonmarket price (e.g., at the original undervalued issuance rate). This may have been one motive for underpricing shares in the United Kingdom. See Vickers and Yarrow, *Privatization: An Economic Analysis*, pp. 180–181.

37. Mancur Olson, *The Logic of Collective Action: Public Goods and the Theory of Groups* (Cambridge, MA: Harvard University Press, 1965).

38. Mancur Olson, *The Rise and Decline of Nations* (New Haven, CT: Yale University Press, 1982), p. 47.

39. Ibid., p. 41.

40. Although Japan's experience in the 1880s is an important exception. For details see T. C. Smith, *Political Change and Industrial Development in Japan: Government Enterprise, 1868–1880* (Stanford CA: Stanford University Press, 1955).

41. Note that in the United States, serious deregulation actually began in the Carter administration.

42. Bermeo, "The Politics of Public Enterprise," p. 9.

43. Horacio Boneo, "Privatization: Ideology and Praxis," in *State Shrinking*, ed. William Glade (Austin: University of Texas, 1986).

44. Leroy Jones and Edward Mason, "Why Public Enterprise?" in *Public Enterprise in Less-Developed Countries*, ed. L. Jones (Cambridge: Cambridge University Press, 1982).

45. Rebecca Candoy-Sekse, *Techniques of Privatization of State-Owned Enterprise*, Vol. 3 (Washington, DC: World Bank Technical Paper No. 90, 1988).

46. John Nellis, "Public Enterprise Reform in Adjustment Lending," *World Bank Policy, Planning and Research Working Paper* No. 233, August 1989).

47. Ibid., p. 16.

48. In addition to Nellis, for the early record see Roger Leeds, "Turkey: Rhetoric and Reality," in Vernon, *The Promise of Privatization*, pp. 149–178. For an update

see John Waterbury, "The Political Context of Public Sector Reform and Privatization in Egypt, India, Mexico, and Turkey," in Suleiman and Waterbury, *The Political Economy of Public Sector Reform and Privatization*.

49. In 1980 the richest MDCs were at about $15,000 per capita, whereas the poorest LDCs were at about $100. The United Nations International Comparison Project tells us that we need to multiply the lowest income countries by a factor of about 4 to adjust for purchasing power differentials, yielding a ratio of 37.5 from top to bottom.

50. Roger Leeds, "Turkey: Rhetoric and Reality," in Vernon, *The Promise of Privatization*, pp. 163–164.

51. For example, Simon Commander and Tony Killick, "Privatization in Developing Countries: A Survey of the Issues," in *Privatization in Less Developed Countries*, ed. Paul Cook and Colin Kirkpatrick (New York: St. Martin's Press, 1988), pp. 91–124.

52. *New York Times*, June 20, 1989, pp. D1–D6.

53. Calculation excludes Taiwan and South Korea as NICs rather than LCDs. Were they to be included, the twenty-nine-nation volume would still be only 70 percent of London volume. International Finance Corporation, *Emerging Stock Markets Factbook: 1989* (Washington, D.C.: IFC, 1989), pp. 16–17.

54. For example, Steve Hanke, "Towards a People's Capitalism," in *Privatization and Development*, ed. Steve Hanke (San Francisco/Panama: International Center for Economic Growth, 1987), pp. 213–222.

55. J. Marshall and F. Montt, "Privatization in Chile," in Cook and Kirkpatrick, *Privatization in Less Developed Countries*, pp. 281–307. Paul E. Sigmund, "Chile: Privatization, Reprivatization, Hyperprivatization," in Suleiman and Waterbury, *The Political Economy of Public Sector Reform and Privatization*.

56. Manuel Tanoira, "Privatization as Politics" in Hanke, *Privatization and Development*, pp. 53–64. Direct quotes from pp. 54 and 56.

Chapter 10

1. The government may have to negotiate many cases, though. There may then be economies of scale in establishing a reputation of being a tough negotiator. Still, the principle will have to hold.

2. As before, we do not specifically deal here with incomplete information and uncertainty faced by the agents and by the evaluator. For the time being we rely instead on sensitivity analysis to simulate the effects of alternative scenarios.

3. See note 25, chapter 9 for references to this literature.

4. This implicitly assumes that either $\lambda_p = 1$ or workers consume all their income.

5. See, for example, the survey by Borcherding, Pommerehne, and Schneider.

6. See, for example, L. Weiss and M. Klass, eds., *Case Studies in Regulation* (Boston: Little, Brown & Co., 1981).

7. See, for example, Vickers and Yarrow, *Privatization: An Economic Analysis*; E. E. Subissati, "Some Evidence Regarding British Telecom's Performance Under Price Cap Regulation," paper prepared for "Telecommunications Costing in a Dynamic Environment" Conference, San Diego, CA, April 5–7, 1989; or L. L. Johnson, "Price Caps in Telecommunications—Regulatory Reform," RAND Note N-2894-MF/RC, Santa Monica, CA, January 1989.

8. Thus one would attribute most, if not all, the change to privatization or pure technical change. This further confounds the picture—pure technical change that may have occurred in the absence of privatization.

9. This is an extreme case. The inflow of funds need not be 100 percent of the purchase price (because it replaces another direct investment by the foreigner or because the foreigner finances part of the purchase in the host country), nor do profits need to be 100 percent repatriated (because they can be reinvested in the enterprise or elsewhere in the host country). Therefore, as discussed in chapter 3, λ_f is quite likely to differ from 0.

10. This phenomenon is not peculiar to cases of privatization. Even in the private sector, there is a strong tendency to "underprice" new issues (in the sense that the stock price tends to rise after completion of the issue) in order to ensure that all shares are in fact sold. For a discussion of why this happens and for references to empirical work supporting this contention see Richard A. Brealey and Stewart C. Myers, *Principles of Corporate Finance* (New York: McGraw-Hill, 1988), chapter 15.

11. Implicitly, Thatcher attached a very high value to λ_p when selling public enterprises with large discounts.

12. Vickers and Yarrow, *Privatization: An Economic Analysis*.

13. This is because consumers will incur rent-seeking efforts to secure the subsidized services, whereas inefficient entry or bypass will occur with respect to the subsidizing services. This is one of the main issues of the U.S. literature on government regulation.

14. In fact this argument underlies the debate on whether or not government should subsidize private investment generally. See J. Mayshar, "Should Government Subsidize Risky Private Projects?" *American Economic Review* 67 (1977): 20–28; and M. B. Stewart, "Should Government Subsidize Risky Private Projects: Comments?" *American Economic Review* 69 (1979): 459–461.

15. S. Peltzman, "Toward a More General Theory of Regulation," *Journal of Law and Economics* 19 (1976): 211–240; Borcherding, "Toward a Positive Theory of Public Sector Supply Arrangements," pp. 99–184; Olson, *The Logic of Collective Action* and *The Rise and Decline of Nations*.

16. See C. B. Blankart, "The Contribution of Public Choice to Public Utility Economics—a Survey," in *Public Sector Economics*, ed. J. Finsinger (London and Basingstoke: Macmillan, 1983), pp. 151–170.

17. Opposition may arise if the methodology yields a prescription for divesiture. At the same time, the methodology gives the losers more precise grounds on which to demand compensation. Thus they may prefer the use of the methodology over the imposition of divestiture.

18. See, for example, N.V. Jagannathan, *Informal Markets in Developing Countries* (New York: Oxford University Press, 1987).

Chapter 11

1. In this summary we use the original numbering of the equations.

2. See Leroy Jones, "Performance Evaluation for Public Enterprise," in *The Elusive Hybrid: Experiments in the Management and Privatization of SOE's*, ed. Ravi Ramamurti and Raymond Vernon (Washington, D.C.: forthcoming).

Bibliography

Abromeit, Heidrun. *British Steel: An Industry Between the State and the Private Sector*. London: Berg Publishing, 1986.

Aharoni, Yair. *The Evolution and Management of State-Owned Enterprises*. Cambridge, MA: Ballinger, 1986.

Aharoni, Yair, and Ray Vernon. *State-Owned Enterprise in Western Economies*. New York: St. Martin's Press, 1981.

Ahmed, Sadiq. "Shadow Prices for Economic Appraisal of Projects: An Application to Thailand." *World Bank Staff Working Paper* No. 609, Sept. 1983.

Ameen, Mansurul. "Study of Divestment of Industries in Bangladesh." Canadian International Development Agency, Mar. 1986.

Arthur Young International. "Financing Privatization Under Limited Capital Conditions." U.S. Agency for International Development, Nov. 1986.

Ascher, Kate. *The Politics of Privatization: Contracting out Public Services*. New York: St. Martin's Press, 1986.

Atkinson, Anthony, and Joseph Stiglitz. *Lectures on Public Economics*. New York: McGraw-Hill, 1980.

Auster, R. "Privatization, Justice and Markets." *Cato Journal* 3 (1983): 869–872.

Austin, James, Lawrence Wortzel, and John Coburn. "Privatizing State-Owned Enterprises: Hopes and Realities." *Columbia Journal of World Business* (Fall 1986): 51–60.

Averch, H., and L. L. Johnson. "Behavior of the Firm Under Regulatory Constraint." *American Economic Review* 52 (1962): 1052–1069.

Aylen, Jonathan. "Privatization in Developing Countries." *Lloyds Bank Review* (Jan. 1987): 15–30.

Ayub, Mahmood, and Sven Hegstad. "Management of Public Industrial Enterprises." *World Bank Research Observer* 2 (Jan. 1987): 79–102.

Balassa, Bela. "Public Enterprise in Developing Countries: Issues of Privatization." World Bank, Report No. DRD292, May 1987.

Baldwin, M. "Thatcherite Panacea." *Dissent* 33 (1986): 283–285.

Ballard, Charles, J. Shoven, and J. Whalley. "General Equilibrium Computations of the Marginal Welfare Costs of Taxes in the United States." *American Economic Review* 75 (Mar. 1985): 128–138.

Barnes, John. "The Failure of Privatization." *National Review* (July 18, 1986).

Becker, Gary. "Competition among Pressure Groups for Political Influence." *Quarterly Journal of Economics* 98 (1983): 371–398.

Becker, Gary. "Why Public Enterprises Belong in Private Hands." *Business Week* (Feb. 24, 1986).

Beesley, M. E., and S. C. Littlechild. "Privatization: Principles, Problems and Priority." *Lloyds Bank Review* (July 1983): 1–20.

Bell, C., and S. Davarajan. "Shadow Prices for Project Evaluation under Alternative Macroeconomic Specifications." *Quarterly Journal of Economics* 98 (Aug. 1983): 457–477.

Bellante, D. "Breaking the Political Barriers to Privatization." *Cato Journal* 3 (1983): 575–580.

Berenyi, Eileen Brettler, and Barbara Stevens. "Does Privatization Work? A Study of the Delivery of Eight Local Services." *State and Local Government Review* (Winter 1988).

Berg, Elliot. "Changing the Public-Private Mix: A Survey of Some Recent Experiences in LDC's." International Monetary Fund, Feb. 7, 1983.

Berg, Elliot, and Mary Shirley. "Divestiture in Developing Countries." *World Bank Discussion Paper* No. 11, 1987.

Bermeo, Nancy. "The Politics of Public Enterprise in Portugal, Spain and Greece." In *The Political Economy of Public Sector Reform and Privatization*. Edited by Ezra Suleiman and John Waterbury. Boulder. CO: Westview Press, 1990.

Bienen, Henry, and John Waterbury. "The Political Economy of Privatization in Developing Countries." *World Development*, forthcoming.

Blankart, Charles. "The Contribution of Public Choice to Public Utility Economics— A Survey." In *Public Sector Economics*, pp. 151–170. Edited by J. Finsinger. London: Macmillan, 1983.

Blankart, Charles. "Elements of an Economic Theory of Privatization." *Schweizerische Zeitschrift für Volkswirtschaft* 123 (Sept. 1987): 329–339.

Blankart, Charles. "Limits to Privatization." *European Economic Review* 31 (Feb. 1987): 346–351.

Blankart, Charles. "Stabilität and Wechselhaftigkeit politischer Entscheidungen—
Eine Fallstudie zur preußisch-deutschen Eisenbahnpolitik von ihren Anfängen bis
zum Zweiten Weltkrieg." *Jahrbuch für Neue Politische Öekonomie* 6 (1987): 74–92.

Boardman, A. E., and A. R. Vining. "Ownership and Performance in Competitive
Environments: A Comparison of the Performance of Private, Mixed and State-
Owned Enterprises." *Journal of Law and Economics* 32 (April 1989): 1–36.

Boneo, Horacio. "Privatization: Ideology and Praxis." In *State Shrinking*: A Comparative Inquiry into Privatization, pp. 40–60. Edited by William Glade. Austin:
Institute of Latin American Studies, The University of Texas at Austin, 1986.

Boorstin, Louis. "Financial Valuation of Companies to be Privatized." Memo,
World Bank. Aug. 15, 1986.

Borcherding, T. E. "Toward a Positive Theory of Public Sector Supply Arrangements." In *Public Enterprises in Canada*, pp. 99–184. Edited by R. Prichard, Toronto:
Butterworth, 1983.

Borcherding, T. E., W. W. Pommerehne, and F. Schneider. "Comparing the Efficiency of Private and Public Production: The Evidence from Five Countries."
Journal of Economics Suppl. 2 (1982): 127–156.

Borins, S. F. "Privatization Theory and Practice: Distributing Shares in Private and
Public Enterprises." *Canadian Public Administration* 24 (1981): 143–145.

Bös, Dieter. "Arguments on Privatization." Bonn University, 1987.

Bös, Dieter. "Privatization and People's Capitalism." Bonn University, 1988.

Bös, Dieter. "Privatization, Efficiency, and Market Structure." In *Sonderforschungs-
bereich 303, Information für die Koordination Wirtschaftlicher Aktivitäten*. Bonn, Nov.
1986.

Bös, Dieter. "Privatization of Public Enterprises." *European Economic Review* 31
(Feb./Mar. 1987): 352–360.

Bös, Dieter. "Privatization of Public Firms: A Government, Trade Union, and
Private Shareholder Game." In *Public Finance and the Performance of Enterprises*.
Edited by M. Neumann. Detroit: Wayne State University Press, 1988.

Bös, Dieter. *Public Enterprise Economics, Theory and Application*. New York: North-
Holland, 1986.

Bös, Dieter. "A Theory of the Privatization of Public Enterprise." *Journal of Economics* Suppl. 5 (1986): 17–40.

Bös, Dieter. "Welfare Effects of Privatizing Public Enterprises." In *Welfare and
Efficiency in Public Economics*, pp. 339–362. Edited by D. Bös, M. Rose, and C. Seidel.
Berlin: Springer-Verlag, 1988.

Bös, Dieter, and W. Peters. "Privatization, Internal Control and Internal Regulation." *Journal of Public Economics* 36 (1988): 231–258.

Bosanquet, Nick. "Is Privatisation Inevitable?" In *Privatisation and the Welfare State.* Edited by Julian Le Grande and Ray Robinson. London: Allen and Unwin, 1984.

Bradford, D. F. "Constraints on Government Investment Opportunities and the Choice of Discount Rate." *American Economic Review* 65 (Dec. 1975): 887–899.

Brede, Helmut, and Ulrich Hoppe. "Outline of the Present Status of the Privatization Debate in the Federal German Republic." *Annals of Public and Co-operative Economy* 57 (April 1986): 205–229.

Browning, Edgar. "The Marginal Cost of Public Funds." *Journal of Political Economy* 84 (April 1976): 283–298.

Browning, Edgar. "On the Marginal Welfare Cost of Taxation." *American Economic Review* 77 (Mar. 1987): 11–23.

Bruce, Colin. "Social Cost-Benefit Analysis: A Guide for Country and Project Economists to the Derivation and Application of Economic and Social Accounting Prices." *World Bank Staff Working Paper* No. 239, Aug. 1976.

Buchanan, J., R. Tollison, and G. Tullock. *Toward a Theory of the Rent-Seeking Society.* College Station: Texas A & M University Press, 1980.

Buckland, B., and E. W. Davis. "Privatization Techniques and the PSBR." *Fiscal Studies* (Aug. 1984).

Butler, Stuart. "Issues in Privatization." *Heritage Foundation* (June 11, 1987).

Campbell, Harry. "Deadweight Loss and Commodity Taxation in Canada." *Canadian Journal of Economics* (Aug. 1975): 441–446.

Candoy-Sekse, Rebecca. *Techniques of Privatization of State-Owned Enterprises,* Vol. III. World Bank Technical Paper No. 90, 1988.

Canning, John B. "Some Divergences of Accounting Theory from Economic Theory." *Accounting Review* 4 (Mar. 1929): 1–8.

Carlsson, Bo. "Public Industrial Enterprises in Sweden." *Annals of Public and Co-operative Economy* 59 (June 1988): 175–195.

Cass, Ronald. "Privatization: Politics, Law and Theory." *Marquette Law Review* 71 (Spring 1988): 449–648.

Caves, D., and L. R. Christensen. "The Relative Efficiency of Public and Private Firms in a Competitive Environment: The Case of Canadian Railroads." *Journal of Political Economy* 88 (1980): 958–976.

Caves, D., L. Christensen, J. Swanson, and M. Tretheway. "Economic Performance of U.S. and Canadian Railroads: The Significance of Ownership and the Regulatory Environment." In *Managing Public Enterprises,* pp. 123–151. Edited by W. T. Stanbury and Fred Thompson. New York: Praeger, 1982.

Caves, Richard. "Privatization and Liberalization in the United Kingdom." Paper presented at ASSA Meetings. Chicago: Dec. 1987.

Center for Privatization. "Country Privatization Strategy." Washington, DC: July 1987.

Center for Privatization. "Privatization Survey for Asia and the Near East." Washington, DC: 1988.

Center for Privatization. "Privatization Survey for Latin America and Caribbean." Washington, DC: 1988.

Center for Privatization. "Privatization Survey for Sub-Saharan Africa." Washington, DC: 1988.

Chamberlain, John, and John Jackson. "Privatization as Institutional Choice." *Journal of Policy Analysis and Management* 6 (Summer 1987): 586–604.

Chambers, R. J. "Income and Capital: Fisher's Legacy." *Journal of Accounting Research* 9 (Spring 1971): 137–149.

Chandler, Alfred. *The Visible Hand: The Managerial Revolution in American Business.* Cambridge, MA: Harvard University Press, 1977.

Charles, S. "The Opportunity Cost of the Sale of Local Authority Rented Accomodation: A Comment." *Urban Studies* 19 (1982): 8.

Chishty, Shamsul Haque "Privatization in Developing Countries: The Experience of Bangladesh." Conference on Privatization Policies, Methods and Progress. Manila: Asian Development Bank.

Cleaver, Kevin. "Economic and Social Analysis of Projects and Price Policy: The Morocco Growth Agricultural Credit Project." *World Bank Staff Working Paper* No. 369, Jan. 1980.

Coburn, John F., and Wortzel Lawrence. "The Problem of Public Enterprises: Is Privatisation the Solution?" Paper presented at the Conference on "State Shrinking." Austin: University of Texas, Mar. 1–3, 1984.

Commander, Simon, and Tony Killick. "Privatization in Developing Countries: A Survey of the Issues." In *Privatization in Less Developed Countries*, pp. 91–124. Edited by Paul Cook and Colin Kirkpatrick. New York: St. Martin's Press, 1988.

Cook, Paul, and Colin Kirkpatrick, eds. *Privatization in Less Developed Countries.* New York: St. Martin's Press, 1988, and Brighton: Wheatsheaf, 1988.

Cowan, L. Gray. "The Anatomy of Government and Market Failures." Washington, DC: Center for Privatization, April 1987.

Cowan, L. Gray. "Assistance by AID to Countries Needing to Privatize the State Owned Sector of the Economy." Washington DC: U.S. Agency for International Development, Dec. 1983.

Cowan, L. Gray. "Divestment and Privatization of the Public Sector." Case Studies of Five Countries (Jamaica, Kenya, Sudan, Indonesia, and Bangladesh). Washington DC: U.S. Agency for International Development, n.d.

Cowan, L. Gray. "Divestment, Privatization and Development." *Washington Quarterly* 8 (1985): 47–56.

Cowan, L. Gray. "A Global Overview of Privatization." In *Privatization and Development*. Edited by S. H. Hanke. San Francisco: Institute for Contemporary Studies, 1987.

Cowan, L. Gray. "Management Contracting as a Means of Reviving Failing State-Owned Enterprises." Washington DC: U.S. Agency for International Development, Dec. 1983.

Cowan, L. Gray. "Performance of State Owned Enterprises." Washington DC: U.S. Agency for International Development, Dec. 1983.

Cowan, L. Gray. "Some Practical Issues of Divestment and Privatization Facing LDC Government." Washington DC: U.S. Agency for International Development, Dec. 1983.

Cowan, L. Gray. "Privatization and Divestment in the LDC's—The Role of AID." Washington DC: U.S. Agency International Development, Dec. 1983.

Cowan, L. Gray, "Privatization: A Technical Assessment." U.S. Agency for International Development, July 1987.

Crampton, Graham. "Subsidies to Urban Public Transport and Privatisation." In Le Grande and Robinson, eds., *Privatisation and the Welfare State.*

Culyer, A. J. "Privatization and the Welfare-State." *Economica* 52 (1985): 533–534.

Dasgupta, P., A. Sen, and S. Marglin. *Guidelines for Project Evaluation.* New York: United Nations Industrial Development Organization, 1972.

Davies, David. "The Efficiency of Public versus Private Firms: The Case of Australia's Two Airlines." *Journal of Law and Economics* 14 (1971): 149–166.

Davies, David, and Peter Brucato. "Property Rights and Transactions Costs: Theory and Evidence on Privately-Owned and Government-Owned Enterprises." *Journal of Institutional and Theoretical Economics* 143 (Mar. 1987): 7–22.

DeAlessi, L. "An Economic Analysis of Government Ownership and Regulation: Theory and Evidence from the Electric Power Industry." *Public Choice* 19 (1974): 1–41.

DeAlessi, L. "On the Nature and Consequences of Private and Public Enterprises." *Minnesota Law Review* 67 (1982): 191–209.

Deru, H. J. "Public-Enterprises in the Netherlands, A Tradition in Privatization." *Annals of Public and Co-operative Economy* 56 (1985): 313–314.

Domberger, S., and J. Piggott. "Privatization Policies and Public-Enterprise: A Survey." *Economic Record* 62 (1986): 145−162.

Donnison, David. "The Progressive Potential of Privatisation." In Le Grande and Robinson, eds., *Privatisation and the Welfare State.*

Dunleavy, Patrick. "Explaining the Privatization Boom—Public Choice versus Radical Approaches." *Public Administration* 64 (Spring 1986): 13−34.

Eckel, Catherine. "The Causes and Consequences of Mixed Enterprise." In *Research in Corporate and Social Performance and Policy*, Vol. 10: International, Comparative and Multinational Studies. Edited by Lee Preston. New York: JAI Press, 1988.

Eckel, Catherine, and Theo Vermaelen. "International Regulation: The Effects of Government Ownership on the Value of the Firm." *Journal of Law and Economics* 29 (Oct. 1986): 381−403.

Eckel, Catherine, and Aidan Vining. "Elements of a Theory of Mixed Enterprise." *Scottish Journal of Political Economy* 32 (1985): 82−94.

Edwards, C., and J. Posnett. "The Opportunity Cost of the Sale of Local Authority Rented Accomodation." *Urban Studies* 17 (Feb. 1980): 45−52.

Evans, C. "Privatization of Local Services." *Local Government Studies* 11 (1985): 97−110.

Finsinger, J., and I. Vogelsang. "Alternative Institutional Frameworks for Price Incentive Mechanisms." *Kyklos* 34 (1981): 385−404.

Fixler, P. E., and Poole, R. W. "The Privatization Revolution; What Washington Can Learn from State and Local Government." *Policy Review* 37 (Summer 1986): 68−72.

Frieden, Karl. "Public Needs and Private Wants: Making Choices." *Dissent* (Summer 1987).

Gallinge, I. "The Denationalization of the Thatcher Government." *IPW Berichte* 11 (1982): 61.

Glade, William, ed. *State Shrinking: A Comparative Inquiry Into Privatization.* Austin: Institute of Latin American Studies, University of Texas at Austin, 1986.

Gomez-Ibanez, Jose, and John Meyer. "Urban Bus Deregulation and Privatization in Britain." Prepared for the Urban Mass Transportation Administration. Washington, DC: US Department of Transportation, Sept. 30, 1987.

Gray, Clive. "On Measuring the Shadow Price of Uncommitted Fiscal Resources in Africa." *World Development* 17 (Feb. 1989): 213−221.

Hanke, S. H. *Privatization and Development.* San Francisco: Institute for Contemporary Studies, 1987.

Hanke, S. H. "The Privatization Debate, An Insider's View." *Cato Journal* 2 (1982): 653—662.

Hanke, S. H. "Privatization, Justice and Markets, A Reply." *Cato Journal* 3 (1983) 873—874.

Hanke, S. H. "Strategies Employed in Successful Privatization." U.S. Agency for International Development, Paper presented at the International Conference on Privatization, Feb. 1986.

Hanke, S. H. "Toward a People's Capitalism." In *Privatization and Development*, pp. 213—222. Edited by Steve Hanke. San Francisco: International Center for Economic Growth, 1987.

Hanke, S. H., ed. *Prospects for Privatization*. New York: Academy of Political Science, 1987.

Hansson, Ingemar, and Charles Stuart. "Tax Revenue and the Marginal Cost of Public Funds in Sweden." Mimeo, University of California at Santa Barbara, Jan. 1983.

Heald, D. A. "Privatization: Analyzing Its Appeal and Limitations." *Fiscal Studies* 5 (Feb. 1984): 36—49.

Heald, David. "Privatization and Public Money." In *Privatizing Public Enterprises*. Edited by D. Heald and D. Steel. London: Royal Institute of Public Administration, 1984.

Heald, D. A. "The Relevance of UK Privatization to LDC's." In Cook and Kirkpatrick, eds., *Privatization in Less Developed Countries*. New York: St. Martin's Press, 1988, and Brighton: Wheatsheaf, 1988.

Heald, D. A. "Will the Privatization of Public-Enterprises Solve the Problem of Control." *Public Administration* 63 (1985): 7—22.

Heald, D. A., and D. R. Steel. "Privatizing Public Enterprises: An Analysis of the Government's Case." *Political Quarterly* 53 (July 1982): 333—349.

Helpman, E., and P. Krugman. Market Structure and Foreign Trade. Cambridge, MA: MIT Press, 1985.

Hemming, Richard, and Ali Mansoor. "Privatization and Public Enterprises." *IMF Working Paper*, Feb. 25, 1987.

Hepple, B. A. "The Transfer of Undertakings (protection of employment) Regulation." *Industrial Law Journal* 12 (1984): 29—40.

Hills, J. "What Is the Public Sector Worth?" *Fiscal Studies* 5: 18—31.

Hirshhorn, Ron, and Arthur Kaell. "A Framework for Evaluating Public Corporations." *Annals of Public and Co-operative Economy* 59 (1988): 141—156.

Hueth, D., R. Just, and A. Schmitz. *Applied Welfare Economics and Public Policy.* Englewood Cliffs, NJ: Prentice-Hall, 1982.

Ikenberry, John. "The International Spread of Privatization Policies: Inducements, Learning and 'Policy Bandwagoning.'" In Suleiman and Waterbury, eds., *The Political Economy of Public Sector Reform and Privatization.*

International Monetary Fund. *International Financial Statistics Yearbook: 1986.* Washington: IMF, 1986.

Jagannathan, N. V. *Informal Markets in Developing Countries.* New York: Oxford University Press, 1987.

Johnson, Gordon. "Privatization in Developing Countries." *Statement for the President's Commission on Privatization.* Washington, DC: Center for Privatization, Jan. 8, 1988.

Johnson, L. L. "Price Caps in Telecommunications—Regulatory Reform." Santa Monica, CA: Rand, Note N-2894-MF/RC, Jan. 1989.

Jones, Leroy. "Performance Evaluation for Public Enterprise." In *The Elusive Hybrid: Experiments in the Management and Privatization of Soe's.* Edited by Ravi Ramamurti and Raymond Vernon. Forthcoming.

Jones, Leroy. "Public Enterprise for Whom? Perverse Distributional Consequences of Public Operational Decisions." *Economic Development and Cultural Change* 33 (Jan. 1985): 333–347.

Jones, Leroy, and Edward Mason. "Why Public Enterprise?" In *Public Enterprise in Less-Developed Countries.* Edited by L. Jones. Cambridge: Cambridge University Press, 1982.

Jones, Leroy, and Ingo Vogelsang. *The Effects of Markets on Public Enterprise Conduct; And Vice Versa.* Ljubljana: ICPE, 1983.

Just, Richard, Darrell Hueth, and Andrew Schmitz. *Applied Welfare Economics and Public Policy.* Englewood Cliffs, NJ: Prentice-Hall, 1982.

Kay, John. "The Privatization of British Telecommunication." In D. Heald and D. Steel, eds., *Privatizing Public Enterprises.*

Kay, J. A., and Z. A. Silberston. "The New Industrial Policy—Privatization and Competition." *Midland Bank Review* (Spring 1984): 8–16.

Kay, J. A., and D. J. Thompson. "Privatization: A Policy in Search of a Rationale." *Economic Journal* 96 (Mar. 1986): 18–32.

Kay, John, Colin Mayer, and D. J. Thompson. *Privatization and Regulation: The U.K. Experience.* Oxford, Oxford University Press, 1986.

Kielland, E. "Privatization, A Many-Headed Monster." *Tidsskrift for Samfunnfurskning* 27 (1986): 195–216.

Kolderie, Ted. "The Two Concepts of Privatization." Hubert Humphrey Institute of Public Affairs, Jan. 1986.

Koo, Bon-Ho. "Privatization in Developing Countries: The Experience of the Republic of Korea." Conference on Privatization Policies, Methods and Progress. Manila: Asian Development Bank.

Kornai, Janos, and Agnes Matits. "The Softness of Budgetary Constraints—An Analysis of Enterprise Data." *Eastern European Economics* 25 (Summer 1987): 1–34.

Krueger, Anne. "The Political Economy of the Rent-Seeking Society." *American Economic Review* 64 (1974): 291–303.

Labour Research Department. "Public or Private, the Case Against Privatization." London: Labour Research Department, 1982.

Lancaster, Kelvin. "A New Approach to Consumer Theory." *Journal of Political Economy* 74 (April 1966): 132–157.

Lee, T. A. *Income and Value Measurement: Theory and Practice.* Baltimore: Baltimore University Press, 1975.

Leeds, Roger. "Malaysia: Genesis of a Privatization Transaction." Cambridge, MA: JFK School of Government, 1988.

Leeds, Roger. "Turkey: Rhetoric and Reality." In *The Promise of Privatization: A Challenge for American Foreign Policy.* Edited by Raymond Vernon. New York: Council on Foreign Relations, 1988.

Le Grande, Julian, and Robinson, Ray. "Privatization and the Welfare State: An Introduction." in Le Grande and Robinson, eds., *Privatisation and the Welfare State.*

Levy, Santiago, and Sean Nolan. *Trade and Foreign Investment Policies under Imperfect Competition: Lessons for Developing Countries.* Boston: Institute for Economic Development Discussion Paper No. 1, Nov. 1989.

Lind, Robert. "A Primer on the Major Issues Relating to the Discount Rate for Evaluating National Energy Options." In *Discounting for Time and Risk in Energy Policy,* Edited by Robert Lind. Washington, DC: Resources for the Future, 1982.

Linn, Johannes. "Economic and Social Analysis of Projects: A Case Study of Ivory Coast." *World Bank Staff Working Paper* No. 253, 1977.

Lissner, W. "The Rush towards Privatization." *American Journal of Economics and Sociology* 45 (1986): 402.

Little, I. M. D., and J. A. Mirrlees. *Project Appraisal and Planning for Developing Countries.* London: Heinemann, 1974.

Littlechild, S. C. "Regulation of British Telecom's Profitability." London: Report to the Secretary of State, Department of Industry, Feb. 1983.

Littlechild, S. C. "Ten Steps to Denationalization." *Journal of Economic Affairs* 2 (1981): 11–19.

Marchand, Maurice, Henry Tulkens, and Pierre Pestieau, eds. *The Performance of Public Enterprises*. New York: North-Holland, 1984.

Marshall, J., and F. Montt. "Privatization in Chile." In Cook and Kirkpatrick, eds., *Privatization in Less Developed Countries*, pp. 281–307.

Mashayekhi, Afsaneh. "Shadow Prices for Project Appraisal in Turkey." *World Bank Staff Working Paper* No. 392, May 1980.

Mayshar, J. "Should Government Subsidize Risky Private Projects?" *American Economic Review* (1977): 20–28.

Millward, R., and D. M. Parker. "Public and Private Enterprise: Comparative Behavior and Relative Efficiency." In *Public Sector Economics*, pp. 199–273. Edited by R. Millward et al. London: Longman, 1983.

Molyneux, Richard, and David Thompson. "Nationalized Industry Performance: Still Third-Rate?" *Fiscal Studies* (Feb. 1987): 48–82.

Mueller, Dennis. *The Determinants and Effects of Mergers: An International Comparison*. Cambridge: Oelgeschlager, 1980.

Nankani, Helen. "Bangladesh; Nationalisation and Denationalisation." Annex III in Berg, "Changing the Public-Private Mix."

Nankani, Helen. "Malaysia; Addressing the Indigenization Problem." Annex VI in Berg. "Changing the Public-Private Mix."

Nellis, John. "Contract Plans and Public Enterprise Performance." *World Bank Discussion Paper* No. 48, 1989.

Nellis, John. "Public Enterprise Reform in Adjustment Lending." *World Bank Policy, Planning and Research Working Paper* No. 233, August 1989.

Nellis, John, and Sunita Kikeri. "The Privatization of Public Enterprise." Washington, DC: World Bank, 1988.

New York Times. (June 20, 1989), pp. D1/D6.

Niskanen, W. A. *Bureaucracy and Representative Government*. Chicago: Aldine, 1971.

Ohashi, Theodore. "Privatization in Practice: The Story of the British Columbia Resources Investment Corporation." In *Privatization in Practice*, pp. 1–110. Edited by Theodore Ohashi and T. Roth. Vancouver: Fraser Institute, 1980.

Ohashi, Theodore. "Selling Public Enterprises to the Taxpayers: The Case of The British Columbia Resources Investment Corporation." In *Managing Public Enterprises*. Edited by W. T. Stanbury and Fred Thompson. New York: Praeger, 1982.

Ohasi, Theodore, and T. Roth. *Privatization in Practice*. Vancouver: Fraser Institute, 1980.

Olson, M. *The Logic of Collective Action: Public Goods and the Theory of Groups.* Cambridge, MA: Harvard University Press, 1965.

Olson, M. *The Rise and Decline of Nations.* New Haven: Yale University Press, 1982.

Osborne, M., and M. Costello. "Selling Off the Public Estate: A Broker's View." *Public Money* 3 (1984): 457–59.

Pakkasem, Phisit. "Privatization in Developing Countries: The Experience of Thailand." Conference on Privatization Policies, Methods and Progress. Manila: Asian Development Bank.

Page, John M. "Shadow Prices for Trade Strategies and Investment Planning in Egypt." *World Bank Staff Working Paper* No. 521, 1982.

Park, Y. C. "Reform of Public Enterprise Sector in Korea." World Bank, Public Sector Management Division, Aug. 1985.

Patton, William, and A. Littleton. *An Introduction to Corporate Accounting Standards.* American Accounting Association, 1967.

Paul, S. "Emerging Issues of Privatization in the Public Sector." *World Bank Policy, Planning, and Research Working Payer* No. 18, Sept. 1988.

Peltzman, S. "Toward a More General Theory of Regulation." *Journal of Law and Economics* 19 (1976): 211–240.

Pendse, D. R. "The Role of Donor Agencies in the Privatization Process." Conference on Privatization Policies, Methods and Progress. Manila: Asian Development Bank.

Pendse, D. R. "Some Reflections on the Role of Donor Argencies in the Privatization Process." *National Westminister Bank Quarterly Review* (Nov. 1985): 2–18.

Penman, Stephen H. "What Net Asset Value?—An Extension of a Familiar Debate." *The Accounting Review* (April 1970).

Perry, J. L., and T. T. Babitsky. "Comparative Performance in Urban Bus Transit: Assessing Privatization Strategies." *Public Administration Review* 46 (1986): 57–66.

Pickering, Craig. "The Mechanics of Disposal." In Heald and Steel, eds., *Privatizing Public Enterprises.*

Radin Soenarno, and Yusof, Zainal. "Privatization in Developing Countries: The Experience of Malaysia." Conference on privatization Policies, Methods and Progress. Manila: Asian Development Bank.

Ray, Anandarup. *Cost-Benefit Analysis: Issues and Methodologies.* Baltimore: John Hoplins University Press, 1984.

Richards, M. "Public Transport and Privatization." *Transporation* 12 (1983): 1–2.

Ritter, Jay. "The Costs of Going Public." *Journal of Financial Economics* 19 (1987): 269–281.

Rose, Richard. "Privatization: A Question of Quantities and Qualities." Conference on "A Supply-Side Agenda for Germany?" Cologne: June 1988.

Rosen, Harvey. "The Measurement of Excess Burden with Explicit Utility Functions." *Journal of Political Economy* 86 (April 1978): s121–s135.

Sappington, David, and Joseph Stiglitz. "Privatization, Information and Incentives." *Journal of Policy Analysis and Management* 6 (Summer 1987): 567–582.

Sato, Seizaburo. "Privatization in Industrialized Countries: The Experience of Japan." Conference on Privatization Policies, Methods and Progress. Manila: Asian Development Bank.

Savas, E. S. "Municipal Monopolies vs. Competition in Delivering Urban Services." In *Improving the Quality of Urban Management*. Edited by W. D. Hawley and D. Rogers. Beverly Hills: Sage Publications, 1974.

Savas, E. S. "Policy Analysis for Local Government: Public vs. Private Refuse Collection." *Policy Analysis* 3 (Winter 1977): 49–74.

Savas, E. S. *Privatization: The Key to Better Government*. Chatham, NJ: Chatham House, 1987.

Schohl, Wolfgang. "Estimating Shadow Prices for Colombia in an Input-Output Table Framework." *World Bank Staff Working Paper* No. 357, Sept. 1979.

Shapiro, C., and J. E. Stiglitz. "Equilibrium Unemployment as a Worker Discipline Device." *American Economic Review* 74 (1984): 433–444.

Shapiro, C., and Robert Willig. "Economic Rationales for the Scope of Privatization." In Suleiman and Waterbury, eds., *The Political Economy of Public Sector Reform and Privatization*.

Sharkey, W. W. "Outline of a Positive Theory of Regulation." *Proceedings from the Tenth Annual Telecommunications Policy Research Conference*. Edited by J. Ordover and O. Gandy. Norwood, NJ: Ablex Publishing, 1983.

Shepherd, William. "Increased Competition: Causes and Effects." Paper presented at the 9th EARIE Conference. Louvain, Belgium: Sept. 1982.

Sherman, R. "Pricing Behavior of the Budget-Constrained Public Enterprise." *Journal of Economic Behavior and Organization* 4 (1983): 381–393.

Shirley, Mary. "Divestiture of State-Owned Enterprises in Developing Countries." World Bank, Draft, July 30, 1985.

Shirley, Mary. "The Experience with Privatization." *Finance and Development* (Sept. 1988).

Short, R. P. "The Role of Public Enterprises: An International Statistical Comparison." In *Public Enterprise in Mixed Economies—Some Macroeconomic Aspects*, pp. 110–196. Edited by R. Floyd, C. Gray, and R. Short. Washington, DC: IMF, 1984.

Sigmund, Paul. "Chile: Privatization, Reprivatization, Hyperprivatization." In Suleiman and Waterbury, eds., *The Political Economy of Public Sector Reform and Privatization.*

Smith, T. C. *Political Change and Industrial Development in Japan: Government Enterprise, 1868–1880.* Stanford: Stanford University Press, 1955.

Spindler, Zane. "Breaking-up Government Bureaus and Crown Corporation; The Economics of Privatization." In Ohashi and Roth, eds., *Privatization in Practice*, pp. 153–182.

Squire, Lyn, and Herman van der Tak. *Economic Analysis of Projects*. Baltimore: John Hopkins University Press, 1975.

Squire, Lyn, I. M. D. Little, and M. Durdag. "Application of Shadow Pricing to Country Economic Analysis with an Illustration." *World Bank Staff Working Paper* No. 330, June 1979.

Steel, David. "Government and the New Hybrids." In Heald and Steel, eds., *Privatizing Public Enterprises.*

Steel, D. R. "The Privatization of Public Enterprises, 1979–83." In *RIPA Policy Initiatives Project.* Edited by P. M. Jackson, London: RIPA, forthcoming.

Steel, David, and David Heald. "The New Agenda." In Heald and Steel, eds., *Privatizing Public Enterprises.*

Stewart, M. B. "Should Government Subsidize Risky Private Projects? Comment." *American Economic Review* 69 (1979): 459–461.

Stigler, G. "The Theory of Economic Regulation." *Bell Journal of Economics and Management Science* 2 (1971): 3–21.

Stigler, G. "The Xistence of X-Efficiency." *American Economic Review* 66 (Mar. 1976): 213–216.

Stiglitz, J. E. "The Corporate Tax." *Journal of Public Economics* 5 (1976): 303–311.

Stiglitz, J. E. "The Role of Discount for Benefit-Cost Analysis and the Theory of the Second Best." In Lind, ed., *Discounting for Time and Risk in Energy Policy*, pp. 151–204.

Stuart, Charles. "Welfare Costs per Dollar of Additional Tax Revenue in the U.S." *American Economic Review* (June 1984): 352–362.

Subissati, E. E. "Some Evidence Regarding British Telecom's Performance under Price Cap Regulation." San Diego: Conference on Telecommunications Costing in a Dynamic Environment, April 5–7, 1989.

Suleiman, Ezra, and John Waterbury, eds. *The Political Economy of Public Sector Reform and Privatization.* Boulder, Co: Westview Press, 1990.

Tandon, Pankaj. "A Note on Optimal Pricing of Publicly Produced Intermediate Inputs." *Atlantic Economic Journal* 17 (Sept. 1989): 43–46.

Tanoira, Manuel. "Privatization as Politics." In Hanke, ed., *Privatization and Development*, pp. 53–64.

Teal, R. F., and Nemer, T. "Privatization of Urban Transit, the Los Angles Jitney Experience." *Transportation* 13 (1986): 5–22.

Thomas, David. "Employment, A New Angle Of Privatization." *New Society* 72 (1985): 132.

Thomas, D. "Privatization and the Unions." *New Society* 68 (1984): 478–479.

Thomas, David. "The Union Response to Denationalization." In Heald and Steel, eds., *Privatizing Public Enterprises.*

Tirole, Jean. *The Theory of Industrial Organization.* Cambridge, MA: MIT Press, 1989.

Trivedi, Prajapati. "Theory and Practice of the French System of Contracts for Improving Public Enterprise Persformance: Some Lessons for LDC's." *Public Enterprise* 8 (1988): 28–40.

Tullock, Gordon. "Rent-Seeking." In *The New Palgrave: A Dictionary of Economics*, p. 149. London: Macmillan, 1987.

Tullock, Gordon. "The Walfare Costs of Tariffs, Monopolies and Theft." *Western Economic Journal* 5 (1968): 224–232.

Turvey, R. "How to Judge When Price Changes Will Improve Resource Allocation." *Economic Journal* 84 (1974): 825–832.

Umar, B. "Bangladesh, Denationalisation of Industries and Houses." *Economic and Political Weekly* 20 (1985): 2203.

Unido. *Guide to Practical Project Appraisal: Social Benefit Cost Analysis in Developing Countries.* New York: United Nations, 1978.

Vernon, Raymond, ed. *The Promise of Privatization: A Challenge for American Foreign Policy.* New York: Council on Foreign Relations, 1988.

Vickers, John, and George Yarrow. *Privatization: An Economic Analysis.* Cambridge, MA: MIT Press, 1988.

Von Weizsäcker, C. C. "Was leistet die Property Rights Theorie für aktuelle wirtschaftspolitische Fragen?" In *Ansprüche, Eigentums—Und Verfügungsrechte*, pp. 123–150. Edited by M. Neumann. Berlin: Duncker & Humblot, 1984.

Vuylsteke, Charles. "Some Legal Aspects of Divestiture." Annex I in Berg, "Changing the Public-Private Mix."

Vuylsteke, Charles. "Techniques of Privatization of State-Owned Enterprises—Methods and Implementation." *World Bank Technical Paper* No. 88, 1988.

Wagner, R. E. "Pressure Groups and Political Enterpreneurs: A Review Article." In *Papers on Non-Market Decision Making*, Vol. 1, 1966, pp. 161–170.

Walker, Alan. "The Political Economy of Privatisation." In Le Grande and Robinson, eds., *Privatisation and the Welfare State*.

Walters, Alan Rufus. "Privatization: A Viable Policy Option?" Conference on Privatization Policies, Methods and Progress. Manila: Asian Development Bank.

Waterbury, John. "The Political Context of Public Sector Reform and Privatization in Egypt, India, Mexico and Turkey." In Suleiman and Waterbury, eds., *The Political Economy of Public Sector Reform and Privatization*.

Webb, M. G. "Energy-Policy and the Privatization of the UK Energy Industries." *Energy Policy* 13 (1985): 27–36.

Webb, M. G. "Privatising and the UK Energy Industries." *Economic Review* 1 (1984): 1–5.

Webb, Michael. "Privatization of Electricity and Gas Industries." In Heald and Steel, eds., *Privatizing Public Enterprises*.

Weiss, L., and M. Klass, eds. *Case Studies in Regulation*. Boston: Little, Brown & Co., 1981.

Williamson, O. E. *Markets and Hierarchies*. New York: The Free Press, 1975.

Willig, R. D. "Consumer's Surplus without Apologies." *American Economic Review* 66 (1975): 589–597.

Wiss, Marcia A. "Divestiture of State-Owned Enterprises in Sri Lanka." Annex VII in Berg, "Changing the Public-Private Mix."

Yarrow, George. "Privatization In Theory and Practice." *Economic Policy* 2 (April 1986).

Index